D1616892

ORIGINS OF THE
GULAG

ORIGINS OF THE
GULAG

The Soviet
Prison Camp System
1917-1934

MICHAEL
JAKOBSON

THE UNIVERSITY PRESS OF KENTUCKY

Copyright © 1993 by The University Press of Kentucky

Scholarly publisher for the Commonwealth,
serving Bellarmine College, Berea College, Centre
College of Kentucky, Eastern Kentucky University,
The Filson Club, Georgetown College, Kentucky
Historical Society, Kentucky State University,
Morehead State University, Murray State University,
Northern Kentucky University, Transylvania University,
University of Kentucky, University of Louisville,
and Western Kentucky University.

Editorial and Sales Offices: Lexington, Kentucky 40508-4008

Library of Congress Cataloging-in-Publication Data

Jakobson, Michael.
    Origins of the GULAG : the Soviet prison-camp system, 1917-1934 /
Michael Jakobson.
        p.   cm.
    Includes bibliographical references and index.
    ISBN 0-8131-1796-8 (alk. paper)
    1. Prisons—Soviet Union—History.   2. Concentration camps—Soviet
Union—History.   3. Forced labor—Soviet Union—History.   4. Soviet
Union—Politics and government—1917-1936.   I. Title.
HV9712.J35   1993
365'.45'094709041—dc20   92-10711

Прощайте же мать и жена
И вы мои милые дети
Знать горькую чашу до дна
Пришлося испить нам на свете

Farewell my mother and wife
And you my dear children.
It seems that we are doomed
To drink the bitter cup to the very end.

Пишет сыночку мать:
"Сыночек мой родной,
Ведь и Россия вся -
Это концлагерь большой".

A mother writes to her [imprisoned] son
"My dear beloved son,
You know that all Russia is
A big concentration camp."

CONTENTS

TABLES AND FIGURES

ACKNOWLEDGMENTS

This book could hardly have been written without the help of my teachers, friends, and colleagues. I am grateful to John Thayer and James Tracy of the University of Minnesota, whose intellectual influence and guidance cannot be overstated.

Terence Emmons of Stanford University, Robert Conquest and Robert Hessen of the Hoover Institution, and Basil Dmytryshyn made extremely valuable suggestions for improving my manuscript. I am deeply indebted to them for their generosity.

Peter H. Solomon, Jr., of the University of Toronto and Alexander Feldman called my attention to pertinent new materials. Alexander Vologodsky and Jack van Doorn of the Second World Center, Amsterdam, Ellen Scaruffi of Bakhmeteff Archive, and Serge Gleboff of the New York Public Library assisted me in finding photographs. Thomas Sgovio allowed me to use his painting as an illustration for the book. Ronald Bulatoff, Duncan Kincaid, Nada Stoy, and Sondra Bierre of the Hoover Institution Archives helped me with computers, archival searches, and, most important, friendship and support. I am also grateful to my colleagues at West Virginia University and at the University of Toledo for creating an atmosphere conducive to research. I would like to thank my old friends Thomas A. Kohut of Williams College and Glenn J. Ames of the University of Toledo for their interest in my work.

I am especially grateful to my teacher and friend John L. Scherer, who actually corrected every sentence of the manuscript. His intellectual contribution to this work is also enormous.

Any mistakes are, of course, my own.

ABBREVIATIONS AND ACRONYMS

Cheka	*See* Vecheka
Dal'stroĭ	Far Eastern Construction Administration
GPU	State Political Administration
GTU	Main Prison Administration
GUGB	Main Administration of State Security
GUITLTP	Main Administration of Corrective Labor Camps and Labor Settlements
GUITU	Main Administration of Corrective Labor Institutions
GULAG	Main Administration of Camps
GUMZ	Main Administration of Places of Confinement
GUPR	Main Administration of Forced Labor
IAO	Corrective Prisons
Narkompros (NKP)	People's Commissariat of Education
NEP	New Economic Policy
NKĬU	People's Commissariat of Justice
NKVD	People's Commissariat of Internal Affairs
OGPU	Unified State Political Administration
OPR	Department of Forced Labor
OPT	Society of Prisons' Trustees
RSDRP	Russian Socialist-Democratic Labor Party
RSFSR	Russian Soviet Federated Socialist Republic
SLON	Northern Special Purpose Camps; Solovetskiĭ Special Purpose Camps
SNK	Council of People's Commissars
Spetsotdel	Special Department
STD	Council for Prison Affairs
TO	Prison Branch
TSITO	Central Corrective Labor Department
TSKO	Central Penal Department
USLAG	Administration of the Solovetskiĭ Camps
USLON	Administration of Northern Special Purpose Camps
	Administration of the Solovetskiĭ Special Purpose Camps

Vecheka	All-Russian Extraordinary Commission for Combatting Counterrevolution and Sabotage
VKP(b)	All-Union Communist Party (Bolshevik)
VTSIK	All-Russian Central Executive Committee

INTRODUCTION

The collapse of Stalinism in the Soviet Union encourages a reexamination of the origins of the system that emerged under Stalin's rule. The places of confinement were the distinguishing feature of the Stalinist system. These include all the institutions that housed inmates—prisons, transit prisons, concentration camps, forced labor camps, and corrective labor camps. Almost no other subject in Russian and Soviet history has attracted so much public and so little scholarly attention. Hundreds of books and thousands of articles, pamphlets, and leaflets have appeared, yet few scholars have attempted to describe systematically the structure and activities of the agencies that ran the camps and prisons.

Three studies must be mentioned. The Soviet historian Mikhail Gernet prepared *Istoriĭa tsarskoĭ tiur'my,* a history of the prisons in Imperial Russia.[1] Viacheslav Artem'ev, a deputy chief of corrective labor camps in Kazakhstan during the 1930s, surveyed camps in the USSR from the mid-1930s to the 1950s in *Rezhim i okhrana ispravitel'no-trudovykh lagereĭ* (The Regime and the Security of Corrective Labor Camps).[2] Kurt Baehrens and other German scholars collected unique materials from former German POWs in the Soviet Union in the 1940s and 1950s. These materials, unjustifiably ignored in the United States, are included in the multivolume work *Zur Geschichte der deutschen Kriegsgefangenen des zweiten Weltkrieges.*[3] Prior to this present study, however, nothing has described the structure and activities of prison agencies from the October Revolution in 1917, when the old prison system was destroyed, to October 1934, when all places of confinement were consolidated under a single agency.

The lack of any systematic investigation of this crucial eighteen-year period has resulted in confusion in other histories. David Dallin and Boris Nicolaevsky, for example, claimed that the People's Commissariat of Justice ran the places of confinement during the mid-1920s.[4] Yet it had no such responsibility at the time; most camps and prisons were then run by the People's Commissariat of Internal Affairs. Further, Aleksandr I. Solzhenitsyn said in *Arkhipelag-Gulag* (*The Gulag Archipelago*) that immediately after the

October Revolution the relevant subagency of the People's Commissariat of Justice was called the "prison administration" (t͡iuremnoe upravlenie).[5] Yet the agency was actually called the Main Administration of Places of Confinement, having been so named by the Provisional Government. The Bolsheviks disbanded this agency in April or May 1918 and replaced it with the Central Penal Department in July 1918. "Prison administration," merely a generic term for a prison agency, had been used by the People's Commissariat of Justice in two decrees in December 1917; apparently Solzhenitsyn mistook the generic term for an agency title. The same error was made by George Legget in his detailed study of the Soviet secret police and by Jacques Rossi in his one-volume encyclopedia of the history and culture of Soviet prison camps.[6] The terminology in documents during the first few years after the Revolution remained confusing because the Bolsheviks had no experience in compiling official papers. The foregoing works, nonetheless, are still the best to be found on the subject. On the other hand, the article "Labor Camps in the Soviet Union" in The Modern Encyclopedia of Russian and Soviet History contains numerous factual errors.[7] All such mistakes, major or minor, reflect the limited knowledge of so fundamental a question in Soviet history.

The major sources used in this study are government decrees, Russian and Soviet periodicals, memoirs of former inmates, and materials from the Hoover Institution Archives at Stanford University. Government decrees published in the multivolume Sobranie uzakoneniĭ i rasport͡iazheniĭ Rabochego i krest'i͡anskogo pravitel'stva (Collection of Laws of the Workers' and Peasants' Government) illustrate the attempts to create a system based on Marxist ideas of crime and punishment. They also show how financial and other considerations influenced the implementation of Bolshevik and Communist theories. These decrees were my major source of information about the first five years of the Soviet penal system. Inescapably, they emphasized the bureaucratic and the institutional rather than the human element. Careful attention to each decree, however, provides insights into the disputes and problems of the Soviet prison system, and this documentary approach is essential to an understanding of its development.

The most important periodicals used in this study are the Ezhenedel'nik Sovetskoĭ I͡usti͡tsii (Weekly of Soviet Justice) and Sovetskoe gosudarstvo i revoli͡ut͡siia prava (The Soviet State and the Revolution of Law), both issued by the People's Commissariat of Justice; and Vlast' sovetov (The Power of the Soviets) and Administrativnyĭ vestnik (The Administrative Herald), published by the People's Commissariat of Internal Affairs. These commissariats ran most of the places of confinement, and their journals contain reports and minutes of conferences on various aspects of the prison system, reflect the struggle for control among the various agencies involved, and detail problems and conditions.

The journals of the Cheka, the GPU, and the OGPU (the secret police), which had their own detention facilities, are not available. Memoirs of former inmates, who customarily wrote about the conditions of their confinement, contain information of institutional developments as well; these have proved to be the major source of knowledge about the Cheka's prisons.

The Hoover Institution has unpublished memoirs of former inmates who left the USSR during World War II, as well as a sizable collection of government documents smuggled out during the war, reports from socialists in the Soviet Union to colleagues abroad, and messages from officers in the Imperial Russian intelligence service, which was still operating in the early 1920s. All such materials have been consulted extensively.

This work investigates three major areas: the structure and interrelations of prison agencies; Bolshevik views of crime and punishment and inmate reeducation; and prison self-sufficiency, particularly the employment of inmates and the funding of the places of confinement.

In Imperial Russia, the Ministries of Justice and Interior were primarily responsible for the prisons. Most were controlled by Justice, but it was unable to run local facilities without the assistance of Interior. The revolutionaries particularly hated the Ministry of the Interior, which supervised the Department of Police. When they took power in February 1917, most of that ministry's subagencies were abolished immediately. Without Interior, however, the Ministry of Justice simply lost control of a number of its places of confinement. The People's Commissariat of Justice acted hastily again during the first months after the October 1917 Revolution, disbanding pre-Revolutionary prison agencies before establishing its own. When the new government finally set them up, it took a long time to reestablish connections with local prisons, which, without a strong central agency, failed either to guard or to employ inmates efficiently. Most prisoners did not work; many simply escaped.

The failure of the People's Commissariat of Justice to bring order out of chaos led to the formation of two other prison systems. The Cheka was given responsibility for guarding the most dangerous enemies of the regime; the People's Commissariat of Internal Affairs was charged with employing inmates considered less dangerous. Justice monopolized the prison system for several months after the October Revolution. It ran some places of confinement from 1917 to 1922, and again, from 1930 to 1934. Internal Affairs administered some camps and prisons from 1919 to 1930, and the secret police was responsible for a number of facilities during 1918-34. These agencies operated through subagencies whose titles often changed.

Competition among the agencies affected the conditions at the places of confinement. In trying to prove that it could operate at less cost than Justice, the People's Commissariat of Internal Affairs reduced the budget for its camps so drastically in the spring of 1922 that thousands of inmates died of starvation.

Officials of the People's Commissariat of Justice of the RSFSR. Above left, Pëtr I. Stuchka, who disbanded the prison agency in May 1918, leaving it without a center for three months—a blunder that led to the establishment of a rival prison system under the Cheka. Above right, Nikolaĭ V. Krylenko, who led the Commissariat in the crucial year 1934, when Justice lost its places of confinement to the USSR's Commissariat of the Interior; it never regained them. Krylenko was arrested and executed in 1938. Below right, Leonid A. Savrasov, who antagonized his superiors by demanding that his

prison agency become independent of the commissariat. He was replaced by a more flexible bureaucrat, Evseĭ Shirvindt, in 1922.

Competition also reflected the struggle at the top. During the political battling between Stalin and Nikolai Bukharin in 1928-29, the People's Commissariat of Justice claimed that Internal Affairs was too liberal toward inmates because it had supported Bukharin. When Stalin won, the Commissariat of Internal Affairs was disbanded, and its places of confinement were transferred to the Commissariat of Justice. In 1934, however, Internal Affairs was re-established and given all the camps and prisons, including those previously under the secret police and Justice. This change, requested by "moderates" in the Politburo to curb the power of the secret police, ironically increased police power. During the 1930s, the secret police actually controlled Internal Affairs and its facilities, which housed two to six million inmates.

According to Bolshevik theory, crime was the product of the injustices of the capitalist sytem; it would simply not occur under socialism. This view limited Bolshevik planning: prison institutions, it was thought, would soon become unnecessary.

The Bolsheviks naively believed in the reform of all inmates. Persons who had been habitual criminals under capitalism should be reeducated under special conditions at the places of confinement. The Bolsheviks even thought they knew how long such reeducation would take. In 1918 they determined that the maximum sentence for all offenses considered criminal would be just five years. In July of that year the government also established special agencies called Distributive Commissions and charged them with the task of reforming prisoners. The state considered their work so important that it financed the commissions even at times when funds were desperately scarce. This decision, if exemplary, proved irrational: there was too little food for inmates, and not even enough for some prison guards and warders. Yet while many died from starvation, the commissions went on with their work.

The concept of inmate reeducation was changed, adjusted, and twisted but not abandoned until the late 1930s. It was restated as late as 1936 in a book published by the USSR Academy of Sciences, *Ot prestupleniìa k trudu* (From Crime to Productive Labor) by I. L. Averbakh.[8] The idea disappeared from public discussion only after the Old Bolsheviks, who had originated and shared the belief in the reeducation of prisoners, were removed from power.

Solzhenitsyn has dismissed the Bolshevik views on crime and reeducation as propaganda. He has attributed the Soviet prison system to Marxist ideology and discovered the seeds of the GULAG Archipelago that emerged after the mass arrests of peasants during 1929-32, in two ideas promoted by the People's Commissariat of Justice in 1917 and 1918: that all healthy inmates work, and that the places of confinement be financially self-sufficient. The error and the irony here, for both Bolsheviks and Solzhenitsyn, are that neither idea was ever realized, yet the GULAG Archipelago emerged anyway.

Many inmates never worked. In 1918 and 1919 only 2 percent were

Officials of the Vecheka-GPU-OGPU. Above left, Feliks E. Dzerzhinskiĭ was the first chairman of the organization. He apparently saved the GPU penal system when the government tried to dismantle it in 1922. After his death he was replaced by Vĭacheslav R. Menzhinskiĭ, below, who supervised the OGPU during its unprecedented expansion. He was less involved, however, in the activities of the camps than was his deputy, Genrikh G. Iagoda, above right, who replaced Menzhinskiĭ after his death in 1934. Iagoda supervised the OGPU camps beginning in the 1920s and was the first of eight GULAG officials to receive the Order of Lenin after completion of the White Sea-Baltic Sea Canal. He was arrested and executed in 1938. Dzerzhinskiĭ photo courtesy of the Hoover Institution Archives.

Gleb I. Bokiĭ, above left, head of the Cheka-GPU-OGPU prison agency 1921?-1930, was replaced by Matveĭ D. Berman, above right, and was arrested in 1937. Under Berman's tenure, the GULAG monopolized the penal system in the Soviet Union and housed more inmates than the total in all the prisons and camps in the rest of the world. Berman was arrested in 1938 and executed the following year. Semën G. Firin,

below right, Deputy Head of the GULAG 1930-1937, was in charge of the camps whose inmates constructed the White Sea-Baltic Sea and Moscow River-Volga River canals. In 1937 he met the same fate as many of his fellow GULAG officials—arrest and, apparently, execution.

employed, and during the 1920s less than half—very close to the percentage in Imperial Russia. Even in the 1930s, when the government included prisoner output in its Five-Year Plans, the proportion of working inmates hardly exceeded 75 percent.

There is no question that the Bolsheviks wanted the prisons to be self-supporting. Financial considerations were often decisive, as in 1922, when the government transferred the places of confinement from Justice (which had merely offered to reeducate inmates) to Internal Affairs (which had promised to make the camps and prisons self-sufficient). But Internal Affairs never met its goal of self-sufficiency; it received government subsidies, which grew as the inmate population increased. Hence, at the end of 1930 the People's Commissariat of Internal Affairs was disbanded, and its places of confinement were handed back to Justice.

Deputy People's Commissar of Justice Pëtr I. Stuchka first claimed that the Soviet penal system was financially independent in 1931. Competition with the Cheka for control of the system was acute, and Stuchka hoped to convince the government that could take over some Cheka camps and prisons and make them self-supporting. His revenues came not from inmate labor, however, but from persons sentenced to forced labor without deprivation of freedom, who paid a percentage of their wages to the People's Commissariat of Justice; these payments turned out to be enough to reimburse the government for its subsidies and to provide the agency with some surplus income. Nevertheless, a sizable number of former inmates and Western researchers have accepted Stuchka's claim about profitability, apparently because it appears to explain the proliferation of prisons and camps holding millions of inmates.

There were in fact many reasons, not just one, for the existence and expansion of the Soviet prison system. They are examined in the ensuing nine chapters. One ironic, tragic factor was Western public opinion. A campaign began in the West in 1930 to boycott Soviet lumber on the grounds that it was produced by forced prison labor. The Soviet government responded to this threat by replacing prison inmates in some parts of the timber industry with "free" exiles—and inmates who had worked as lumberjacks suddenly found themselves building the White Sea–Baltic Sea Canal, the first in a series of huge construction projects achieved with prison labor. Subsequently, these projects required an endless supply of inmates, and many prisoners concluded that they had been arrested for no other reason.

The first chapter of this study describes the prison system under the Tsar and the Provisional Government; the second discusses the Bolshevik theory of crime and punishment; and the remaining chapters deal with the Soviet prison system. The list of acronyms that follows here, the organizational charts (Figures 1-10) accompanying the text, and additional information in the Appendix should help readers follow the administrative changes in the Russian and Soviet prison systems. Besides these fundamental issues of structure and development, other questions are considered implicitly in the narrative: Did Marxism or the Bolshevik Revolution or Leninism necessarily, inexorably, lead to this camp and prison system? Did Stalin really matter? And were the origins of the system—or, for that matter, the origins of Soviet totalitarianism—truly evil, or merely banal?

1 THE IMPERIAL RUSSIAN PRISON SYSTEM

Before the 1917 October Revolution, the rate of increase in the Russian prison population soared beyond the rate of natural population growth. The average daily Russian prison population more than doubled between 1900 and 1914. During the same period (before Russia lost territory in World War I), the total Russian population grew 18 percent, from 138 million to 168 million.[1] The prison population increased from 85,000 in 1900 to 184,000 in 1912, decreased to 169,000 in 1913, then increased again to 177,000 in 1914. It fell to 157,000 in 1915, and even further, to 142,000, in 1916.[2]

Soviet scholars have attributed the extraordinary growth of the prison population to the partial dissolution of the peasant communes, which had controlled the behavior of their members, and to the rapid expansion of cities and towns. The urban population swelled from 18.4 million in 1897 to 28.5 million in 1913.[3] City dwellers were also arrested at a higher rate than peasants. The decrease in the number of prisoners in 1913 was related to the war: young Russian males, the age group most likely to commit crimes, were drafted in immense numbers.[4]

Most prisoners were poor peasants, young and male. In 1914, 1,859,314 people were arrested on various charges. A Russian prisoner spent an average of ten days behind bars. Prison terms varied from one day to life. Ninety-three percent of the prisoners were male; 60 percent were younger than forty. The average daily numbers of political prisoners fluctuated between 1 and 2 percent of the total prison population. About 50 percent of the political prisoners were nobles, who constituted less than 2 percent of the total Russian population. The average daily number of prisoners convicted of crimes against the state and/or against religion (religious sacrilege, disobedience to the police, etc.) grew from 16,000 in 1910 to 30,000 in 1914, and then to 35,000 in 1915. Sixty-five percent of these convicts were peasants, who made up over 80 percent of the Russian population. Twenty-five percent were city dwellers, who accounted for 18 percent of the total population, and 10 percent belonged to the privileged classes. The percentage of nobles serving terms as common criminals, as distinct from political prisoners, was negligible.[5]

Prison life reflected the divisions within Russian society. Prisoners belonging to the privileged classes, unless the courts stripped them of their titles, retained certain rights in most places of confinement. Unlike inmates from the nonprivileged classes, they could buy their own food, wear their own clothes, and live apart from commoners. Women were segregated from men, juveniles from adults, and usually, the military from civilians, clergy from laity, and political prisoners from common criminals.[6]

Prisoners were further separated on the basis of the seriousness of their crimes. Those convicted of murder and armed robbery were confined in high-security facilities called *katorga* prisons. Their daily population averaged 29,300 in 1914. Prisoners convicted of less serious crimes were sent to corrective prisons (*ispravitel'no arestantskoe otdelenie*, or IAO in its Russian acronym). They totaled 34,750 in 1914. The rest were in ordinary prisons, military prisons, jails (*arestnoe pomeshchenie*) of the lower courts, police stations, detective police stations (*zhandarmskoe upravlenie*), political police stations (*sysknoe upravlenie*), and corrective juvenile prisons (*ispravitel'noe otdelenie dlia nesovershennoletnikh*).[7] The capacity of the Tsarist Russian prison system totaled more than 200,000 inmates. Many prisons were not full, but some, especially *katorga* prisons, were seriously overcrowded.[8]

Only prisoners in the *katorga* and corrective systems had to work. Prison labor elsewhere was optional, except for those convicted of theft and embezzlement.[9] There appears to have been no general rule regulating prisoners' wages, which varied from one prison to another.[10] There was a rule, however, which allowed prisoners to receive only a portion of their salaries. *Katorga* prisoners were given 10 percent of what was left after deductions for their food and clothing. Those held in corrective prisons ended up with 30 percent, and inmates in ordinary prisons, 40 percent. What was left of the salaries was divided equally between the prison and the government.[11]

Prison system data are available only for 1899. In that year the income from prisoners totaled 1,462,950 rubles, or about 10 percent of the prison budget. Inmates received 499,221 rubles, from which were deducted 145,721 rubles for food and clothes. Prisons received 435,807 rubles, and 389,200 went to the government.[12] Prisoners were not paid for performing community services or for working as janitors, cooks, and laundry persons in the institutions; instead, one day was deducted from their term for each day of free labor. About 40 percent of the prison population worked; the rest did nothing.[13]

Some Tsarist government officials believed that the prisoners should contribute more to maintain the system. Minister of Justice Nikolai V. Murav'ev even proposed that the prison system be made financially independent, but no attempt was made to implement his suggestion. The idea of self-supporting prisons became popular only after the 1917 October Revolution.[14]

During the first years of the twentieth century, there was one warder for every ten prisoners and one military guard for every fifteen prisoners. One year, the staff totaled 18,080 warders—including 658 females—and 11,802 military guards. These jobs were generally considered undesirable, because Russians traditionally sympathized with prisoners. Of 7,719 newly hired warders, 3,167 quit and 1,142 were fired their first year, despite significant government benefits.[15] The starting salary for a warder was 150 percent higher than that of a worker of comparable education and skills. The salary was raised 33 percent for every five years of employment. After fifteen years a warder's wages had doubled, increasing about 25 percent more rapidly than the wages of other government workers. Warders also enjoyed annual bonuses, and retired privates and noncommissioned officers who had been hired as warders retained their military pensions.[16]

All prisoners, warders, and military guards were under the jurisdiction of five agencies. The Ministry of Justice controlled about 85 percent of the prisoners; the Ministry of the Interior, the Ministry of War, the Ministry of the Marine, and the Holy Synod were responsible for the rest.[17] The Ministry of the Interior supervised the jails of the lower courts, police stations, and detective and political police stations. The Ministry of War controlled the prison fortresses (such as Petropavlovskaĭa krepost'), military prisons, and military punishment detachments (*distsiplinarnaĭa chast'*). Its places of confinement were primarily for military personnel, though some politicals and criminals were kept in the prison fortresses. The Ministry of the Marine retained jurisdiction over naval prisons and punishment detachments. The Holy Synod was responsible for prison monasteries, which held convicted clergy and some female juveniles.[18] The rest of the prisons were under the jurisdiction of the Ministry of Justice or, more accurately, under two of its subagencies: the Main Prison Administration (*Glavnoe tĭuremnoe upravlenie*, or GTU) and the Council for Prison Affairs (*Sovet po tĭuremnym delam*, or STD). The GTU had executive powers, whereas the STD had merely advisory functions. A third agency, the Society of Prisons' Trustees (*Obshchestvo popechitel'noe o tĭur'makh*, or OPT), assisted the Ministry of Justice in operating its prisons. The OPT was an independent administration.[19]

The Main Prison Administration had been established in 1879 when the prison system was centralized under the Ministry of the Interior. It was transferred to the Ministry of Justice in 1895.[20] Its structure, however, did not change between 1879 and April 1918, five months after the Revolution, when the entire system was abolished.[21] The GTU's personnel consisted of a chief, two deputies, inspectors, two specialists (an architect and a statistician), and clerks. The Ministry of Justice appointed the administrative personnel and the

Figure 1

The Russian Prison System before 1917

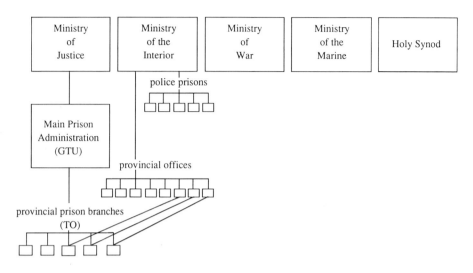

Prisons of the Ministry of War, the Ministry of the Marine, and the
Ministry of the Interior ceased to exist soon after February 1917;
monasteries of the Holy Synod stopped being used as prisons
shortly after 1905. Provincial branches of the prison system of the
Ministry of Justice received funds and orders from the Ministry of
Justice, but administratively were subordinate to the provincial
offices of the Ministry of the Interior.

specialists; the Tsar selected the chief from a list compiled by the Minister of
Justice, and announced his appointment in a special edict to the Senate.
Inspectors supervised some individual prisons and all the GTU provincial
prison offices or branches (*tiuremnoe otdelenie*, or TO). Each TO comprised a
provincial prison inspector (*gubernskiĭ tiuremnyĭ inspektor*), his deputies,
and clerks. The TOs controlled most individual prisons. The staff of each
prison included a superior warder (*smotritel'*), his deputy, senior and junior
warders, a priest, a doctor, and subordinate medical personnel. Some prisons
also had military guards. The GTU determined the number of warders and
guards for each prison. The priests and medical staff were controlled by the
TOs but funded by the Society of Prisons' Trustees.[22]

The system did not eliminate administrative anomalies. The Ministry of
the Interior, which had controlled the GTU before 1895, retained some authority over them after they were transferred to the Ministry of Justice: although
the branches received funds and orders from the Main Prison Administration,
they were also agencies of the provincial administrations and, consequently,

subordinate to the Ministry of the Interior. Governors headed the provinces, and provincial prison inspectors acted as vice-governors who reported to the governors and to the provincial administrations. As a result, the Ministry of the Interior often interfered with the operation of the *katorga* prisons, which were directly controlled by provincial governors. Interior also exercised some control over prisons in Moscow and St. Petersburg through its agents, the city governors, even though these prisons were funded by the Main Prison Administration of the Ministry of Justice. The GTU, in its turn, was able to influence the policies of city and provincial governors through local agencies. In St. Petersburg the GTU agency was called the Observation Commission (*Nabliu-datel'naia komissiia*).[23] The Ministry of the Interior also supervised the prisons under the Ministry of Justice through the chiefs of the local and political police. They had the right to enter any prison, communicate directly with prisoners, and report any violation of procedure to the Minister of the Interior, who could inform the Tsar.

The Ministry of Justice could supervise all places of confinement outside its immediate jurisdiction through procurators and judges, who, in addition to enforcing judicial procedures, supervised the treatment of prisoners. Other agencies retained control over local prisons. The local *zemstvos* (elective district councils) were in charge of supplying and maintaining prisons, and local Cossack governments controlled special Cossack jails. Military authorities became involved if a civilian prison housed military personnel.[24]

The Council on Prison Affairs (STD) discussed changes in the prison system and various related issues at the request of the GTU. For example, it considered proposals to establish new prisons. Subordinate to the Ministry of Justice, the STD had a chairman and eight members appointed by the Tsar; the GTU chief served as its ninth member. The council had no executive power, and its members received no compensation. Its decisions were not binding, but the Minister of Justice reported them to the Tsar.[25]

The Society of Prisons' Trustees (OPT), the third central agency supervising civilian prisons, was independent of any government agency and remained under the protection of the Tsar. Critics claimed, however, that the agency was actually subordinate to the Ministry of Justice because the minister was also its president. The society accepted private donations and solicited money in public places. Members of the OPT were wealthy landowners and merchants who contributed annually to the society. It was an honor to be chosen; members received no money. Members of OPT offices at the county (*uezd*) level were selected from major contributors. They too were unsalaried, but clerks and physicians were paid by the government. The OPT provided food and clothing to prisoners out of government funds; it paid for prison heating and electricity from city revenues.[26]

Despite intense competition between Justice and Interior, neither minis-

Table 1. Russian Prison Budget, 1911–1917

1911	25,912,000 rubles	1915	31,338,000
1912	27,183,000	1916	33,021,000
1913	28,463,000	1917	39,109,000
1914	28,963,000		

try was able to exclude the other from prison administration. Justice controlled the funds, but local offices of Interior were indispensable in running the prisons. Of three sources of money—government funds, income from prisoner labor, and charities—government funds constituted 90 percent. In 1899, the budget totaled 1,462,950 rubles.[27] It grew twenty-eight times during the next eighteen years (see Table 1); by 1917 it amounted to about 1 percent of the total budget of the Russian Empire—4,077,871,071 rubles.[28]

Most of the money was spent to maintain the prisoners. In 1917, 15,776,000 rubles were devoted to that purpose. Some 9,787,139 rubles were provided for the administrative staff and warders; 3,949,276 for military guards; 7,972,000 for rent and upkeep of premises; and 2,053,826 for construction and repair. The remaining 7,443,739 rubles were allocated for central administration, local institutions, the transport of prisoners, and various other items.[29] *Zemstvos,* Cossack administrations, and peasant communes provided additional moneys for rent and maintenance of small local prisons.[30]

The Ministry of Justice spent only about 33 percent of its budget on prisons: 39,109,000 rubles out of 118,967,055 in 1917. The greatest share was allocated to the Russian judicial system.[31] Established in 1864 during the liberal reforms of Alexander II, the judicial system was divided into lower courts with elected judges, and higher courts with appointed judges. In the higher courts, jurors rendered a verdict as to the guilt or innocence of the accused. The jurors were frequently influenced by public opinion. In one famous trial in 1878, jurors acquitted the revolutionary Vera Zasulich, though she had tried to assassinate the governor of St. Petersburg; they deemed her innocent because he had ordered a political prisoner birched.[32] With verdicts like this, and popular sentiment often running against the government, authorities increasingly resorted to administrative arrests of revolutionaries by agencies of the Ministry of the Interior. In 1915 approximately 20 percent of all prisoners had been seized using such administrative measures.[33]

The socialist press naturally condemned administrative arrests. It also criticized corporal punishment in prisons, the rudeness of warders and guards toward prisoners, and the privileges extended to nobles by the jailers. Further, it rallied against the official encouragement given military guards to shoot prisoners during violent incidents, and it was indignant over the working conditions in *katorga* prisons—particularly in Siberia, even though prisoners there were not forced to work during severe weather. It criticized the lack of vocational training for prisoners who were not juveniles. It was unhappy about medical care in prisons, despite the fact that almost everyone received some medical assistance (in 1914 about 8 percent, or 14,351 prisoners, were hospitalized). The socialist press also complained about food, although here too it must be noted that prisoners received soldier's rations.[34]

In 1875, relatives of political prisoners and former prisoners formed the Political Prisoners' Aid Society (*Obshchestvo pomoshchi politicheskim zakliuchënnym*), headed by famous revolutionaries, including Vera Figner and Ekaterina Breshkovskaĭa. Although the Tsarist government never legalized the society, it was able to collect enough funds to assist political prisoners financially and to publish *Vestnik katorgi i ssylki* (Herald of the *Katorga* Prison and Exiles). The journal was printed abroad and smuggled by socialists and anarchists to readers in Russia.[35]

The February Revolution of 1917 changed everything. In early March the new Provisional Government released most of the prisoners. In cases where the Provisional Government acted slowly or released only political prisoners, mobs freed the rest.[36] Only some Cossack and local prisons managed to keep their inmates behind bars.

Soon, however, there were new arrests. The first to be taken into custody were those who had faithfully served the old regime, especially police and military officers. Then, in July 1917, the Provisional Government began to arrest Bolsheviks: that is, members of the Russian Socialist-Democratic Labor Party (RSDRP) headed by Lenin.[37] Still, although precise statistics are not available, the total number of prisoners hardly exceeded 35,000—perhaps one-fourth of the total under the Tsar.[38] Police units were disbanded or were paralyzed by the general disorder, and criminals remained at large. The situation was, quite simply, out of control. Under pressure from the new Petrograd Soviet, composed mainly of former political prisoners, the government had even abolished the Department of Police in June 1917. Agencies set up to replace the department hired an insignificant number of the old employees, and generally proved to be ineffectual. The Provisional Government used military cadets and a few loyal military units to arrest its rivals.[39]

On the other hand, the Main Prison Administration, despised by former political prisoners, was not disbanded; even the old personnel stayed. The GTU was simply renamed the Main Administration of Places of Confinement (*Glavnoe upravlenie mest zakliucheniia*, or GUMZ), and its local agencies became "prison inspections" (*tiuremnaia inspektsiia*) instead of "prison branches" (the local offices of the GUMZ retained the word prison in their name, but it was removed from the title of the central agency). The Council on Prison Affairs, the Society of Prisons' Trustees, and the Observation Commis-

Figure 2
The Prison System, February – October 1917

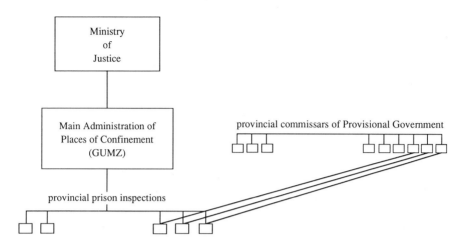

Note the title changes: from GTU to GUMZ, and from "prison branches"
to "prison inspections." Before1917 the Ministry of Justice distributed
funds to its provincial offices through the GTU; after February 1917 such
funds came from provincial commissars of the Provisional Government.

sion of Petrograd suffered no semantic or organizational changes. Special
representatives of the Provisional Government, designated provincial commissars, replaced the provincial governors, however, and all funds from the
Main Administration of Places of Confinement allocated for prison inspections
now went through the commissars' hands.[40]

Some of the old prisons continued to function. Many under the Ministries
of Justice, War, and Navy, as well as local *zemstvo* and Cossack prisons, went
on as usual. When the Department of Police and the Ministry of the Interior
was abolished, however, its places of confinement were closed or transferred
to other agencies.

The Political Prisoners' Aid Society, which had been illegal under the
Tsar, was legalized and helped financially by the government. It focused its
efforts on assisting former political prisoners to return home, and it provided
limited support to some Bolsheviks who had been imprisoned—but none at
all to police, military officers, and supporters of the old regime, who now
found the tables turned.[41]

2 THE BOLSHEVIK JUDICIAL SYSTEM 1917-1922

During the July 1917 uprising instigated by the Bolsheviks against the Provisional Government, a Petrograd publisher received an order for a leaflet. It frantically announced that the *katorzhniks* (high-security convicts) had seized power in Russia.[1] Its author's fears were premature, but his description of the Bolsheviks as convicts was entirely correct. Most of the future leaders of Soviet Russia had attended the Sixth Congress of the Bolshevik Party on 26 July 1917, and Leon Trotsky commented on its composition: "Of 171 delegates who filled out a questionnaire, 110 had spent 245 years in prison; 10 delegates were in *katorga* prisons for 41 years; 24 had spent 73 years in the IAOs; 55 delegates had been in exile 127 years; 27 had been abroad for 89 years; 150 had been arrested 549 times." Further, the Council of People's Commissars (*Sovet Narodnykh Komissarov*, or SNK), the Bolshevik executive government established on 8 November 1917, had fifteen members (four workers and eleven intellectuals), who had all spent many years in prison, exile, and emigration under the Tsar. Five had already been imprisoned by the Provisional Government.[2] Their only experience at governing, someone remarked, was running a prison cell.

While in prison, the Bolsheviks and other revolutionaries had often looked upon criminals as potential allies. Many, including Lenin, expected criminals to side with the Bolsheviks in any uprising against the government. Maxim Gorky, a writer close to the Bolsheviks, had popularized this romantic view in his short story "Chelkash" (1895). Chelkash was a thief, but he was also generous, courageous, and dashing, respected despite or, really, because of his profession. Gorky and other Russian revolutionaries were perpetuating the sentimental notion that the criminal was a victim of society and a natural ally of revolution. Friedrich Schiller, Charles Dickens, and Victor Hugo had written in this Romantic genre outside of Russia, and each had been read widely inside the country.[3]

Prisoners, of course, have always questioned the fairness and effectiveness of judicial and punitive systems. Many Russian prisoners believed that the courts had approached their cases in a formal and bureaucratic manner, without considering their peculiar circumstances. Many felt that society shared the responsibility for their misfortunes.[4] These ideas corresponded to the Marxist view of crime and punishment. Lenin wrote in 1917: "The basic cause of social excess [and a crime is a form of social excess] is the exploitation of the masses [by the capitalists]. The removal of this cause will lead to the withering away of excesses." Viewing the state as an instrument for one class to exploit another, he added that crimes would disappear with the withering away of the state.[5] More specifically, Lenin felt that crime would diminish and eventually cease once Communism had replaced capitalism. Because the environment drove people to crime, there was no individual guilt, only social guilt—the exploitation of workers by capitalists. If society was guilty, there could, of course, be no justifiable or adequate punishment for a crime.[6]

In the Marxist sense, imprisonment was seen not as social retribution exacted on the criminal but as a means of reforming the prisoner. The length of the sentence should, therefore, depend not on the severity of the crime but on the individual prisoner; as soon as a prisoner reformed, he or she was to be released.[7] Such ideas were restated and revised, but never ignored, in major Soviet publications on the judicial and penal systems until the mid-1930s, when most of the Old Bolsheviks imprisoned under the Tsar were out of power or had disappeared in the purges. Once they no longer served the Party, these notions and their authors were consigned by the Soviet press and the juridical literature to the trash heap of history.

While these ideas held sway among Bolsheviks and their left-wing so-cialist-revolutionary allies (the Left Esers), the old criminal code was abol-ished. Unfortunately, nothing was promulgated in its place. (The Left Esers resigned from the government in March 1918 to protest the Brest-Litovsk Peace Treaty.) Meanwhile, however, the Soviet government set limits on pun-ishment for only a single crime in 1917: the failure to pay taxes was punishable by up to five years in prison.[8] Consequently, individual courts meted out "justice" with license. Judges feared reprisals by their political enemies, and communication among the judiciary was nonexistent, further complicating a system termed "extremely arbitrary" by a Soviet jurist. The jurist noted that while petty thieves were executed and some men received long sentences for a "bad attitude" toward their wives and children, murderers were known to have served no more than a month.[9]

Assuming that petty offenders reformed after five years, in 1918 the government set a five-year maximum sentence for all small offenses. Unfor-tunately, the definition of "petty crime" changed several times a year, and the system remained as arbitrary as ever; chaos prevailed until the introduction of the Criminal Code of 1922. No upper limits were established for the punish-ment of political offenses, and the lower limits varied from three to 10 years, but local judges ignored even these limits.[10] Sentences for political offenses were thus left entirely to the discretion of local courts. In 1918, for example, the Moscow Revolutionary Tribunal sentenced to prison a person who had kept the shoulder loops of various uniforms, including those of the White armies. His collection consisted of thirty-nine loops; he got thirty-nine years! Another defendant received nine years for having worked as a warder for nine years prior to 1917. The prosecutor, Nikolai Vasil'evich Krylenko, exulted: "You walked around the prison for nine years, now sit in the same prison for nine more."[11] Krylenko was a prosecutor at this and other major political trials until 1931, when he became the People's Commissar of Justice. He held that post for just under eight years; he was arrested and executed in 1938.

About 15 percent of those accused of political offenses were executed between September and December 1919, at the peak of the Civil War. Amazingly, or perhaps just as one would expect for such times, the same offense was considered political in one region, criminal or merely civil in another. Central law enforcement agencies were vague and inconsistent in dealing with political crimes. The Council of People's Commissars stated on 20 July 1918 that speculation should be considered a criminal offense. Two days later, in connection with other changes in court procedures, the People's Commissariat of Justice (*Narodnyĭ Kommissariat ĭustitsii*, or NKĬU) ordered speculation to be treated as a political crime.[12]

Arbitrariness of sentencing was matched by arbitrariness of release. The government announced eleven amnesties between 1918 and 1921. Various state agencies released prisoners spontaneously because of food shortages or lack of facilities. Fëdor Il'ich Dan, a prominent Menshevik who was arrested repeatedly during the early years of Bolshevik rule, recalled that prisoners never knew at any given moment whether they would be released or executed.[13]

During the height of the Civil War, Bolsheviks had more pressing matters to consider than the caprice of justice. If hooliganism weakened the government, consider hooliganism a counterrevolutionary offense. If someone stole a pencil from a government agency on a tight budget, thus undermining the efficiency of that agency, while a murderer happened to be a revolutionary fighter, then execute the thief and free the murderer. In the early struggle for survival, it was judicious to keep things simple. By the end of 1919, however, when a Bolshevik victory seemed probable, Commissariat of Justice officials felt the need for uniformity and rationalization, not for rational explanation. In theory, crimes were to have diminished after the October Revolution; in fact, the Civil War had resulted in a sharp rise in their number. The discrepancy between theory and fact could no longer be ignored.

The first legislation, "A Leading Principle of Criminal Law," was enacted on 12 December 1919. In writing this law, Deputy People's Commissar of

Justice Pëtr Stuchka restated the Marxist thesis that crimes result from the exploitation of one class by another. He did not mention Lenin's prophecy that crimes would decrease after the October Revolution, and he did not admit that crimes had increased since 1917. Avoiding any short-term predictions and hedging his remarks, Stuchka said that crime would continue in the country throughout "the whole transitional period from capitalism to Communism, the period of the dictatorship of the proletariat." Without guessing the duration of this transitional period, Stuchka asserted that both crime and the state would disappear only after the "final victory of the proletariat over all the bourgeois and intermediate classes."[14] The "intermediate class" was a new element in Marxist theory. An "intermediate class" or "bourgeois class" could hardly have existed in Soviet Russia in 1919, when private enterprise did not exist. Nevertheless, Bolshevik propaganda employed both terms without compunction. Those who fought against the Bolsheviks or committed crimes under Bolshevik rule belonged to the bourgeois or intermediate classes.[15] Stuchka was apparently using the terms in this sense. In fact, he didn't really need new terms. If there were no individual crime in bourgeois society, there could be no guilty persons during the transitional period, only a small guilty class. It followed that anyone who did anything to hinder the new Soviet regime was a counterrevolutionary. All crime was political.

Stuchka also adopted Marxist theory on punishment: since the environment made people commit crimes, there was no individual guilt, and punishment should not be seen as retribution. Stuchka added, however, that during the transitional period from capitalism to Communism, punishment was not merely a reeducational process, as the Bolsheviks had claimed in 1917, but a defensive measure by the state. Stuchka, in fact, asserted that punishment was a political act both in capitalist society and during the transitional period from capitalism to socialism (he was apparently the first to express this notion). In sentencing, judges needed to consider both the personality of the criminal and the degree of danger to the Soviet regime when the crime was committed. Under different circumstances, the same crime had different consequences. Naturally, the punishment for similar crimes should vary with the degree of danger to the state. Everything depended on the political circumstances. In explaining the arbitrariness of the release of prisoners, Stuchka added nothing new. Since the environment turned people into criminals, there was no point in keeping criminals locked up after the disappearance of the circumstances under which the crime had been committed.[16]

Several years later, Krylenko restated Stuchka's idea about the expediency of punishment. He claimed that during 1917-21 the task of the courts was not to guarantee justice but to ensure the survival of the dictatorship of the proletariat.[17] There were, in fact, many other agencies charged with and fired by the task of protecting the dictatorship, among them the Military Revolutionary Committees, which had organized Bolshevik military operations during the October Revolution. Immediately after the Revolution, they functioned as organs to suppress armed resistance to the new state, but their responsibilities soon broadened. Confronted by food shortages in the cities and sabotage by Tsarist bureaucrats, the Council of People's Commissars (SNK) ruled on 15 November 1917 that these committees should arrest any person suspected of speculation, hiding food, or sabotage. Suspects were to be kept in the prison at Kronshtadt, a naval fortress near Petrograd, until a revolutionary court could decide their guilt or innocence.[18] At the moment of the decree, however, revolutionary courts had yet to be established!

On 24 November 1917 the SNK abolished the old courts, which had not functioned since the October Revolution anyway, and instituted a new judicial system. This decree and another by the People's Commissariat of Justice (NKIU) on 19 December 1917 elaborated the rules and regulations of Revolutionary Tribunals and people's courts. The tribunals had jurisdiction over the offenses identified by the government as especially dangerous. These offenses, besides armed struggle against the state, included speculation, hiding food, refusal to pay taxes, hooliganism, and (sometimes) riding a train without a ticket. People's courts were responsible for all other cases. They heard civil suits and dealt with such criminal offenses as petty theft and assault. Judges of both courts were supposed to be elected: local soviets (councils) would choose the judges who sat on the tribunals; the populace would vote for judges on the people's courts. The Bolsheviks claimed that this new system was more democratic than the imperial system, under which low-court judges had been elected, whereas high-court judges had been appointed administratively.[19]

The election of all judges under these new procedures immediately created problems for the Bolshevik government and eventually led to the establishment of a punitive system in which courts played a minor role. There were always conflicts between the local and central authorities, and because elected judges depended more on local governments than on Moscow, they felt constrained to side with local officials. Regional and municipal governments tried to hide food from the central authorities, who had to feed several million people in Moscow and Petrograd. Kursk, Kaluga, and Altai provinces even proclaimed themselves independent republics.[20] The central government desperately required agencies to enforce its decrees in the provinces. Such agencies might have been the Military Revolutionary Committees, which had representatives in most major cities and were proving efficient by the end of November.[21] Unfortunately, they turned out to be too independent for the SNK.

Consequently, on 7 December 1917 the All-Russian Extraordinary Commission for Combating Counterrevolution and Sabotage (Cheka or Vecheka) was established, directly subordinate to the SNK. The Military Revolutionary

Committees were disbanded during the next two months. The head of the Cheka was a former member of the committees, Feliks Édmundovich Dzerzhinskiĭ. By the end of June 1918 the new agency had offices in forty-three major cities.[22] The Cheka was supposed to function as an administrative organ. By July 1918, however, the organization had already executed some people without trial. On 30 August 1918 socialist revolutionaries wounded Lenin and assassinated the chief of the Petrograd Cheka. On 5 September the Council of People's Commissars declared a "Red Terror" in response to the "white terror" of anti-Bolshevik forces.[23] With armed resistance to the Bolshevik government increasing all the while, the Cheka was authorized to arrest, investigate, and sentence persons at the beginning of 1919.[24] There was no right of appeal. With astonishing speed, the Cheka sentenced more than 60 percent of all prisoners and pronounced and carried out over 80 percent of all the death sentences issued during 1919-20.[25]

Attempting to avoid Cheka interference in their affairs, government authorities established their own organs of repression. In 1919 the People's Commissariat of Food Supply, the Commissariat of Internal Affairs (*Narodnyĭ Kommissariat vnutrennikh del,* or NKVD), the Commissariats of Labor, Transportation, and War, and even local soviets set up courts and investigative committees with the power to arrest people. In fact, the number of agencies that had the right to arrest people was greater than the number of agencies that did not. An agency or official lacking such a right had little bureaucratic standing. The most important agencies—the Cheka, the Revolutionary Tribunals, the organs of repression of the People's Commissariats of Food Supply, Internal Affairs, and War—also had the right to execute people.[26]

This gruesome competition had a comic side. In a popular Soviet joke, later used by Nikolaĭ Erdman in his play "The Mandate," a young petty clerk received written permission from authorities to occupy a small government-owned room. The document bore official seals and was titled "The Mandate," deluding the clerk into believing that he was an important person and that he had the right to arrest whomever he wished. Terrified by his growing desire to exercise that power, he ran to his mother and cried, "Hold me, please! Otherwise, I will arrest everybody in this country!"[27]

The distribution of punitive functions among government agencies has traditionally been attributed to the Civil War and to War Communism. To prevent hoarding during a period of extreme need, the policy of War Communism prohibited normal trade in foodstuffs, and special detachments were dispatched from the cities to requisition grain from the villages. This explanation is inadequate, however, because these agencies retained the right to imprison people months after the Civil War ended in November 1920, and arrests continued after the requisitioning of grain stopped in March 1921. The Council of People's Commissars finally revoked the right of arrest for most state agencies on 23 June 1921. It simultaneously decreed that no Communist could be arrested without the permission of the corresponding Party organizations—a fact overlooked in the historical literature. Administrative arrest still threatened the entire non-Party population, but now, at least, only four agencies could employ this measure: the Cheka, the NKVD, local soviets, and the newly established Administrative Commission of Petrograd.[28]

Soviet criminologists have frequently complained that reliable statistics on the number of prisoners during 1918 and 1919 are lacking. Only a few courts and penal institutions kept their records; most documents were destroyed when power changed hands in the regions. More reliable data exist for 1920. Aleksander Solzhenitsyn, who had access to Soviet archives, has noted that by the end of 1920, eighty-four places of confinement under the jurisdiction of the NKVD accommodated 49,736 prisoners; since the NKVD controlled about only 30 percent of such places, the entire system may have held some 180,000 prisoners. Solzhenitsyn believed, however, that the number of prisoners in NKVD custody was understated.[29] There are other, incomplete figures. A published Soviet report noted that 262 places of confinement under the People's Commissariat of Justice (NKIU) housed 55,422 prisoners.[30] Together, then, the NKVD and NKIU institutions accommodated more than 100,000 prisoners. Prisons and camps under the jurisdiction of the Cheka (with 40,000-60,000 prisoners)[31] and in the territories of the six Soviet Republics—Armenia, Azerbaijan, Belorussia, Georgia, Kirgiz, and the Ukraine—and the Bashkir and Tatar Autonomous Soviet Republics (with 10,000-20,000 prisoners) were not included in the report.

The numbers grew. By the end of 1921, NKIU places of confinement held 73,194 prisoners, up about 18,000 from the previous year. The NKVD housed 40,000-60,000.[32] No data exist on the number of prisoners elsewhere. If their numbers did not change from 1920, there may have been 170,000-200,000 inmates by the end of 1921, approximately equal to the maximum number of prisoners ever held in Tsarist jails—184,000 in 1912.[33] By the spring of 1922, prisoners from the Cheka had been transferred to the NKIU, which had 28,577 prison employees, including 10,000 military guards.[34] Prisons had had approximately the same number of staff on their payrolls in 1916, when they held about 142,000 inmates.[35] The NKVD probably housed 60,000. Again, there are no data on the number of prisoners in other places of confinement. If those figures remained constant, the total exceeded an all-time record of 200,000 early in 1922.[36]

Any comparison of the prison populations of Tsarist and Soviet Russia must consider territorial changes and the unprecedented number of executions by the Bolsheviks. In 1918, Soviet Russia lost 12 percent of its territory, 15 percent of its people, and 8 percent of its prisons to the Baltic states, Finland, Poland, and Romania. During their first four years in power, the Bolsheviks executed far more people than had the Romanov dynasty in its entire 300-year reign. Some sources have claimed that the Bolsheviks executed about 15 percent of all political cases between 5 September 1918, when mass executions began, and 20 January 1920, when the death penalty was temporarily abolished. If so, it means that 10 percent of all the sentences issued in Russia were death penalties, and that during the seventeenth-month period of the Great Terror between September 1918 and January 1920 the Bolsheviks executed at least 60,000 persons. And this number does not include many thousands executed without any trial.[37] Further, on the initiative of Stuchka, the NKIU introduced a new form of punishment, called forced labor without deprivation of freedom. Those sentenced in this way remained free but had to pay 25-50 percent of their salaries to the state.[38] This was, in effect, a fine in installments rather than incarceration. Since many persons sentenced to death or to forced labor without deprivation of freedom would have been prisoners in the Tsarist system, for accurate comparison they must be added to Soviet prison population totals.

After declining briefly following the Revolution, the number of prisoners rose to record numbers. During 1918-20 most people arrested were convicted of political offenses, because many criminals remained at large while the government was engaged in a protracted fight against its political enemies.[39] The proportion of political prisoners in the total prison population decreased with the defeat of the White armies, the famine of 1921-22, and the introduction of private enterprise in 1921. After victory and the demobilization of the Red Army, many soldiers joined the militia, and it became more effective than before in arresting criminals. Moreover, famine quite literally weakened the peasant protest against the requisitioning of grain. Peasants had been the majority of political prisoners. The scarcity of grain reduced their consumption of alcohol, and they became less rowdy. In March 1921 the Bolsheviks stopped requisitioning grain, and in that year the number of criminals equaled the number of political prisoners for the first time since February 1917.[40]

Before the Revolution, the Bolsheviks had viewed criminals as their allies. After the Revolution, opponents of the government saw them as their allies. Relations between political prisoners and criminals changed drastically after October 1917. Antagonism grew because the politicals got more food and lived in less crowded cells. They were under the protection of the Political Prisoners' Aid Society, which functioned freely from 1917 until 1922. The society had significant funds, and its representatives had the right to enter the prisons, to communicate directly with prisoners, and to offer food and clothing. The criminals, on the other hand, served their sentences in near-starvation.[41] No love was lost on the politicals.

The problems were exacerbated when prison administrations divided the politicals into two groups. The first group, mainly people who had tried to overthrow the Bolshevik government, was labeled "counterrevolutionary." It included officers and soldiers in the White armies and members of the bourgeois political parties, all of whom were treated as common criminals.[42] The second group comprised people who had protested against certain policies or insisted on sharing power with the Bolsheviks but had not tried to topple the government; they belonged to various socialist parties that had been considered revolutionary under the Tsar. Peasants and city dwellers recognized as dangerous to the Bolshevik government could be found in both groups. All of this was quite arbitrary, and the classification of prisoners often depended simply on who had arrested them.[43]

The prison administration employed some educated inmates to act as warders and guards. At a time when more than 50 percent of the country was illiterate, about 90 percent of the counterrevolutionaries and Group 2 political prisoners could read and write, whereas only a small percentage of common criminals were literate. Yet there was always a shortage of staff. Socialists adhered to the old prison tradition forbidding cooperation with the administration, and refused to serve as warders and guards.[44] The counterrevolutionaries, who as a rule had not been prisoners under the Tsar, did not know or care about the prison code of honor. Jobs as warders and guards let them survive. These jobs also allowed the counterrevolutionaries to exact revenge on the socialists for their previous lack of privileges in confinement and for their political defeat by the socialists in 1917.[45]

The prison administrations did not restrain their violence. Criminals eventually occupied the positions of warders and guards and followed the cruel example set by the counterrevolutionaries. It was natural for Solzhenitsyn and other former political prisoners to portray criminals as monsters and subhuman.[46] Such an attitude, understandably, was a complete reversal from that of pre-Revolutionary days when political prisoners and intellectuals sentimentalized the criminal, even imagining a natural alliance between criminality and political radicalism.

The Soviet prison system rapidly decentralized. Three agencies, the NKIU, the NKVD, and the Cheka, supervised inmates during this period, each with approximately the same number of prisoners.[47] Decentralization was even greater than under the Tsar, whose Ministry of Justice, it may be remembered, had controlled more than 80 percent of all prisoners.[48] Soviet penologists had originally intended to put all prisoners except juveniles under the control of the Commissariat of Justice; they had wanted a centralized prison system.[49] As in so many matters at this time, quite the opposite occurred.

3 THE NKĨU's RISE TO POWER

While struggling to take power before the October Revolution, Lenin insisted that the Bolsheviks already had their own unique form of government: the soviet, or revolutionary council.[1] After the Bolsheviks seized power, Lenin gave the local soviets substantial powers in the provinces. This tactic led to problems for the Bolshevik government in Petrograd. The soviets were elected locally and acted independently during the first months after the Revolution. Several proclaimed that their provinces had become independent republics. In its effort to control these regions, the central government established new agencies to carry out its orders.

The Bolshevik judicial system offered a classic example of this practice. The Cheka replaced the Revolutionary Tribunals and people's courts of the People's Commissariat of Justice (NKĨU), which had functioned partly under the jurisdiction of local soviets. The Cheka would reassert the primacy of the central government, now located in Moscow. With this single, bold stroke, the NKĨU lost its control over the judiciary.[2]

THE NKĨU EXPERIMENT

An undated telegram from the People's Commissariat of Justice apparently written just after the Bolsheviks came to power warned of impending changes in the provincial prison administrations, at the time called "prison inspections." The telegram informed local soviets and provincial prison authorities about a decree of the Council of People's Commissars (SNK) which transformed the inspections into "executive agencies" of the provincial soviets. The post of provincial commissar was abolished. Prison funds previously at his disposal were transferred to the soviets. Henceforth, the soviets would handle all financial transactions between the Main Administration of Places of Confinement (GUMZ) and its local offices, the provincial inspections. The soviets would also regulate the financial activities of the provincial inspectors. The

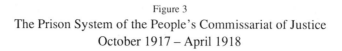

Figure 3

The Prison System of the People's Commissariat of Justice
October 1917 – April 1918

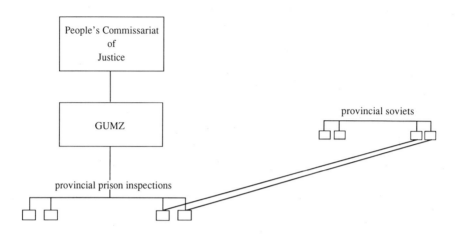

Provincial soviets replaced the provincial commissars of the Provisional Government.

telegram stressed that the Society of Prisons' Trustees and its local offices
would continue their functions, but local soviets would appoint the Directors.
The Council of Prison Affairs was not mentioned. It apparently ceased to exist
after the October Revolution.[3]

Despite many similarities to the SNK decree on the judicial system, this
new SNK decree on the prison system had one distinctive feature. The judicial
system was being decentralized, and the SNK decree disbanded pre-Revolutionary central agencies without establishing new ones; the People's Commissariat of Justice actually lacked any means to control local courts. The
prison system, on the other hand, was supposed to have a central agency, and
the SNK left the Main Administration of Places of Confinement (GUMZ)
intact. This was useful, because the NKIU had experienced personnel who
could control local camps and prisons. But the NKIU had its own ideas. It
intended to disband the GUMZ and to establish a new agency in a general
reform of the Russian prison system.[4]

The NKIU, headed by Left Eser Evgenii Shteĭnberg and his deputy Petr
Stuchka, adopted a policy toward the GUMZ which resembled Trotsky's
slogan about negotiating with the Germans at Brest-Litovsk: "Neither war nor
peace." The NKIU continued to pay the salaries of GUMZ officials but
otherwise ignored them.[5] Except for its telegram to local offices on the SNK
decree, Justice even avoided mentioning the GUMZ by name, instead refer-

ring to it in two enactments of 12 and 19 December 1917 merely as a "prison administration" (tíuremnoe upravlenie).[6] Solzhenitsyn and others have erroneously accepted this term as a legal title.[7] It should be mentioned, however, that terms in government decrees were often arbitrary and confusing after the October Revolution because the new rulers lacked experience drafting official documents.

An NKĨU board assumed the responsibilities of the GUMZ, its five members charged with running the whole Commissariat of Justice. They had no time to develop relations with local prisons. During the seven months that this board functioned as the central prison agency, seven acts were published on the places of confinement—five by the NKĨU, one by the SNK, and one by the People's Commissariat of War. Five dealt exclusively with the Petrograd prisons; the other two concerned the prison system as a whole. The board was simply overwhelmed. The five enactments on the Petrograd prisons tried to solve the most urgent problems. Prisons were overcrowded; there was not enough food; they lacked medicines. On 15 December 1917 the NKĨU ordered that all newly arrested prisoners be transferred from the Bolshevik headquarters in the Smolnyĭ Institute in Petrograd and from a new prison established in the former palace of Grand Duke Nikolaĭ Nikolaevich to six pre-Revolutionary prison facilities in the city. This same decree set up temporary investigative commissions to verify the correctness of charges within forty-eight hours of an arrest: the commissions were either to release a prisoner or to send his or her files to court. On 12 January 1918 another decree established a medical commission to check prisoners' complaints about diseases in the Petrograd prisons. On 19 January the People's Commissariat of War transferred all prison "personnel and property" of the former Ministry of War in Petrograd and Kronshtadt to the NKĨU.[8]

The prisons remained overcrowded. By the end of January 1918, conditions in the Petrograd jails were so desperate that Lenin ordered the People's Commissariats of Justice and Food Supply to distribute food "unconditionally . . . in accordance with the requests of the prisons." He also mandated that one-third to one-half of the inmates be transferred to provincial prisons where the food supply was satisfactory.[9] This order was largely ignored; few local prisons were willing to accept prisoners from Petrograd, and the problem was never really solved. Food has always been inadequate at Soviet prisons. Sometimes it has been withheld purposely; sometimes hunger was merely a fact of Soviet life.

The two additional NKĨU acts on the Russian prison system were general in nature. The problems of individual places of confinement outside Petrograd were not addressed, much less known, in Petrograd and Moscow. The NKĨU's organization of the Prison Commission on 6 January 1918 seemed hopeful. It was supposed to consist of representatives of the People's Commissariats of Labor, Education, and Welfare plus commissars of the Petrograd prisons and commissars from major provincial prison administrations—but no one from the provinces came to its single session, which established a governing bureau. The bureau was given four major responsibilities: (1) to supervise all prison activities; (2) to take drastic action in emergencies, subject to NKĨU approval; (3) to establish the necessary organs for accomplishing specific tasks, such as forming a commission on prison affairs and another on assistance to prisoners who had been released; and (4) to prepare a "broad reform" of the Russian prison system. The bureau set about assuming the functions of the GUMZ and the disbanded Council on Prison Affairs. It had only three members, however, and was merely able to prepare the reform. It chose to do nothing, or simply could do nothing, about the immediate problems at the places of confinement.[10]

On 24 January 1918, the NKĨU bypassed both the GUMZ and the Prison Commission and ordered all able-bodied prisoners, including convicts and suspects—that is, persons arrested but not yet convicted—who were traditionally kept in jail, to be divided into "work teams."[11] In signing the order, Deputy People's Commissar of Justice Left Eser L. Shreider initiated a brutal new era in the Russian prison system.

Afraid that opponents of the government would criticize the new order, the NKĨU at first limited the use of prison labor: the jobs of prisoners were not to be more difficult than the jobs performed by unskilled laborers. This limitation was introduced to prevent prison administrations from creating work merely to punish prisoners. The NKĨU ruled that prisoners' salaries should equal the wages of free workers in similar jobs, and deductions from prisoners' salaries to finance the facilities were not to exceed 33 percent.[12] (Recall that in Imperial Russia the deductions had varied from 60 to 90 percent of salary.) While serving their terms, however, inmates could use only 10 percent of what remained after the 33 percent deduction. The balance was to be returned to them upon their release.[13]

The NKĨU act on "work teams" initially came to nothing because the Commissariat had no way to enforce the order. During 1918-19, hardly more than 2 percent of all NKĨU prisoners worked.[14] In Imperial Russia, the share had been 40 percent, or about 20 times higher.[15] Several authoritative studies have overlooked this NKĨU decree, leaving the impression that the Left Esers did not participate in the creation of forced labor at places of confinement. There was, in fact, no disagreement between the Bolsheviks and the Left Esers on this subject. Leaders of both groups believed that the slogan "He who does not work shall not eat" meant prisoners too.[16]

Faced with extinction, the Main Administration of Places of Confinement simply went on with its business. Isolated from all sources of information by the NKĨU board, the GUMZ was out of touch with reality. It continued to send circular letters to local prisons, including some in Bessarabia as late as April 1918. Bessarabia had been taken over by Romania in January 1918.[17]

In November 1917, prison guards and warders in Petrograd and Moscow dismissed all supervisory staff appointed by the GUMZ before the Revolution, and elected their own supervisors without even consulting the GUMZ. An NKIU official later complained that the elected prison administrators ignored their duties and let the prisons run themselves.[18]

The GUMZ was finally disbanded in April or May 1918. Its demise followed the breakdown of the coalition government: On 15 March, the Left Esers, including People's Commissar Shteinberg, quit the government to protest the ratification of the Brest-Litovsk Peace Treaty. The Bolshevik Petr Stuchka replaced Shteinberg and abolished the GUMZ; its archives and several employees were transferred to Moscow. Bolsheviks would later blame Eser mismanagement for the inefficiency of the prison system in the first months after the Revolution.[19] The Esers, on the other hand, saw their prison policy as more liberal than Bolshevik administration and criticized the harshness of the Bolshevik regimen.[20]

Both were wrong. The NKIU's failure to establish any effective contacts with most of the local prisons persisted not months but years after the October Revolution. The Bolsheviks and Left Esers did not seriously disagree about the GUMZ or how to reform the penal system. Members of both parties had been political prisoners who despised officials of the GTU and GUMZ equally. After the Left Esers departed from the People's Commissariat of Justice, the Bolsheviks did not fundamentally alter the "Temporary Instruction on the Deprivation of Freedom" formulated by the Eser-run Bureau of the Prison Commission during January-March 1918.

The Temporary Instruction introduced sweeping prison reforms in July 1918. It altered the basis for the segregation of inmates, established a new central prison agency, and changed the relations between the agency and its local offices and the places of confinement. Following Lenin's idea that the severity of punishment should not depend on the severity of the crime, the Instruction ended segregation of inmates according to their crimes. Members of the military were incarcerated with civilians, and clergy with laity, though the segregation of men from women and juveniles from adults was preserved, and the Instruction implicitly retained the separation of political prisoners from common criminals and inmates of the privileged classes from the underprivileged. *Katorga* and corrective prisons were abolished, and the places of confinement of the Ministries of Marine and War as well as local prisons under *zemstvo* and Cossack administration were closed.[21]

The new system of segregation sought to reform rather than punish prisoners. New units were organized: (1) prisons, including transit facilities, for most inmates; (2) correctional penal institutions, primarily reformatories and agricultural colonies, for younger inmates, not including juveniles who were under the jurisdiction of the People's Commissar of Welfare; (3) probational institutions for prisoners from the first two categories who behaved; and (4) special prisons, called isolators, for those who didn't. There were also hospitals and mental institutions.[22]

All the pre-Revolutionary penal facilities, except for police stations, fell under the aegis of the NKĨU. The militia of the People's Commissariat of Internal Affairs (NKVD) replaced the police and took control of these stations. Yet despte its broad new powers, the NKĨU failed to use them. The Cheka began to occupy many former prisons. Agencies without any connection with the prison system used some facilities as offices and warehouses. Lenin signed a decree on 5 October 1920 telling agencies to return them to the NKĨU, but most simply ignored the order.[23] Putting Justice at a greater disadvantage in the bureaucratic infighting, the provincial offices of the NKĨU proved even more independent than the rural offices of other central agencies.

To bring order to the system, the Instruction established the Central Penal Department (Tsentral'nyĭ karatel'nyĭ otdel, or TSKO). It assumed the responsibilities of the old Main Administration of Places of Confinement, the Society of Prisons' Trustees, and the Observation Commission. The chief was supposed to be the People's Commissar of Justice or a member of the Commissariat board, which appointed all TSKO members.[24]

The Central Penal Department had nine divisions.[25] The first was concerned with applying the penitentiary theories of what was known as Consultative Body #1 (see below). This division established colonies and institutions, organized work outside the prisons, and set wages. It tested the impact of various jobs, rewards, and punishments on inmate behavior; provided general and vocational education for prisoners; and organized seminars and workshops for teachers and staff at the places of confinement.

The second division distributed prisoners according to instructions from the first and processed data from questionnaires. It was charged with locating the places of confinement, and with helping local agencies find administrators and teachers. It supervised the regime at penal institutions and reviewed prisoner complaints and petitions.

Third, a technical division, established shops and supplied tools and equipment to the places of confinement. It was also responsible for the vocational training of inmates. This duty conflicted with the responsibilities of the first division, but the Instruction did not clarify who was to do what. The fourth was the agricultural division, charged with setting up agricultural colonies and training centers, assisting local offices to find specialists, and supplying agricultural equipment to the colonies. It too sometimes encroached on the responsibilities of the first division. The fifth, the medical division, was to cooperate with the Commissariat of Public Health in organiz-

Figure 4
The Prison System of the People's Commissariat of Justice
July 1918 – October 1922

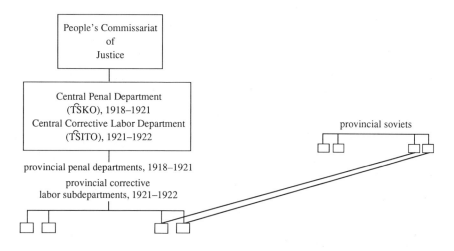

Provincial penal departments were incorporated into provincial soviets.
The Agency and its provincial offices were renamed in the spring of 1921.
In October 1922 the confinement facilities of the NKIÛ (Justice) were
transferred to Internal Affairs (NKVD).

ing medical services at places of confinement. It set up hospitals and outpa-
tient clinics, supplied medical equipment, determined occupational health
standards and diets, and processed prison records.

Sixth, the Supply Division was to provide prisoners and staff with their
food and clothing; it also armed the convoy guards. Seventh, the construction
division built or rented and maintained facilities to hold prisoners. The eighth
division, the convoy guards, organized teams to transport prisoners and
supplied the guards with housing, food, and clothing. The ninth division,
charged with assisting prisoners who had been released, established offices
in various localities and organized conferences and workshops for office employees.

The Penal Department also set up three permanent consultative bodies.
Consultative Body #1, which dealt with theory, consisted of the chiefs of the
first, second, fifth, and ninth divisions and their deputies. Consultative Body
#2, which concentrated on practical problems, included chiefs and deputies
of the first, second, third, fourth, and fifth divisions. Consultative Body #3,
concerned with supply and maintenance, included chiefs and deputies of the
third, fifth, sixth, and seventh divisions. These groups frequently heard from

specialists invited by the divisional chiefs. They were entirely consultative and had no legal power. By their very existence, however, they limited the authority of the chief of the Central Penal Department.[26]

Local penal departments were established in the fifty-nine provinces of Russia. Each had a representative in the NKĨU office or the court department in the provincial soviets. Each soviet appointed the chief of the provincial penal department (though the NKĨU could veto the choice), and the chief selected other members of the department with the approval of the NKĨU provincial office. Each department included specially trained teachers or psychiatrists to help with the "rational" distribution of prisoners. These psychiatrists, along with engineers, technicians, agricultural specialists, and medical doctors, made up the consultative body of the provincial penal department, which was supposed to advise the department chief. The chief conveyed these recommendations to a Distributive Commission in each province, which included the chief of the provincial penal department, his deputy or someone selected by the provincial soviets with the approval of the Department, directors of prison facilities in the province, and a few specialists.[27]

The Distributive Commission had broad responsibilities. In addition to distributing prisoners among the provincial places of confinement, it could petition a local court for a parole or, for an inmate still under interrogation, with the corresponding interrogative commission. The time spent behind bars was not as important to the parole board as the class origin and personality of an inmate. The commission had the exclusive right to isolate in a punishment cell any prisoner who refused to work or otherwise transgressed the rules. It could also ask a local people's court or Revolutionary Tribunal to keep in prison an inmate who had finished his or her sentence; that person could be classified a hooligan or a nonreforming recidivist and be detained until he or she reformed. The commission even controlled aspects of daily prison life. Although rules prohibited prisoners from receiving food above the ration, the commission could and did permit inmates to get packages from the outside. The additional food could not be eaten solely by the inmate but had to be distributed among other prisoners. This rule reflected the tradition of the political prisoners in Imperial Russia.[28]

Provincial penal departments possessed the right to set the rules for regional prisons. Because the July 1918 Instruction was so vague, provincial departments used the rules and regulations of pre-Revolutionary codes, if they "had not been abolished by the Revolution and did not contradict the present Instruction." The provincial departments controlled all the prisons in the province except those directly supervised by the Central Penal Department. Such institutions were apparently intended for enemies of the regime.[29]

The staff at each place of confinement included a director (*nachal'nik* or *direktor*), one to two deputies, a head of the technical subdivision, with an instructor for each major trade, a head of the corrective subdivision with corrective assistants for each group of inmates, and a head of the educational subdivision with teachers and some medical personnel.[30] As previously mentioned, inmates were divided into groups on the basis of their personalities and class origins. This was not considered the same as segregating nobles from commoners in pre-Revolutionary Russia. It was simply felt that class determined consciousness, and consciousness fixed personality.[31]

The director, the deputies, the heads of the subdivisions, and the medical personnel constituted a board responsible for all activities at the place of confinement. The provincial penal departments appointed the directors with the approval of the provincial NKIU office, and the directors selected the rest of the employees. Directors had the unique right to petition local people's courts to give an inmate a leave of absence up to one year "in case of the death of a father, mother, spouse, child or another close relative or for some other serious reason."[32] There is no record of how this rule was applied.

All able-bodied inmates were required to work. A physician and work manager determined their ability to perform various jobs. Labor compensation was to conform to trade union rates established for similar work in regions where the jails were located. Inmates received one-third of their salaries, and the TSKO took the remainder: that is, the Instruction doubled the deduction established by the NKIU law on work teams of 24 January 1918, bringing it close to pre-Revolutionary rates, which varied from 60 to 90 percent.[33] The two-thirds deduction was said to be temporary, lasting only "until the exact cost of keeping an inmate in a place of confinement was calculated."[34]

Inmates were supposed to work on a piece-rate basis. This allowed the administration to control their productivity. The Instruction tried to protect working prisoners from excessive demands by the prison administration. It stipulated that inmates were to participate in the commission which set the norms.[35] Letting the inmates sit on the commission was part of the tendency after the October Revolution to establish worker control of industry. Labor legislation of 1917-18 stressed that free workers should join in establishing production norms. Productivity, not surprisingly, began to fall throughout the country, and by the beginning of 1919 the government had criticized the practice. By the middle of the year, workers' control of industry had ended, and forced labor was introduced throughout Russia.[36] In prisons, however, the July Instruction's provision for inmate participation in establishing production norms had no practical significance, because hardly 2 percent of all inmates worked.[37] The next NKIU statutes, issued 15 November 1920, failed to mention this provision at all. The omission is particularly interesting because it showed that the government did not distinguish between working inmates and free workers during the first years after the October Revolution.

The Instruction did provide, however, that inmates who refused to work could be incarcerated indefinitely; recalcitrant prisoners would not be released until they had repaid the prison for everything spent on their upkeep. For an inmate who performed badly, the food ration could be reduced, or he or she could end up in a punishment cell. Finances were paramount in the Instruction. It encouraged many small places of confinement to close, and combined the smaller guard convoys from towns with larger teams from cities. It further decreed that all places of confinement be financially self-sufficient. Funds were to be deducted from the salaries of inmates, or, for those whose health did not permit them to work, obtained by confiscating their personal property.[38]

By the time it went into effect, however, the Instruction on reforming prisoners was out of date, less than useless. The bureau of the Prison Commission had begun to compile the document before the Civil War, and it was published at a time when the Bolsheviks faced considerable armed resistance. Consequently, by July 1918 the government was concerned about keeping its foes locked up, not reeducating them. There were more problems. Foremost was the crucial fact that the People's Commissariat of Justice was unable to guard its charges. In disbanding the Main Administration of Places of Confinement before establishing the Central Penal Department, Justice had cut all legal ties with individual places of confinement and needed to establish them all over again. In any case, the individual prisons were not interested in renewing relations with the NKĨU, primarily because it could not support them; the NKĨU actually had hoped to be financed partly *by* them.[39]

The center did not hold. Individual places of confinement had to scrounge for their own income. Guards, warders, and even administrators had to take additional jobs to survive. Many guards carried on illegal businesses with prisoners, and almost all ignored their prison duties. A Colonel Nekrasov of the Tsarist army, who was held in a Petrograd prison from December 1917 to January 1918 on charges of high treason, recalled that inmates came and went at will. Homeless people entered the prison at night for the warmth and left in the morning, unnoticed by the prison administration. Stuchka said that in 1918 only those prisoners did not escape who did not try.[40]

The same conditions apparently prevailed at the special places of confinement supervised by the TSKO and housing political opponents. This was at the height of the Civil War, and the government needed to reassert its authority. Central officials found they could no longer rely on the NKĨU, and the Instruction was out of touch with reality. In desperation, the Bolsheviks turned to the Cheka. It was given control over some old prisons and acted quickly to establish new places of confinement. These were concentration camps.

The Cheka Prisons and Concentration Camps

Following the October Revolution, agencies that arrested opponents of the Bolshevik regime put them in their own prisons. The Military Revolutionary Committees, which assumed police functions during and for several weeks after the Revolution, imprisoned at the Smolnyĭ Institute the cadets who had defended the Provisional Government; the institute even housed a few members of the Provisional Government itself. Prisons of the Military Revolutionary Committees existed in other cities as well. And by the end of November 1917 the new Revolutionary Tribunal had set up its own prison in the former palace of Grand Duke Nikolaĭ Nikolaevich in Petrograd. Such facilities, established as the need arose, did not challenge the authority of the NKĨU prison agency; they were considered temporary. Neither the Council of People's Commissars nor the All-Russian Executive Committee (*Vserossiĭskiĭ Tsentral'nyĭ Ispolnitel'nyĭ Komitet*, or VTSIK) had issued any decrees to instruct the NKĨU. On 15 December 1917, the NKĨU board ordered all prisoners moved from temporary prisons to facilities in Petrograd under its jurisdiction and the temporary prisons in the city closed.[41] Facilities of the Military Revolutionary Committees elsewhere were shut down when the committees disbanded in the beginning of 1918.

The Cheka places of confinement differed from those of the Military Revolutionary Committees. Although the decree of July 1918 transferring NKĨU prisons to the Cheka and authorizing the formation of its concentration camps is unavailable, it is known that both Lenin and the Council of People's Commissars had approved of the camps from the outset. Lenin was clear on this matter. He sent a telegram 9 August 1918 to Evgeniĭa Bosh, a Cheka official, and to the executive committee of Penza province, where there was a revolt against the Bolshevik government, telling them to put everyone whose behavior was "suspicious" into "the concentration camp outside the city." The SNK Decree on the Red Terror of 5 September 1918 restated Lenin's command by ordering class enemies to be isolated in the concentration camps.[42]

The Cheka's main agency was called the All-Russian Cheka (*Vserossiĭskaĭa Cheka*, or Vecheka). No available document describes the structure or even the title of the Vecheka organ that ran the prisons and camps. It has been assumed by scholars that from 1918 to 1921 it was called Komendatura, because this was the name given the Cheka prison offices in the provinces in 1918. More information on the name of the agency is available for the later period. A former Chekist, E. Dumbadze, who joined the Cheka only in 1921, termed its main prison agency the Operational Department and Komendatura (*Operativnyĭ otdel i Komendatura*); it is possible that this title had been used from the beginning. Another former, Chekist G. Agabekov, reported that from 1921 the agency was named the Special Department (*Spetsial'nyĭ otdel* or Spe-

Figure 5

The Prison System of the Vecheka, GPU, and OGPU
July 1918 – April 1930

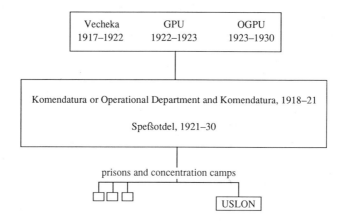

In 1922 the Vecheka became the GPU; in 1923, the OGPU. In 1920 the northern concentration camps were called Northern Special Purpose Camps, or SLON, administered by USLON; in 1922 or 1923 they were apparently renamed the Solovefskiĭ Special Purpose Camps. The acronym of both titles is SLON.

t͡sotdel).[43] The word "Komendatura" is the only major difference between these two titles. The adjectives "operational" (Dumbadze's version) and "special" (Agabekov's version) are so general that they can be interchangeably applied to Cheka subagencies. Memoirs of former inmates provide the major source for the history of the Cheka places of confinement. The inmates, of course, hardly knew the structure of the Komendatura, but their memoirs do reveal the composition and structure of the administration of individual prisons and camps. They also describe the expansion of these places and depict their living conditions.

The Cheka concentration camps grew rapidly. Ten months after they were formed, the Cheka set up another place of confinement—the forced labor camp. By mid-1919 the Cheka had established one or more prisons and camps in all major cities of Russia (Moscow had five), usually using the buildings of the katorga prisons (as it did at Ĭaroslavl', Kholmogory, Moscow, and Orël) and the large, ordinary prisons of the former Ministry of Justice. Prison facilities were still too few, so the Cheka converted some monasteries in Moscow, Kholmogory, and Solovki and took over the buildings of the former city government at Petrograd and private companies in Moscow and Rostov-na-Donu.[44]

Nothing succeeds like success. The Cheka had the exclusive right to send prisoners to its own places of confinement. Since the Cheka courts committed many more people than the camps could absorb, the organization was allowed to send its prisoners to NKĨU places of confinement, and, in April 1919, to the forced labor camps of the Cheka-NKVD. Statistics are available only for 1920. Cheka camps and prisons could probably hold 40,000-60,000 inmates, but that year Cheka courts sentenced some 100,000 people to prison. The Cheka sentenced about 50 percent of the prisoners in NKĨU facilities in 1919, and about 30 percent in 1920; it sentenced 44 percent of the prisoners in forced labor camps in 1921.[45]

The security problems at NKĨU facilities (discussed above) resulted in their transfer to the Cheka, which was determined to retain control over them and offered its guards greater compensation than NKĨU guards had received, primarily in the form of military rations. These larger rations had previously been given to officers and soldiers of the Red Army and to Chekist troops, whereas NKĨU guards had received only meager civilian rations. Now they benefited from the competition: in February 1919 the guards started to receive the same rations as Chekist soldiers.[46]

The Cheka used military terminology to identify its prisons and concentration camps as well as applying to its prison agency the military term Komendatura. The chief of an individual place of confinement was a commandant (*komendant*) instead of the traditional NKĨU terms supervisor (*smotritel'*), chief (*nachal'nik*) and director (*direktor*). A warder (*nadziratel'*) was now known as a military guard (*karaul'nyĭ*). The Cheka also used military terms to describe relations between the commandant and other employees.[47]

Because military rations were still significantly lower compensation than guards and warders had received in Tsarist Russia, Chekist guards—like their NKĨU counterparts—had to take additional jobs, engage in illegal businesses, frequently with inmates, and, by and large, ignore their duties. Hence, inmates escaped from the Cheka facilities almost as easily as they had fled those of the NKĨU. The escape rate was especially high for work camps near major cities in European Russia, where most large Cheka and the NKĨU prisons were located. The escape rates were much lower from places of confinement in the northern parts of Russia, where climate and vast, unpopulated spaces made flight virtually impossible. To reduce the number of escapes, the Cheka decided in November-December 1918 (1) to prohibit prisoners in large cities from working, and (2) to move more concentration camps to northern parts of the country, mostly to Arkhangel'sk province.[48]

Both decisions contradicted NKĨU policy. Certainly the Cheka was not bound by NKĨU directives, but Cheka administrators had followed NKĨU procedures for three months after the July 1918 Instruction, which stated that all healthy inmates must work. Few inmates in its institutions actually did, but the NKĨU had planned to introduce universal forced labor and to require prisoners to pay for the upkeep at all its places of confinement. The Cheka decision to prevent some security risks from working openly contradicted the intentions of the Commissariat of Justice.[49] It was, however, too late for the NKIU to do anything about it.

The literature on the Soviet forced labor system has traditionally portrayed the Cheka as its founder. It was actually the NKIU, and the Cheka in fact played a countervailing role in 1918. Wherever and whenever it could, it sabotaged NKIU policy. It is true, however, that the Cheka created the most difficult living and working conditions that ever existed at Russian places of confinement, the very conditions that gave the Soviet camps their sinister character. These conditions developed after the Cheka decision to transfer large numbers of inmates from its concentration camps in central Russia to northern camps in Arkhangel'sk province. Recall that the NKIU Instruction of July 1918 clearly stated that the jobs of inmates should not be more taxing than work performed by free laborers and that the salaries of inmates should equal the wages of free laborers doing similar work. The transfer of many inmates to concentration camps in the north rendered the Instruction meaningless.[50]

Forestry was the major industry of northern Russia. In Tsarist days it provided mainly winter employment because roads in the swampy Russian forests were impassable the rest of the year, particularly during the spring and autumn. Local peasants held these jobs. They ate their own food, wore their own clothes, and used their own tools to cut the trees. Peasants also provided the horses to transport lumber to the banks of rivers. During the summer, special teams tied the logs to big rafts and moved the rafts downriver to mills. Peasants were paid according to the forest conditions in the region.[51]

Inmates of the concentration camps, on the other hand, worked in the forest the year around. The camp administrators had no experience organizing the industry, no model to follow, and no efficient way to supply prison workers with the food, clothing, and medicines they needed to survive. The supply problems were exacerbated by the lack of roads from central to northern parts of the country. To reach the northern camps it was necessary to travel the rivers by boat or raft in summer and the snowbound roads by sled in winter. In Spring and autumn, torrents closed the region. The Cheka appears to have been the most efficient organization in Russia at the time, but even the Cheka could not supply so many things to so many people under these conditions. As a consequence, inmates died from starvation, exposure, and disease. The Cheka could not even organize forestry operations. Prisoners lacked tools to cut dry trees for bonfires when the temperatures fell to minus 40 or lower, and few inmates had clothing that could protect them in such extreme cold.[52]

Mortality reached 30 percent in the northern camps, ten times the rate at prisons in Tsarist Russia and about four times the rate at Cheka and NKIU camps in central Russia.[53] This high mortality rate, combined with the conditions of the Civil War, increased the hostility between the administration and inmates and among the inmates themselves. The death of one prisoner meant the survival of another; the survival of one meant the death of another. These conditions, with minor modifications, persisted in the northern places of confinement until the 1950s, when they improved slightly.

Reports written by the few survivors of Cheka prisons and concentration camps, especially survivors of the northern camps, are characteristically dry and unemotional. This was apparently the only way survivors could speak with any dignity of their ordeal. The reports seem as shocking as the photographs of the human skeletons in Nazi camps. A former prisoner describes the northern camp in Kholmogory in 1921:

> Of 1,200 [prisoners], 442 died from May to October [1921]: 12 in May, 20 in June, 30 in July, 80 in August, 110 in September, 190 in October (110 from dysentery and 80 from starvation). . . . The mortality rate increased when the weather got colder. The deaths were caused not only by diseases but by lack of food and by cold weather. Hungry prisoners ate everything [they could chew] and often got stomach diseases which their weakened organisms could not fight. Many recovered from typhus [800 of 1,200 had typhus] only to die from starvation. . . .
>
> Every morning the corpses were taken by a team of gravediggers, a former lawyer and two former students, who buried them in unmarked pits outside the city.

The summer conditions were "easier":

> On the way to work, prisoners begged for food and instantly ate everything they got, even raw potatoes. They tried to steal turnips from the gardens [of free people], and no punishments could prevent them from doing that. Quite a few were shot and killed by the guards while they attempted to run to the gardens. [Explaining the death of the prisoners], the guards reported that the prisoners "were killed during their attempts to escape." Prisoners really only wanted to stuff their empty stomachs.
>
> In addition to physical deprivations, the prisoners lived in an atmosphere of permanent fear of being abused and beaten by the administration. The previous Commandant Bachulis [1920] even shot and killed prisoners [for violation of discipline]. It was said he divided the prisoners into teams of tens and punished the whole team for any transgression by one of the team members. It was also said that when one prisoner escaped, Bachulis executed the rest of the team. When the escapee was caught, he was beaten and buried [alive]. Later on Bachulis became commandant of the camp in Portalinsk, 60 miles north from Arkhangelsk. . . . where Bachulis fully showed his cruelties. Of 200 prisoners who had been sent to Portalinsk from Kholmogory, only few remained alive [several months later].
>
> To disobey any demand of the administration was unthinkable: the prisoners were intimidated to such an extent that they endured all of the humiliation and [beating] without any murmur.

The conditions of women prisoners were both better and worse. The administration had complete power over them. [The women were required to have sex with the administration.] Only a few refused. . . . One of them was . . . shot and killed [for such a refusal]. The women begged another to agree—they were afraid that all of them would be punished [by the angry administration].

Prisoners were executed near the village of Koskovo. The people of the village heard the shots of machine guns, shouts, and moans. They said that 8,000 prsoners were executed over a period of several years.

The author of the report concluded if prisoners did not die, the conditions of the camp "turned them into pitiful, intimidated slaves."[54]

Other Cheka prisons and camps were not much better:

[In Imperial Russia] all prisoners received at least the basics—2.5–3 pounds of rye bread. [After the Revolution] nobody received more than a pound [of so-called bread]. In 1921 the bread of Orel prison was made from millet husk with small additions of oat and rye flour. The husk cracked in the mouth, stuck in gums, caught between the teeth. In the Vladimir prison the inmates received sunflower oilcake instead of bread.

[In Iaroslavl', during the summer 1921,] the prisoners received as much food during a week as they used to receive during one single day before the revolution. The kitchen of socialists [the most privileged category of prisoners] was near the toilet. . . . While going to the toilet, the prisoners jumped into the kitchen and took garbage (intestines of fishes, spoiled potatoes, onion peels) . . . and ate it. Emaciated, lacking any living color in their skin, the prisoners looked like skeletons.[55]

Inmates of city facilities—such as the Tagankskaia prison in Moscow in the winter of 1918-19—also suffered:

The [political] prisoners' food consisted of ¾ of a pound of bread (sometimes prisoners got only ¼ pound of bread.) They also received so-called soup, which consisted of warm turbid water with one or two potatoes. The conditions of criminals were even worse. But I hesitate to say what tortured prisoners more: hunger or cold. The prison was not heated during the winter: the heating system was out of order, and firewood could not be delivered to prison from the railway because the prison did not have a horse.[56]

The Butyrskaia prison hospital, also in Moscow, was no better during the winter of 1919-20:

The barracks had neither heat nor running water. [Because of lack of medical personnel,] the criminals who had recovered after typhus took care of patients. . . . The patients were covered with dirt and insects. They were lying on the [cement] floor like pieces of firewood. . . . The mortality rate was extremely high. Prisoners had the same paralyzing fear of getting sick, and therefore of being transferred to the hospital, as they had [of their executioner].[57]

In the Saratov prison, mistreatment was common:

In some rare cases the prisoners survived their physical and mental torture. Their disfigured bodies and their gray hair (which changed its color not from aging but from the fear and torture they experienced) witnessed more convincingly than any words what they had passed through. . . . Ivan Ivanovich Kotov, a member of the Constituent Assembly, was brought to his execution with an arm and leg broken and without an eye.[58]

The Ekaterinodar prison was no better either:

During four months of my imprisonment, I washed my hands and my face two times. The prison regulations did not stipulate that the administration should allow us to take baths. . . . The one-inch-thick dirt covered all of us. Herds of lice, fleas, and bedbugs crawled over us. . . . A bucket in the corner of the cell was the place where the prisoners took care of their biological needs. . . . The number of prisoners in one cell varied between 148 and 160. . . . More often than not they were thirsty. . . . The food was delivered in the same buckets that were used for washing toilets. No medical help was available. When one prisoner complained that his eyes hurt, the administration answered, "You do not really need your eyes in the prison."[59]

Ironically, some Bolsheviks who were responsible for the existence of the northern and other camps had vehemently criticized the Tsarist government for its cruel treatment of prisoners only a few years before. The irony was enhanced by the fact that during the Stalinist terror of the 1930s, some of these same Bolsheviks would themselves die in the northern camps. In fact, most administrative workers and guards at these camps were only marginally better off than the inmates. Because it was almost impossible to find people who would willingly work there, the Cheka had to use inmates as guards—mostly imprisoned officers and soldiers of the defeated White armies and former Chekists who had committed crimes. The strange circumstances of who controlled whom only hardened the feeling between the administration and the inmates.[60]

The northern concentration camps were given a new title in 1920: Northern Special Purpose Camps (*Severnye lageriﾑa osobogo naznacheniﾑa*, or SLON). The name change, for whatever reasons it occurred, stressed the special role these camps had in the history of Soviet prisons. The title applied only to camps in Arkhangel'sk province; other Cheka concentration camps continued to function under their original names until July 1922, when they were transferred to the NKĨU. At that time, the Cheka was replaced by the Main Political Administration (*Glavnoe politicheskoe upravlenie*, or GPU).[61]

Meanwhile, however, by transferring inmates to the north, the Cheka succeeded in reducing the total number of escapes. Although more inmates escaped each year from Cheka prisons and camps in central Russia than from a similar number of places of confinement in Tsarist Russia before the February 1917 Revolution, security at Cheka installations was better than at NKĨU facilities. The Soviet government became aware of the Cheka success in reducing escapes at the beginning of 1919. It decided to use the Cheka to correct another deficiency of the NKĨU penitentiary system: namely, the failure of the Central Penal Department to employ its inmates.[62]

THE CHEKA AND NKVD JOINT VENTURE

The NKĨU introduced the term "forced labor" (*prinuditel'nye raboty*). It initially had no connection with the places of confinement or with the two agencies destined to run the forced labor camps—the Cheka and the NKVD. Deputy People's Commissar of Justice Petr Stuchka proposed to the NKĨU Board in December 1917 that Soviet courts be given the option to sentence petty offenders to labor without deprivation of freedom; such persons would continue to work at their jobs or be assigned other positions by the courts, and pay a percentage of their salaries to the NKĨU prison agency. Without being very specific, Stuchka claimed he had borrowed the idea from Swiss jurists and adapted it to Russian conditions.[63]

The People's Commissariat of Justice objected that such sentences would be unenforceable. The Central Penal Department (TSKO) had too little power in the provinces. Nevertheless, the NKĨU did incorporate the proposal in the Instruction of July 1918. The idea of forced labor at places of confinement had appeared in the January 1918 law on work teams, a month after the Stuchka proposal, but the term "forced labor" was used in connection with the camps and prisons for the first time in the NKĨU Instruction.[64]

The NKĨU was right: it could not enforce sentences of labor without deprivation of freedom. By the end of 1918 it had to ask the People's Commissariat of Internal Affairs (NKVD) for help. The NKVD was willing, but it wanted to retain the deductions from salary of those sentenced to forced labor without deprivation of freedom.[65] The NKĨU, understandably, refused to accept this plan: it needed the deductions to support its own places of confinement, otherwise, it did not care whether the sentences were enforced.[66]

At the beginning of 1919, the Council of People's Commissars (SNK) and the All-Russian Central Executive Committee (VTSIK), agreed that the NKĨU would be unable to enforce sentences and looked for another agency to do the job. There were three candidates: the Cheka, the NKVD, and the People's Commissariat of Labor. The recent NKIU appeal to the NKVD for help and the Cheka success in strengthening security at the concentration camps made the choice easier.

The VTSIK published two decrees establishing forced labor camps on 15 April and 17 May 1919.[67] The decision authorizing the NKVD to supervise persons serving sentences of forced labor without deprivation of freedom was made at the same time but published somewhat later. The language and organization of these documents have left room for various interpretations. The decree of 15 April stated that the provincial Cheka offices should organize the camps, run them awhile, and then transfer them to the administrative departments of the executive committees of the provincial soviets. The administrative departments were local agencies of the NKVD. The decree of 17 May also authorized the provincial Cheka to set up camps but did not say who should run them. It simply repeated that having organized them, the Cheka was to transfer the camps to the administrative departments. In a provision dealing with the camp commandants, the decree stated that as a rule they should report eventually to the administrative departments of provincial soviets (the NKVD provincial offices) but temporarily to the provincial Cheka. This "temporary" measure lasted about three years: the Cheka ran some forced labor camps until the end of 1921.

The two decrees were inconsistent in naming the central agency of the forced labor camps and in identifying the role of the Cheka. The 15 April decree called the agency the Central Administration of Forced Labor Camps (*Tsentral'noe upravlenie lageriami prinuditel'nykh rabot*); the decree of 17 May called it the Department of Forced Labor (*Otdel prinuditel'nykh rabot*, or OPR).[68] The latter was the name that stuck and in fact more aptly corresponded to the tasks of the agency, because the OPR was responsible not only for inmates in forced labor camps but also for persons sentenced to forced labor without deprivation of freedom.

A year later, in May 1920, the name was changed to the Main Administration of Forced Labor (*Glavnoe upravlenie prinuditel'nykh rabot*, or GUPR). In the same month, its title was probably altered to the Main Administration for Public Work and Labor Conscription (*Glavnoe upravlenie obshchestvennykh rabot i povinnostei*). This subagency reverted to the name GUPR late in 1920, however, and kept the title until October 1922, when the NKVD absorbed all NKIU places of confinement.[69]

The role intended for the Cheka is unclear. The decree of 15 April stated that the central agency of the forced labor camps should be established "within" the NKVD with the "cooperation" of the Cheka. The decree of 17 May also stressed that the central agency should be established "within" the

Figure 6
The Prison System of the People's Commissariat of Internal Affairs
May 1919 – October 1922

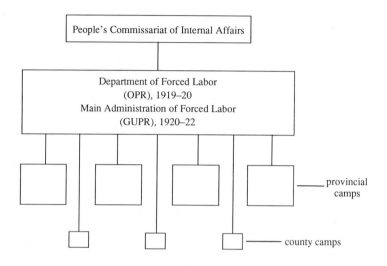

The Agency responsible for forced labor was renamed in May 1920.

NKVD but failed to say anything about Cheka cooperation.[70] Maybe this didn't really matter. At the time, the NKVD and the Cheka were extremely close. Feliks Edmundovich Dzerzhinskiĭ, who had spent eleven years in Tsarist prisons for his revolutionary activities, was both chairman of the Cheka and People's Commissar of Internal Affairs. Other officials of the Cheka also worked in the NKVD. The duties of many officers in these agencies overlapped.[71] However the decrees were worded, some cooperation was assured between the Cheka and the NKVD in establishing and running the forced labor camps.

The Cheka's role can shed light on the structure of both forced labor and concentration camps. We have a description of the Department of Forced Labor and its individual camps from the decree of 17 May 1919. No available document describes the structure of both the Komendatura and the individual concentration camps, but the memoirs of former inmates, portraying those camps in the smallest detail, indicate that the structure of the concentration camps was identical with that of the forced labor camps.[72] The Cheka merely used the concentration camps as a model when it set up the Department of Forced Labor–Main Administration of Forced Labor Camps (OPR-GUPR) and the individual forced labor camps. There is evidence that financial pressures induced the Komendatura and the OPR to merge—*de facto,* if not *de jure*—in June–July 1919, when various other departments of the NKVD and the Cheka combined.[73] The OPR-GUPR and the Komendatura were separated again in December 1921, several months before the government transferred the Cheka's places of confinement to the NKĨU. This was an administrative tactic to weaken the NKĨU claim that the forced labor camps had belonged to the Cheka and should now revert to the NKĨU along with the other Cheka places of confinement.

At some point during 1921, the Cheka apparently started to call its prison agency Spetsotdel. The Spetsotdel, which was also responsible for keeping state secrets and compiling and deciphering secret codes, was headed by an Old Bolshevik, Gleb Ivanovich Bokiĭ, a graduate of the Petersburg Mining Institute. Bokiĭ's deputy was Ĩa. P. Fel'dman.[74]

The pre-Revolutionary Main Prison Administration (GTU) of the Ministry of Justice had controlled about 80 percent of all places of confinement in Russia. None of the three Soviet agencies (the TSKO of the NKĨU, the Komendatura-Spetsotdel of the Cheka, or the OPR-GUPR of the NKVD-Cheka) had as large a share, though each of these three agencies had more control over its facilities than had the Tsarist agency. Before February 1917, several other agencies exerted some influence on the decisions of the GTU; these were shut down during 1917-18.[75] According to the July 1918 Instruction, no agency outside the NKĨU could control Central Penal Department activities. Furthermore, the Cheka was independent, and no agency outside of the Cheka was permitted to interfere in the activities of its Komendatura-Spetsotdel.

The VTSIK decree of 17 May 1919 forbade agencies outside the jurisdiction of the Cheka and the NKVD to control the Department of Forced Labor–Main Administration of Forced Labor. The OPR-GUPR was solely responsible for the forced labor camps. It compiled instructions, rules, and regulations; it estimated camp budgets, distributed prisoners among the facilities, and organized prison labor. The OPR, of course, reported periodically on camp activities to some unnamed agency, probably the NKVD board or, temporarily, the Cheka. The head of the OPR was a member of the NKVD board.[76]

The OPR-GUPR structure was more centralized than that of the Central Penal Department. Three consultative agencies, whose members were the chiefs of the nine TSKO divisions, had limited the powers of the TSKO chief. There were no such limitations on the chief of the OPR-GUPR, which had only three divisions. Its Administrative Division was responsible for personnel, statistics, and "all other issues that were not the responsibilities of the two other divisions." The Organization and Instruction Division was charged with setting up the camps, training and supervising personnel, "etc." The Mainte-

Table 2. Cheka Forced Labor Camp Statistics, 1921–1922

	Camps	Prisoners
1 January 1921	107	51,158
1 September 1921	117	60,457
1 December 1921	120	40,913
1 October 1922	132	60,000 (approx.)

George Legget, *The Cheka: Lenin's Secret Police* (Oxford: Clarendon Press), 178.

nance and Supplies Division was responsible for the construction and repair of camp buildings and the organization of prison labor.[77]

Control over the camps in the provinces nominally belonged to the administrative departments of the provincial soviets, which were subordinate to the NKVD. Power, however, belonged to the provincial Cheka, which was to establish forced labor camps in all provincial cities. Counties (*uezdy*) might also establish camps with the permission of the OPR. Each camp had to accommodate no fewer than 300 prisoners, since smaller units were considered uneconomical.[78]

It took the Cheka more than a year to fulfill these tasks in the provinces. At the beginning of 1920, eight months after the VTSIK decree, it had thirty-four camps with 8,660 inmates; near the end of the year, there were eighty-four camps with 49,736 inmates, and by September 1921 their population exceeded 60,000 (see Table 2). The number of prisoners decreased in late 1921 (perhaps because more convicts and political prisoners were sent to NKIU places of confinement) but rose again in 1922.[79]

All the pre-Revolutionary prison buildings filled quickly, and the VTSIK let the Cheka establish forced labor camps in monasteries and on county estates. (As previously mentioned, the Cheka had already converted several monasteries into prisons and even set up concentration camps in them. The idea of using county estates, however, was new.) The commandant of each camp was elected by the local executive committee and approved by the OPR-GUPR. Every two weeks, the commandant had to report to the administrative department of the provincial soviet or to the provincial Cheka, listing arrivals and departures, escapes, and any other extraordinary events.[80] These reports were mere formalities: neither the administrative departments of the provincial soviets nor the provincial Cheka had time to control the commandant.

The situation was different under the TSKO. Its provincial offices had no responsibilities other than supervising their places of confinement; hence, despite other failings, they managed to check on at least some of the activities of the TSKO provincial directors. The power of commandants of forced labor camps and concentration camps was not legally limited by any organization, whereas the directors of TSKO camps and prisons had to report to a board.

Thus, the commandant of a forced labor or concentration camp had undivided authority over all the inmates and employees. Responsible for all of the operations of the camp, he could punish prisoners and hire or fire employees.[81]

The commandant had two deputies. One was responsible for camp supplies and maintenance. The second was charged with organizing forced labor inside and outside the facility: setting up shops, providing tools and equipment, finding contractual jobs for inmates, and locating specialists among the prisoners at the request of various Soviet governmental enterprises. Clerical personnel consisted of a senior clerk, a bookkeeper, one clerk for each 100 prisoners, and one typist for every 300 prisoners. Routine supervision of the inmates was in the hands of a guards division consisting of a chief, two deputies, heads of two subdivisions, and guards. The number of guards depended on the number of inmates: two guards for every fifteen inmates in camps of no more than 300 prisoners; one guard for every ten inmates in camps of more than 300. Guards were subdivided about equally into the camp guard, which supervised inmates within the camp, and the convoy guard, which watched them outside the facilities. The military term "camp guard," like "commandant," had been introduced by the Cheka at concentration camps in August 1918, and camp guards of both forced labor and concentration camps had received military rations ever since the camps were founded.[82]

Provincial departments of public health provided medical services for inmates in the forced labor camps. Compared with pre-Revolutionary medical care, services were everywhere substandard—though inmates of forced labor camps got better medical treatment than prisoners in the TSKO places of confinement, simply because the administrative departments of local soviets had better relations with the public health departments of the provincial soviets. The VTSIK decree of 17 May 1919 stated that a doctor should visit forced labor camps at least twice a week, and a nurse should be stationed at camps permanently. Each camp was to have a casualty ward with fifteen beds for every 300 inmates.[83] The reality was something else. Forced labor camps had no qualified nurses; physicians did not visit regularly; and only a few camps had casualty wards. The situation was even worse at the northern concentration camps, where inmates had no medical assistance whatsoever.

The VTSIK decree restated two fundamental conditions of the NKIU Instruction of July 1918: it demanded that all inmates in forced labor camps work and that their labor cover all camp expenses. The only difference in the decrees was that the VTSIK enactment was more specific. It stressed that inmate labor should even pay the wages of administrators and guards. Both inmates and administrators would be held responsible for the failure to make the camp economically self-sufficient. A special instruction, which is not available, determined punishments for any camp budgetary deficit.[84]

As early as the beginning of 1919, NKIU officials had argued that places of confinement could never, in principle, become self-sufficient.[85] The uncompromising language of the VTSIK decree was apparently a response to such arguments. Nevertheless, the decree of 1919 did not tell camp officials to achieve self-sufficiency at any cost; it actually limited the exploitation of inmates, just as the Instruction had done. The decree sought to regulate the working conditions of inmates by using the same rules governing free workers in the country. Inmates needed to work only eight hours a day, mainly a day shift. Overtime and night shifts were allowed in accordance with the Labor Code. The salaries of inmates were to equal the wages of free workers doing similar jobs. Regional trade unions had determined the salaries of free workers. Both NKIU Instruction and VTSIK decree stated that workers were to perform physical labor assigned to them by administrators. The OPR-GUPR might allow some inmates to perform intellectual and clerical work. The concentration camps also employed prisoners as guards.[86]

The documents differed in two major points. First, the VTSIK decree increased the deduction from the salaries of prisoners from the two-thirds established by the Instruction to three-fourths. Second, it dropped the request found in the Instruction to hold inmates at the places of confinement until they could repay all the money that had been spent on their upkeep, and also mercifully omitted the requirement that prisoners who were unable to work pay their expenses from savings.[87] In any case, these last two provisions of the Instruction were unrealistic: the camps were already overcrowded, with no room even for new prisoners; and almost none of the inmates had any savings.

The VTSIK decree introduced rewards for good work. Prisoners who performed exemplary labor were allowed to live in private quarters outside the camps. They came in to the camp to work and went home at night. The NKIU Instruction had not included such a provision. Good work could also bring early release. Those incarcerated by an administrative order might obtain release from the OPR-GUPR by appealing to the administrative department of the provincial soviet. Those sentenced to the camps by a court could be released according to rules established under the NKIU Instruction: that is, in the same way that inmates at NKIU places of confinement could obtain their freedom.[88]

The most striking differences between the decrees appeared in the rules for segregation of prisoners, punishments, and relations between the administration and the inmates. In fact, the VTSIK accepted the rules and regulations established by the Cheka in its concentration camps. The 1919 decree had abolished the elaborate NKIU system of segregation based on class and personality; all that remained was segregation based on sex and age—though in some Cheka prisons and concentration camps, it must be added, men and women recognized as political prisoners were allowed to be together.[89]

A special instruction establishing punishments for transgressing camp rules is not available. The VTSIK decree itself specified punishments only for escapes. Just as at Cheka places of confinement, escapes were severely punished. For an initial attempt, the sentence was increased ten times: for a prisoner who had been serving a five-year sentence, the new term became fifty years! For a second attempt, the Revolutionary Tribunal would determine the punishment, which could be execution. A system of mutual responsibility was introduced whereby all inmates or a group of inmates at a camp were punished if a single prisoner attempted to escape. Inmates were to elect a monitor from their group to mediate between the prison administration and the prisoners, and inmate complaints were channeled through the monitor.[90] Before the February Revolution, political prisoners had struggled for the right to elect monitors in order to deal with the administration as a united group rather than separately; then, however, prison administrations had resisted the idea, preferring to deal with inmates on an individual basis.[91]

The NKIU refused to allow any monitors in its places of confinement. Elective monitors did serve in Cheka institutions among the politicals, but counterrevolutionaries and common criminals were not permitted to elect representatives.[92] The Cheka-NKVD may have accepted the idea to reduce the cost of supervising inmates. The system of collective responsibility seems to confirm that this apparent concession was actually a money-saving measure.

Just as in other places of confinement, the majority of inmates came from peasant and worker families. Of 17,000 camp inmates for whom statistics were compiled on 1 November 1920, peasants made up 39 percent and workers 34 percent. Of these 17,000, about 4,500 were imprisoned for counterrevolutionary activities; 3,500 for criminal offenses; 3,000 for speculation; another 3,000 for military desertion; and 2,000 for the misuse of authority.[92]

The forced labor camps were filled with people sentenced or ordered there by the Cheka. Even in 1921, when the people's courts and Revolutionary Tribunals regained some of the authority they had exercised in 1917 and early 1918, the Cheka still supplied the forced labor camps with 44 percent of their inmates. The agency was always looking for young, hard-working males. Thanks to Cheka policies and careful selection, the forced labor camps needed smaller government subsidies than the NKIU places of confinement. The people's court and Revolutionary Tribunals under the People's Commissariat of Justice had been unable to cooperate long enough to send many healthy young men to NKIU camps. Further, both courts and tribunals depended on the local soviets for their financial support, and the soviets were closely allied with the NKVD, which ran the forced labor camps with the Cheka.[93] The fact that the forced labor camps were somewhat more productive than the NKĨU places of confinement probably determined the outcome of the rivalry with the NKVD. In October 1922 the People's Commissariat of Internal Affairs absorbed almost all the camps and prisons in the country.

But in 1919, this outcome was by no means clear. Many government officials guessed that the NKĨU would monopolize the prison system. Both the Cheka and the NKVD were supposed to run their places of confinement temporarily: the role of the Cheka was to end with the Civil War, and the NKVD was to relinquish its responsibilities as soon as the NKĨU strengthened its ties with the provincial offices. The trouble was that the NKĨU lost battle after battle. Its problems had begun in the winter of 1917, when it disbanded the pre-Revolutionary prison agencies before organizing its own—an astonishing bureaucratic error and one from which the NKĨU never fully recovered.

4 REEDUCATION VERSUS FINANCIAL SELF-SUFFICIENCY

While it monopolized control of the Soviet places of confinement between November 1917 and July 1918, the People's Commissariat of Justice (NKIU) introduced four new ideas. It declared that (1) all able-bodied inmates must work; (2) courts could sentence suspects to forced labor without deprivation of freedom; (3) inmates must pay their own upkeep by deductions from their salaries or savings; and (4) the administrations of all penal institutions should reeducate prisoners.

The All-Russian Central Executive Committee (VTSIK) decree of 17 May 1919 authorized the Department of Forced Labor–Main Administration of Forced Labor (OPR-GUPR) to implement all these ideas except the reeducation of prisoners, which it simply failed to mention.[1] The Civil War had contributed to sharp increases in the number of crimes, and many former inmates committed new offenses as soon as they were released. The VTSIK apparently felt that this was no time to speak about reeducating inmates.

The NKIU understood this fact but could do little to advance its own interests. Justice had been unable to compete with the Cheka in preventing escapes, nor had it utilized inmate labor as efficiently as the Cheka-NKVD. The NKIU still had to compete for control of the camps and prisons, so it stressed reeducation as its unique contribution to the penitentiary system. The tactic backfired and was the major reason that the government transferred the NKIU places of confinement to the NKVD in 1922. The NKIU doubted it could make its own facilities self-sufficient; the NKVD expressed no doubts.

The NKIU as a Competitor, 1919-1920

The People's Commissariat of Justice had claimed that its Instruction had provided the structure and outlined the purposes of the Distributive Commissions. They were the only agencies corresponding to Lenin's idea about reeducating prisoners. But although the commissions were supposed to be functioning by July 1918, they still existed only on paper in June 1919. The NK﨎U complained that it lacked money to start operations but assured skeptics that the commissions would reduce recidivism. The V﨑SIK had its doubts, but Lenin backed the NK﨎U proposal. The decree of the Council of People's Commissars of 18 June 1919 restated all the provisions on the Distributive Commissions found in the July 1918 Instruction. It added a provision specifying that the government completely subsidize commission activities. Inmate labor as a source of revenue for the budget of the commissions was not mentioned at all.[2]

Lenin's support encouraged the NK﨎U. On 9 September 1919 it succeeded in upgrading the status of the Central Penal Department to an All-Russian agency, putting it on the same administrative level as the OPR-GUPR. The law was applied retroactively from 1 February 1919, or four months before the OPR was established. The Central Penal Department was to be called the Central Penal Department of the Russian Soviet Federated Socialist Republic (T﨑KO RSFSR), and each local office was termed a department (*otdel*) rather than a branch (*otdelenie*). These changes meant that employees of the T﨑KO RSFSR and its local offices would have the same political status and financial privileges as employees of the OPR-GUPR.[3]

Differences remained. Since the employees of the forced labor camps belonged to the Cheka, they received the larger food ration given Red Army soldiers, and they were exempt from military service. The personnel of the T﨑KO RSFSR, on the other hand, got civilian rations and might at any time be drafted. A decree of 1 October 1919 of the Council of Workers and Peasants Defense (*Sovet raboche-krest′ianskoĭ oborony*) eliminated these inequalities by exempting from the draft all employees of the penal departments, including the military guards who had worked for a department at least nine months. Simultaneously, or perhaps within a month or two, military guards at the NK﨎U places of confinement started receiving the military ration.[4]

Within nine months, however, the T﨑KO RSFSR began to lose bureaucratic ground. The losses did not result from the intrigues of its main rivals, the Cheka and the People's Commissariat of Internal Affairs (NKVD), or from any failure of the T﨑KO, but from interference by the People's Commissariat of Education (*Narodnyĭ kommissariat prosveshcheniia, or Narkompros*). Since its formation in 1917, the Narkompros had argued that all educational activities, including those at places of confinement, should fall under its jurisdiction. The Narkompros, in turn, was challenged by a private group called Proletkult, which claimed to represent the proletariat and wanted to control worker education. Proletkult based its arguments on orthodox Marxism, and its spokesman was the respected Old Bolshevik Aleksandr Aleksandrovich Bogdanov. Lenin nonetheless opposed turning over any administrative functions to a nongovernmental organization. He decided to strengthen the Narkompros at the expense of the NKĨU.[5]

The Council of People's Commissars (SNK) decree of 30 June 1920 transferred all educational institutions and activities (schools, libraries, lectures, and theatrical performances) at the places of confinement from the T̂SKO RSFSR of the People's Commissariat of Justice to the Narkompros (the forced labor camps and Cheka prisons did not have any educational institutions at this time). The move was a stunning defeat for the NKĨU, but the Commissariat of Justice was not completely excluded. In fact, the June decree created an educational system that encouraged its cooperation with the Commissariat of Education. The Narkompros and the NKĨU Board of the Places of Confinement (*Kollegiĩa mest lisheniĩa svobody*) were ordered to develop educational programs jointly. There is no information available on the composition of the board, but it certainly included the chief of the T̂SKO. The provincial penal departments retained their right to hire and fire teachers. They were compelled, however, to select the teachers from a list compiled by the Narkompros and to dismiss them only with the approval of the board. The departments had to adjust the educational activities of the Narkompros to the rules and regulations of the places of confinement.[6]

As a result, the T̂SKO lost those funds allotted by the government for education at the camps and prisons. This was a devastating blow, and the NKĨU fought vigorously to regain these moneys and its monopoly on education. It succeeded only in April 1922.[7] The entire history of the T̂SKO RSFSR was a series of budget cuts and futile attempts to procure government funds. The Statutes of 15 November 1920 reflected this financial dilemma.[8] The Instruction of 1918 had been temporary and was supposed to be superseded by the Statutes. The NKĨU, however, was unable to draft a comprehensive document on its penitentiary system, and the Statutes merely supplemented the Instruction. In particular, they failed to mention the structure and composition of the T̂SKO and its provincial departments, suggesting that both retained their structures. Individual places of confinement, on the other hand, were described in detail, whereas their structure and composition had been ignored by the Instruction.

The goal was to reduce expenses. The Instruction of 1918 had stated that each director of an individual place of confinement was to have one or two deputies. The November Statutes ruled that directors of small facilities should have no deputies. It also abolished some of the corrective subdivisions established by the Instruction, leaving the director with three: educational, labor, and medical (the Instruction had not mentioned that the medical staff should constitute a subdivision).[9]

The head of an educational subdivision was responsible for schools, libraries, lectures, and theatrical performances. As mentioned earlier, these activities came within the purview of the Narkompros on 30 June 1920.[10] TSKO Chief Leonid Arkad'evich Savrasov subsequently asserted that the provincial penal departments had to continue their education activities at the places of confinement because the Narkompros was doing absolutely nothing. In any case, the Narkompros could not fund the Departments.[11]

The November Statutes more than the 1918 Instruction saw labor as a corrective measure. The Instruction had stressed that inmate labor must cover the expenses of the penal system.[12] The head of the labor subdivision was required to organize work at the places of confinement so that it benefited both inmates and the various localities around the prisons.

The Statutes restored the pre-Revolutionary division into junior and senior warders (a distinction the Instruction had abolished) hoping thereby to attract educated people to begin administrative careers at the places of confinement. Junior warders were further divided into two categories. Even junior warders of the lower, second category were to be at least twenty-five years old, physically developed, literate, and educated.[13] Within a year, Savrasov complained that such requirements were unrealistic, that places of confinement were lucky to find anybody, let alone the literate and educated, to serve as guards and warders. The Main Prison Administration (GTU) had considered employee turnover a "plague" on the prison system during pre-Revolutionary times, but labor turnover during the Soviet period was significantly greater.[14] Nevertheless, to attract literate employees, the authors of the Statutes offered them certain privileges. An applicant who had graduated from one of the special penitentiary schools could become a junior warder in the first category without experience as a warder in the second. The provincial penal department controlled promotions to senior warder, and applicants had to pass a test administered by the department. It should be mentioned that the illiterate, poor people who were the absolute majority of warders and guards learned quickly—how to abuse their power! The Statutes stressed that employees at places of confinement were forbidden to have personal relations with prisoners or to use prisoners as their servants.[15] The warning had little effect.

The authority of the directors of NKIU places of confinement was vague. There were two conflicting tendencies. The Instruction gave directors the power to select all employees, who would subsequently be confirmed by the provincial penal departments. It stipulated, however, that the directors were not authorized to resolve general problems at the individual camps or prisons without staff approval. The Statutes made directors more dependent on the provincial penal departments and less on their employees: the deputy directors and the heads of the subdivisions could be appointed by the provincial penal departments. In case of a disagreement with senior employees, who made up the board at a place of detention, the director could ignore the opinion of the board—although if that happened, the board could appeal to the provincial penal department, which might overrule the decision of the director. The Statutes increased the authority of the directors compared with their powers under the Instruction. Their authority, however, still fell far short of that wielded by Commandants at the concentration and forced labor camps, whose power was not limited by any central or provincial agency.[16]

The Statutes did not alter the kinds of places of confinement established by the Instruction of July 1918, but they did set formal criteria for dividing inmates into three groups: (1) those convicted of crimes without pecuniary motives (*korystnyĭ kharakter*); (2) those convicted of crimes with mercenary motives; and (3) recidivists in both groups. The Statutes also established four regimes at each place of confinement: (1) a regime for inmates under close observation by the camp administration (*razriad ispytuemykh*); (2) a regime for inmates being reformed (*razriad ispravliaiushchikshsia*); (3) a regime for model inmates (*obraztsovyĭ razriad*); and (4) a punishment regime. Upon arriving at the prisons, all inmates were put under close observation. The inmates of the recidivist group were supposed to remain there for half their terms before they could transfer to the regime for inmates being reformed. Those who had committed crimes for pecuniary reasons had to serve a third of their sentences under close observation, and inmates guilty of offenses without pecuniary motives were to spend one-fourth of their terms, but not less than three months, under the first regime (the board at the place of confinement could petition the corresponding Distributive Commissions to reduce this term). Then, after serving under the regime for reforming inmates, a prisoner might move to the regime for model inmates. A prisoner who broke the rules went on the punishment regime.[17]

Those on punishment were often sent to solitary, though in some prisons, solitary confinement did not exist, and some prisoners were exempted from isolation because of their health. Prisoners on the fourth regime performed the most undesirable jobs, such as cleaning cesspools. They received one-fourth of their salaries after deductions, and the rest of their pay was held in a reserve fund. Once a month they could receive two packages, buy additional food, see their relatives, and write one letter. They had to serve a minimum of one month on the punishment regime before returning to observation. Inmates under observation were put either in solitary or in the general cellblock. These prisoners were allowed to spend half of their remaining money after the deductions from salary for prison maintenance. Once every week, they could receive a package, send a letter, buy additional food, and see relatives. Those serving under the regime to reform prisoners could choose solitary confinement cells or general cells. They could spend up to three-fourths of their wages after deductions, and twice a week they were permitted to receive a care package, but supplementary food, see relatives, and post a letter. They could also take a leave of absence for up to seven days every year, and the Board could petition the provincial court to parole such inmates after they had served one-fourth of their sentences. Model inmates lived in special facilities separated from other prisoners. They were not locked up during the day; they could use all of their wages after deductions and were allowed the other privileges three times a week; and they enjoyed two leaves of absence for up to seven days a year. The board could petition a court for parole after an inmate had spent one month on this regime.[18]

There were two major criticisms of these procedures. On the one hand, those who wanted to restore the pre-Revolutionary system, where the punishment fit the crime, claimed that the Statutes treated prisoners unfairly. For example, before being considered for transfer to the regime for improving inmates, a thief had to serve a longer term under observation than someone convicted of murder without mercenary motives.[19] On the other hand, orthodox Marxists could see segregation on the basis of the crime as a retreat from the Instruction of 1918, which had abolished such segregation. Those Bolsheviks who had been political prisoners in Imperial Russia might also object to the provision that allowed prisoners to receive care packages without having to share them with other prisoners. This provision violated a long tradition of sharing food in the political prisons of Tsarist Russia.[20]

The Statutes of 15 November 1920 changed the rules on compulsory universal labor. The Instruction had stated that all healthy inmates, both suspects and convicts, had to work. The Cheka revised this rule at its facilities, preventing some inmates from working for security reasons. The OPR-GUPR, with no prisons or imprisoned suspects of its own, put everyone to work; it was understood that inmates at all places of confinement had no choice of assignments. The Statutes ruled that convicts had to work where they were told but could choose any job that was available. The prison administration was supposed to weigh their individual work experience, evaluate the opportunities to put this experience to use outside the camps, and consider the needs of the region. Inmates might work inside the camps—at factories, shops, agricultural colonies, farms, and as support staff—or they could be employed outside them. In assigning outside work, the administration was obliged to consider who was likely to try to escape, and to build facilities that would allow guards to keep the inmates under observation. Despite these precautions, more than 50 percent of the 2,000 escapes at NKIU facilities occurred from job sites outside the compounds.[21] The November 1920 Statutes also restated the provisions in the VTSIK decree of 1919 and the NKIU Instruction of 1920 on forced labor camps. Inmates were to work the same hours and get the same pay as free workers in similar positions. The Statutes said that prisoners should work eight hours a day, Mondays through Fridays, and until lunchtime on Saturdays.[22]

The biggest change made by the Statutes involved camp upkeep. The VTSIK decree and the Instruction had insisted that prisoners pay for their own maintenance; the Statutes merely said they should pay "insofar as possible" (po vozmozhnosti).[23] In 1920 the NKIU had employed only 50 percent of its inmates. In forced labor camps, 60 percent worked. Trade unions resisted attempts by the government to employ more inmates, because so many free union members were unemployed. Many NKIU officials openly doubted that the work of prisoners could cover the expenses of their confinement. In any case, the major efforts of bureaucrats of the TSKO, the Komendatura-Spetsotdel, and the Department of Forced Labor–Main Administration of Forced Labor were directed not toward raising inmate labor productivity but toward getting funded.[24]

THE NKIU IN 1921

The NKIU's effort to stress the corrective or reeducational nature of the places of confinement culminated in the spring of 1921. It managed to convince the All-Russian Central Executive Committee to change the name of the Central Penal Department to Central Corrective Labor Department (Tsentral'nyĭ ispravitel'no-trudovoĭ otdel, or TSITO) and to call the provincial penal departments the provincial corrective labor subdepartments (Ispravitel'no-trudovye podotdely).[25] By selecting the words "corrective labor" instead of "forced labor," the NKIU appeared to claim that it had not made its places of confinement as productive as the forced labor camps because it was more concerned with inmate reeducation. The NKIU insinuated that the OPR had ignored this goal.

This was clever semantics. The word combination "corrective labor" proved to be the NKIU's most enduring and successful linguistic find. It appealed to the government for its propaganda value. From that time on, most places of confinement in the Soviet Union were called corrective labor institutions (uchrezhdeniĭa). What had propagandistic value for the government, however, was the target of sarcasm for the inmates. They called the TSITO the "Central Extermination (istrebitel'nyĭ) Labor Department" instead of the Central Corrective (ispravitel'nyĭ) Labor Department.[26] Some inmates felt that the administration was intentionally mocking them with this word play. If the Soviet places of confinement were to be called "corrective institutions," the Cheka should be renamed the "Commission of Mutual Trust."

The most significant document to describe the places of confinement was a report of the TSITO NKIU RSFSR in late 1921. It was signed by the RSFSR's People's Commissar of Justice Dmitriĭ Ivanovich Kurskiĭ and TSITO Chief Savrasov, and was printed by the publishing house of the Taganskaia Prison in Moscow. It identified the major problem of the NKIU penal system as a lack of funds. The central TSITO, its subagencies, the provincial corrective labor departments, and all places of confinement were in financial straits. The TSITO "significantly" reduced its staff from an unspecified number to 166 employees, but because of "incredibly" low salaries it could not fill many positions. Even jobs as heads of the TSITO departments remained vacant until November 1921. From its beginning as the TSKO in July 1918 until November 1921, 386 people had worked for the agency. Only seventy-one had stayed longer than one year. Labor turnover was notably higher than for most government agencies. The number of provincial corrective labor departments grew from fifty-one to fifty-nine in 1921 and created a total of 1,159 positions—which, as the report lamented, were "far from being filled." It was the usual reason: no money. [27]

The financial situation of the guards at the individual places of confinement deteriorated in 1921. By March they had been deprived of their military ration, though guards at the Cheka and NKVD camps and prisons continued to get theirs. The NKIU ration was meager and not always supplied on schedule. In many provinces, guards simply starved; in others, they ignored their responsibilities and tried to improve their own conditions by doing business illegally with the inmates. Under these conditions, only 72 percent of the guard positions were filled; in Arkhangel'sk, Kursk, Moscow, and Petrograd provinces, never more than 50 percent. Warders and guards were recruited from inmates and from people facing starvation in the provinces. Inmates performed their guard duties adequately, as best they could, but the TSITO felt this practice was improper. Nonetheless, the Cheka was doing it; the NKVD did it; the TSITO realized it had no choice. People brought in from the provinces "had neither experience, nor clothes, nor shoes, and could not work due to emaciation." [28]

The loss of the military ration meant the loss of military status. The Main Artillery Administration used this circumstance to stop supplying NKIU guards with the revolvers traditionally given only to agencies with military status, such as the Cheka and the people's militia. Instead, guards received rifles, which were more cumbersome than revolvers. The TSITO needed more food, uniforms, shoes, underwear, arms—literally everything. Without the military ration and status, the agency was helpless. [29]

In 1921, all the NKIU places of confinement employed 16,000 free workers as supervisory personnel and warders. The salary of a free worker in the NKIU penitentiary system was one-ninth the wage of a factory mechanic. This was a starvation wage, and there were not many takers. The salaries of clerks

Table 3. TSITO Places of Confinement, 1921

Accommodations	No. of Institutions	% of Total
more than 1,000	9	3.4
700-1,000	12	4.6
500-700	12	4.6
400-500	10	3.8
300-400	23	8.8
200-300	21	8.0
100-200	75	27.9
50-100	73	27.1
less than 50	32	11.8

were no higher than those of warders. As a result, they left the employ of camps and prisons in great numbers, and the administration was forced to rely on prisoners to perform these jobs.[30]

Despite the severe problems with staffing, the number of TSITO places of confinement grew in 1921 from 262 to 267: twenty-two new ones opened, eleven closed, and six transferred to the jurisdiction of the Autonomous Republics. Altogether, the 267 prisons and camps could accommodate 60,468 inmates (see Table 3). An average facility could house about 225 persons. The smallest, in Lodeinopol'sk, had space for 23; the largest, located in Irkutsk, for 1,436. But overcrowding became acute in 1921, as the number of inmates at TSITO facilities grew from 55,422 in January to 73,194 in November. This represented an increase from 93.4 to 121 inmates per 100 available accommodations. The thirty-six most crowded places of confinement housed 15,678 prisoners, or 254 for every 100 accommodations. Male-to-female proportions remained the same as before the February Revolution: 92 percent of all inmates were adult males, 7 percent females, and 1 percent juveniles.[31]

Convictions by the Cheka decreased in the early 1920s. In 1919, the Cheka had convicted about half of all NKIU inmates. The percentage dropped to 30.2 in 1920. In 1921, 31.6 percent had been sentenced by people's courts, 40.2 by Revolutionary Tribunals, only 21.2 percent by the Cheka, and 7 percent by other agencies. This decline resulted partly from the fact that fewer political offenders were being sent to NKIU places of detention, as shown by the figures in Table 4.[32]

The TSITO report of late 1921 described the food situation at places of confinement as catastrophic. Both the Instruction of July 1918 and the Statutes of November 1920 had stated that prisoners were to be given adequate amounts of food: about 2,500 daily calories for nonlaboring inmates and more for those who worked. It is doubtful that prisoners ever got this much food after the October Revolution. With hunger rampant in the countryside in the

Table 4. Crimes of Inmates at NKĨU Facilities, November 1921

	No. of Inmates	% of Inmates
Violent crimes	2,269	3.1
Property crimes	18,810	25.7
Speculation	3,587	4.9
Counterrevolutionary activities	8,637	11.8
"Office delinquencies" (embezzlement, bribes)	8,198	11.2
Other crimes (desertion, refusal to pay the tax in kind, etc.)	31,163	43.3

1920s, the official ration for prisoners was reduced "drastically" to an unspecified number of calories. The report laconically called the new rations "half-starving" and "starving." It said that if additional funds were not forthcoming, the starving ration would have to be reduced by one-third.[33] Were the writers joking?

The staple was bread. In many places of confinement, inmates got nothing but a half-pound of bread a day; in some, only a quarter-pound. Prisoners at the Samara Provincial Corrective Labor Camp were described as torpid from hunger; they spent their days scrounging the garbage for bones. A telegram from the Ufa Prison reported that from six to eleven inmates died there from starvation every day. Messages from many provinces spoke about the increase of disease and epidemics of typhus. The TSITO repeatedly threatened and pleaded with the People's Commissariat of Food Supplies about its urgent needs, and the Commissariat ordered its local offices to give food to the NKĨU, but the local offices time and again replied that they had nothing to give. The TSITO tried to grow its own food at the camps, but there was not enough land or tools or horses or seeds. The bureaucracy hoarded or confiscated whatever resources were available. Inmates were not merely hungry; they were ill-clothed and dirty. The People's Commissariat of War appropriated all TSITO inmates' clothes for Red Army soldiers; the People's Commissariat of Education took the inmates' soap for babies at the maternity hospitals under its jurisdiction. The report calculated that the TSITO would have been able to feed, clothe, and wash its inmates only if everything taken by other agencies were returned.[34]

Facing starvation, many inmates turned to escape. The few guards, fending for themselves, made flight easy. During a ten-month period in 1920, 2,315 prisoners escaped; in the nine months from January through September 1921, the number jumped to 2,762. Of these, 783 got away from the places of confinement, 1,644 from work sites outside the prisons, and 95 from hospitals; 240 fled while in transit. Ironically, the only thing that prevented all the inmates from escaping was hunger: in prison they usually got some food, however meager, whereas free people in certain areas were dying of starvation at higher rates than did the inmates.[35]

Soviet scholars often exaggerate the role of Lenin in establishing government agencies. One fact is indisputable: Lenin signed the decrees—but others enforced them. In the midst of the hunger and disorder the Distributive Commissions, established by Lenin's order in June 1919, worked effectively, and the educational system at NKIU places of confinement was relatively efficient. According to data from forty provinces, the Distributive Commissions in the RSFSR held 575 sessions during the first months of 1921. They discussed (1) 888 cases concerning the transfer of inmates from ordinary places of confinement to the NKIU agricultural colonies; (2) 1,229 cases about commuting sentences from deprivation of freedom to forced labor without deprivation of freedom; (3) 2,312 requests for prisoners to work outside the camps; (4) 1,767 petitions for inmate leaves of absense; (5) 3,744 requests for transfers to other facilities; (6) 2,707 petitions for parole; (7) 1,980 petitions for a change of regime; and (8) 175 appeals for probation. The Central Corrective Labor Department (TSITO) also made an effort to eradicate illiteracy. It hoped to raise the literacy of most prisoners to the level of first and second graders in Soviet elementary schools. Almost all places of confinement had some classes for political education, and a few even gave instruction in political economy, natural science, literature, hygiene, the history of culture, agronomy, and foreign languages. Many facilities offered art, acting, and music classes (some inmates participated in theatrical performances), and most had small libraries. These received books from the local departments of education, Party committees, and TSITO bookstores, though Savrasov complained that the supply of books did not satisfy the demands of the inmates.[36]

The report fully reflected the evolution of the NKIU view on inmate labor. The Instruction of 1918 declared that prisoner labor should make the NKIU places of confinement completely self-sufficient. The Statutes of 1920 stated that inmates should pay as much as possible for their maintenance and stressed that labor should be viewed as a form of education.[37] By the time the VTSIK changed the name of the Central Penal Department to the Central Corrective Labor Department early in 1921, the differences between the NKIU and the NKVD were clear. The NKVD still referred to its places of confinement as forced labor camps, whereas the TSITO report of November 1921, though it mentioned the desirability of higher labor productivity, never stated that NKIU places of confinement would or should be self-sufficient.[38]

Data on labor are available for 144 out of the 267 TSITO places of confinement, or 31,409 of the total 73,194 prisoners. The proportion of inmates who worked increased from 50 percent in 1920 to 55 in 1921. Some 17 percent worked outside; 10.8 percent were employed in shops within the camps and prisons; and 0.6 percent labored inside as cooks, janitors, maintenance personnel, and even as teachers, actors, musicians, artists, and lecturers. The government appreciated the political value of the shops to train the future proletariat. Inmates were employed as carpenters, cabinet-makers, shoemakers, painters, and metalworkers. In 1921 the number of shops grew from 184 to 471. By November, they were operating at 135 of the 144 facilities. The new shops were small, however, and apparently not very productive. The percentage of NKĨŬ inmates working in them rose from 2.5 in 1919 to 10 in 1920, and marginally to 10.8 in 1921. The 7,500 prisoners in the shops sold their products for 3,815,343 rubles in October 1921, a sum equaling the monthly salaries of just 1,000 free mechanics at factories.[39]

The TSITO blamed other agencies for not providing the tools for expanded production. It complained that the wages of shop workers were too low. They actually decreased in 1921, and inmates who possessed skills kept this fact to themselves in order to be sent to work outside the places of confinement, where salaries were higher. The TSITO was defeated by a kind of circular logic: if the TSITO lacked tools, it did not need more shop workers; if it couldn't attract more shop workers because of the low wages, it didn't need more tools. Whatever the logic, the agency knew it needed more resources and higher salaries. (Someone proposed improving management by deducting a percentage of inmate salaries for bonuses to be awarded to administrators, guards, and warders.) Inflation was the primary reason for the inadequate salaries. When the New Economic Policy reintroduced private enterprise in Russia in 1921, inflation soared. The fixed wages of inmates and prison workers could not keep up with the gains in private industry. In order to stimulate productivity, the TSITO passed a law on 23 August 1921 lowering the deductions on inmate salaries as their wages rose, and on 6 September 1921 it linked inmate salaries to the wages of free workers in similar jobs in private enterprise. As a result, inmate wages increased 100 percent during 1921 but still could not keep pace with the salaries paid free workers.[40]

The NKĨŬ had decided in 1918 that its agricultural colonies and cattle-breeding farms would eventually produce enough to feed the entire prison population. Workers also engaged in mining, transport, forestry, and peat extraction, but the colonies were considered the greatest resource. When the NKĨŬ abandoned the idea of self-sufficiency in 1920, these notions were scrapped—yet the report of 1921 still portrayed the colonies as models in reeducating inmates. The agency needed to demonstrate that its agricultural colonies and farms did better at reeducating prisoners than the industrial shops, though ideologically, one would have expected the opposite. Although the colonies and farms failed to feed all the NKĨŬ inmates, they did feed everyone who worked on them; in fact, they were the only NKIU institutions where inmates did not starve. The NKIU sent prisoners to the colonies and farms as a reward for demonstrating good behavior and for possessing proper attitudes, and inmates released from these institutions committed fewer crimes than inmates freed from any other place of confinement. The number of agricultural colonies and farms increased rapidly but remained a small proportion of the total: there were four in 1918, seventeen in 1919, thirty in 1920, and forty-one in 1921. By the end of the year they housed about 6,500 inmates, or some 1,000 fewer than worked in shops. The TSITO complained that it could have established more farms and colonies had it controlled the land and resources, or even received additional cooperation from the agencies that did control these resources.[41]

UNIFICATION, 1922

The struggle among the NKIU, Cheka, and NKVD to control the places of confinement was a natural bureaucratic rivalry. One factor made the competition especially intense and prevented cooperation among agencies: Lenin and other Soviet officials believed that all the places of confinement should be controlled by one agency. NKIU, NKVD, and Cheka officials expected an eventual consolidation of sorts. The introduction of private enterprise in 1921, somewhat ironically, strengthened a trend toward governmental centralization. The state tried to counteract the relaxed economic policy by tightening administrative controls.[42]

By the end of 1921, the government had decided to consolidate the prison system. Since the Cheka was the most centralized agency in the country, it might have been expected to head the revamped system. Actually, it had the least chance, for its dreadful image did not suit the government's policy of economic liberalization. Lenin wanted new restrictions placed on the Cheka and envisaged the development of rule by law. The Politburo of the Russian Communist Party of the Bolsheviks limited Cheka operations on 1 December 1921. Lenin told the ninth All-Russian Congress of Soviets on 23 December that the Cheka's work should be confined to "political tasks." The Congress resolved on 27 December that the NKIU, not the Cheka, should deal with lawbreakers.[43] Many officials anticipated that the Cheka would lose its places of confinement. But to whom? To the NKIU or to the NKVD?

The NKVD, as it had many times before, stressed that it could make the inmates more productive. The NKIU promised to reeducate inmates more quickly. The NKVD maintained that it could absorb the Cheka places of confinement with less disruption than the NKIU; the People's Commissariat of Internal Affairs previously had run the forced labor camps with the Cheka and knew its methods. The NKIU argued that Cheka places of confinement and forced labor camps had been established as a temporary measure for the specific conditions of the Civil War, so it was natural that the Commissariat of Justice should regain its monopoly over these places when the fighting ended. Lenin, once again, sided with Justice and its efforts to reform prisoners.[44]

The People's Commissariat of Justice held its Fourth Congress in January 1922 to formulate theses on the economic relaxation in the country and to put new restrictions on the Cheka. Commissar of Justice Kurskiĭ expressed his hope that the Congress would develop a comprehensive program to strengthen the NKIU's position. The Congress, however, split over every vital issue. In his report to the deputies, Savrasov restated the major points of the TSITO policy, asserting that reeducation was its most important goal. He stressed that the TSITO already had a reeducational policy, while the GUPR had none. Consequently, Savrasov continued, all the places of confinement should be concentrated in the hands of the TSITO. It, rather than local soviets, should appoint all the directors, and it should have complete authority to control everyone sentenced to forced labor without deprivation of freedom. Such convicts were currently under GUPR supervision.[45]

These were traditional demands and arguments. Savrasov, unfortunately, added a few of his own, much to the embarrassment of NKIU officials. The TSITO's pre-Revolutionary predecessor, the Main Prison Administration, had never been an independent agency and had never demanded independence. Savrasov, nonetheless, claimed that reeducation at places of confinement had nothing to do with the NKIU; therefore, the TSITO should be made an independent agency, not a subagency of the NKIU. He also reinterpreted the position of the People's Commissariat of Justice on the self-sufficiency of places of confinement. In 1921, the NKIU had thought this goal beyond reach. The government viewed such an attitude as negative and pessimistic. Savrasov, putting the best foot forward, stated that self-sufficiency was both desirable and attainable. The TSITO would need engineers, agronomists, managers, and other specialists; to attract them, it required salaries higher than these professionals could obtain in other industries. That plea was accompanied by another request to increase the wages of all workers at the places of confinement. Savrasov insisted that only bright and dedicated people could reeducate inmates. Again, it came down to a question of higher salaries for prison workers. Savrasov was reiterating comments in the TSITO report to the Ninth Congress of Soviets in December 1921, which had described the extremely difficult economic conditions at the camps. Savrasov did more than describe them, however. He demanded that deductions from inmates' wages be used first to feed and clothe the prisoners. Only well-fed inmates would be able to work hard enough to make their places of confinement self-sufficient.[46]

The congress supported Savrasov's request for more money but rejected his demand for TSITO autonomy. The NKIU board did not like the latter idea, nor did representatives from the TSITO provincial offices. Most stressed the fact that the TSITO had failed to establish working relations with the provincial corrective labor departments, especially those in Siberia, and without the support of those offices the agency was powerless in the provinces. Some speakers, carried away in their criticisms of Savrasov, lost their sense of bureaucratic purpose. They pointed out that the TSITO could not possibly be responsible for those sentenced to forced labor without deprivation of freedom bcause it had no way of enforcing the sentences. Their argument, of course, undermined any NKIU hope of putting all convicts under its supervision.[47]

The Main Administration of Forced Labor (GUPR) took advantage of the bluntness and disunity of the NKIU. Its representatives to the Fifth All-Russian Congress of the Chiefs of the Administration Departments of the Provincial Soviets, held in February 1922, asserted that as the NKIU Congress had already demonstrated, the TSITO could not assume the responsibility for all the places of confinement in Russia. The NKIU needed funds that the government could not, or would not, provide. The GUPR was smarter and took another tack. It did not ask for any funds at all but told the government that it would operate the forced labor camps and, if necessary, all the places of confinement without any subsidies. Inmates would simply be informed that they could pay for their crimes only through productive labor; if they failed to fulfill production norms, they would get neither food nor clothes. Pressing its advantage, the GUPR emphasized that while it and the TSITO had both believed in the principle "He who does not work shall not eat," the injunction had not been enforced with the proper zeal. The GUPR promised to change all that.[48]

The Main Administration of Forced Labor eventually failed to achieve prison self-sufficiency, but it did reduce the cost of operating forced labor camps. In March 1922 the government had provided 18,000 rubles in subsidies to the GUPR; the amount was cut to 16,800 rubles in April, and the subsidies continued to decrease.[49] There is no information on the conditions of the forced labor camps during this period when the GUPR struggled for survival; inmates were starving even before the agency's budget began to fall. But whatever the human cost, the campaign to reduce expenses allowed the GUPR to retain control of the forced labor camps throughout the spring of 1922, when the government seriously considered turning over all the places of confinement to the NKIU. Then, in May, Moscow issued two laws that preserved the division of these places between the NKIU and the NKVD.

The law "On the Question of Review of Government Agencies of the RSFSR" of 2 May 1922 stated that all concentration camps under the temporary custody of the NKVD should revert to the NKIU. The camps were to be included in the NKĨU penitentiary system as general places of confinement for petty offenders. This transfer was to be completed before 1 July 1922. The State Political Administration (GPU) would keep one prison each in Moscow and Petrograd and some facilities at NKĨU institutions in each province; GPU agents would help guard these locations. (This provision reflected the VTSIK's distrust of the ability of the People's Commissariat of Justice to guard its inmates; one may recall that this distrust had been the major reason the concentration camps had been established in July 1918.) The law did not mention Cheka prisons or the Northern Special Purpose Camps in the concentration camp system. Both were apparently transferred to the NKĨU. In July 1922 the places of confinement of the People's Commissariat of Justice employed 18,557 persons and 10,000 guards. About the same number of employees and guards had served in the GTU in 1916, when the number of prisoners totaled 142,000.[50]

The VTSIK and the SNK issued the second law on 24 May 1922. It described the structure of the NKVD, which had changed with the introduction of private enterprise. The changes did not affect the GUPR, however; like its predecessor, the OPR, this organization had full authority over everyone sentenced to forced labor with or without deprivation of freedom. The Main Administration of Forced Labor (GUPR) had three departments. The law specified that the provincial offices be called subdepartments of forced labor; like the OPR provincial offices, they were subagencies of the administrative departments of the provincial soviets. They too had three divisions. GUPR county offices could be established with the permission of the NKVD and local soviets.[51]

One can easily argue that NKVD offices had replaced the local soviets much earlier. This law, in any case, made it official; the NKVD became "an executive agency" of the VTSIK.[52] The soviets were out of the picture, and the NKVD was stronger than ever in its quest to control the places of confinement in Russia. Its position was consolidated when Lenin, who had supported the NKĨU during the first five years of its existence, became ill. He suffered his first stroke in May 1922; it incapacitated him until the end of the year and, in effect, paralyzed the NKĨU.

Under the circumstances, the NKĨU request for more money was especially annoying to the government. Commissariat of Justice continued to maintain that the self-sufficiency of places of confinement could not be achieved except, perhaps, at the agricultural colonies, and it continued to publish reports on the poverty of workers in the NKĨU judicial system. The reports were pathetic. Some county judges had neither shoes nor clothes nor access to transportation (not so much as a bicycle) to travel in judicial districts encompassing more than 1,000 square kilometers. A few judges had to work as laborers for rich peasants in order to support their families.[53] While this was true enough, the government simply didn't want to hear it. The NKĨU was always begging for more money, whereas the NKVD said it could function without government support. Whether it could or not, and by what means, was unimportant. What mattered was money.

The Council of People's Commissars decided on 25 July 1922 to transfer almost all the places of confinement in the country to the NKVD. This occurred two months after Lenin's stroke and less than one month after the NKĨU had received Cheka facilities. A law of 12 October 1922 specified that in order to establish unity in administering the prison system, the responsibilities of the NKĨU Central Corrective Labor Department and its local offices were to be taken over by the new NKVD Main Administration of Places of Confinement (*Glavnoe upravlenie mestami zakliucheniia*, or GUMZ) and its local offices. The Main Administration of Forced Labor was abolished and its functions delegated to the GUMZ.[54]

Now came the turn of the NKVD to monopolize the administration of the places of confinement. It never lacked zeal.

5 THE NKVD MONOPOLY
1922-1930

NKVD control of the places of confinement occurred in two phases. The first phase (1922-27) corresponded to the New Economic Policy, when the government permitted limited private enterprise. The second phase (1928-30) was connected with the collectivization of agriculture and the end of the NEP.

During the first phase, the People's Commissariat of Internal Affairs (NKVD) prison agency, known as the Main Administration of Places of Confinement (GUMZ), attempted to destroy the revolutionary legacy of 1917-21, when prisons had been controlled by the Central Corrective Labor Department (TSITO) of the People's Commissariat of Justice (NKIU) and the Main Administration of Forced Labor (GUPR) of the NKVD. This legacy consisted of two major ideas: (1) the self-sufficiency of the places of confinement, and (2) the reeducation of inmates. The GUMZ continued to speak in these terms but interpreted them in such a way that they lost their revolutionary meaning. GUMZ policies, in fact, resembled those defended by liberal penologists in pre-Revolutionary Russia. Even the agency's title had been introduced by the Provincial Government in May 1917, only to be abolished by the Bolsheviks in July 1918. This process of restoring pre-Revolutionary values at the places of confinement was sometimes contradictory, occasionally indirect, but there is no doubt that it happened.

All of this stopped abruptly in 1928. Collectivization and its turmoil led to (1) the revival of the ideas of self-sufficiency of the places of confinement and the complete reeducation of inmates; (2) the retransfer of facilities from the NKVD to the NKIU in 1930, after the NKVD was accused of supporting the anti-Stalinist group that opposed collectivization; and (3) the rapid growth of camps and prisons under the State Political Administration–Unified State Political Administration (GPU-OGPU).

The New Economic Policy, 1922-1927

The New Economic Policy began in March 1921, but had little impact on the prison agencies (the T͡SITO of the NKI͡U, the GUPR of the NKVD, and the Special Department of the Cheka) during its first eighteen months. Competition among the agencies prevented the abandonment of policies traditionally supported by the government. The NKVD had claimed it could make all of the places of confinement self-sufficient by forcing inmates to work hard. The NKI͡U had promised eventually to make such places unnecessary by reeducating the inmates.[1] The NKI͡U had first introduced the idea of self-sufficiency in 1918 but openly began to doubt its feasibility in 1919. By 1922 neither the NKI͡U nor the NKVD believed the ideas it espoused, but each had to stand for something in order to compete for funds.[2] The government, in extreme financial difficulties, opted for the NKVD program, and the places of confinement were united under the Commissariat of Internal Affairs. Yet two groups of bureaucrats continued to battle during the first year after unification. The rivalry between agencies became a struggle within the NKVD. Only the forms of struggle changed.

The Council of People's Commissars (SNK) decree of 25 July 1922 and the joint NKVD-NKI͡U enactment of 12 October 1922 ruled that the T͡SITO and its facilities should come under the jurisdiction of the NKVD. At the time of the transfer, the NKVD lacked a prison agency because its Main Administration of Forced Labor (GUPR) had been disbanded.[3] The SNK failed to foresee difficulties involved in enforcing its decision. There were many.

The officials of the old GUPR wanted their jobs back. They argued, reasonably enough, that since the government preferred their policy over that of the T͡SITO, they should be the ones to implement the policy. A potential crisis was avoided mainly by the political skill of Evseĭ Gustavovich Shirvindt. Shirvindt was a 1914 graduate of the law school of Odessa University and had been a member of the NKI͡U board from 1917 to 1919, when he joined the Communist Party. From 1920 to 1922 he was a Deputy People's Commissar of Justice in the Ukraine. In 1922 he had moved back to Moscow to replace the confrontational Savrasov as head of the NKI͡U RSFSR prison agency, just before that agency was transferred to the NKVD. As chief of the new GUMZ, he was given the authority to select his most important deputies.[4]

Shirvindt's attitude turned out to be unexpectedly cautious. He favored T͡SITO people, but he did not want to antagonize former GUPR personnel. Having had some experience at places of confinement, Shirvindt doubted that they could ever become self-sufficient, and his first memorandum requested additional government funds. Neither the SNK nor the All-Russian Central Executive Committee (VT͡SIK) viewed such requests favorably. Shirvindt

Figure 7
The Prison System of the People's Commissariat of Internal Affairs of the RSFSR
October 1922 – December 1930

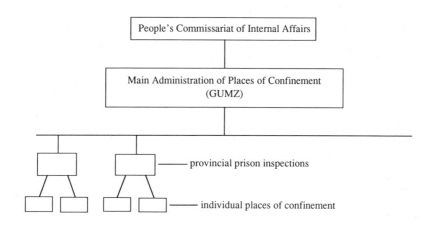

Provincial prison inspections were attached to the local soviets but acted independently.

feared that if he were to exclude all GUPR officials from running the places of confinement, they would hinder his efforts to get more money.[5]

Shirvindt, the consummate bureaucrat, sought compromise. He established five departments: a Secretariat, an Administrative-Penitentiary Department, a Labor Department, a Maintenance Department, and a Convoy Guards Department (five happened to be the average between the TSITO's nine departments and the GUPR's three). He also created nine subdepartments. This plan provided sixteen important posts (two deputies, five heads of departments, and nine heads of subdepartments) in the GUMZ—enough to absorb the most influential personnel of the rival former agencies, TSITO and GUPR. Shirvindt next changed the names of some places of confinement. The new titles reflected the TSITO thesis that inmates should be reeducated rather than the GUPR idea that the camps and prisons become self-sufficient. Prisons were called "corrective houses"; probational institutions were identified as "transitional corrective houses." Shirvindt kept the names of the agricultural and industrial colonies.[6]

Former GUPR people were unhappy about the compromise. When the First All-Russian GUMZ Conference convened on 21 November 1922, there was nothing but conflict and tension. The conference was supposed to formulate principles for the GUMZ on the places of confinement and to choose members for a Statutes Commission, which would then draft comprehensive statutes for the penitentiary system. (No such statutes had been compiled during the first five years after the October Revolution; the places of confinement had operated according to the fragmentary rules set forth in the Temporary Instruction of July 1918 and in the NKIU Statutes of 15 November 1920.) Twenty-six people had been invited to the session, but there was so much interest that another six people showed up. Shirvindt used all his power and skill to control the meeting. He detailed the principles of GUMZ policies in an introductory statement. He argued that under the difficult economic conditions in the country, inmate labor should be viewed not merely as corrective but also as possessing "a certain material value." The country needed immediate material support, so it followed that inmate labor should take precedence over reeducation.[7]

Shirvindt did not expressly promise to achieve any of these goals. His opponents understood this reticence as a refusal to commit the GUMZ either to self-sufficiency or to reeducation. Critics claimed Shirvindt had reversed and abandoned the policies of both the TSITO and the GUPR. Shirvindt, of course, replied that he was only continuing their programs. His critics were right. Shirvindt was not interested in either the TSITO plan for inmate reeducation or the GUPR goal of prison self-sufficiency; he was more influenced by the TSITO criticisms of prison self-sufficiency and GUPR complaints about the infeasibility of corrective labor. He was also concerned about upgrading security at the special places of confinement that housed political prisoners. He feared that the Main Political Administration (GPU) would exploit security problems at the camps and eventually acquire control—just as lapses in NKIU security had led to the establishment of Cheka places of confinement in July 1918. The GPU was legally subordinate to the NKVD, but it acted independently, and under the circumstances Shirvindt decided to be cautious. He wanted his ideas accepted at the conference without discussion or debate. He stressed that this was the only way to deal with these issues under the current conditions. Conference participants interpreted this as an order, and dutifully obeyed.[8]

Shirvindt was unable to stop debate on the selection of people for the Statutes Commission, however. Interest was heightened by the fact that commission members would receive additional income. A delegate named Tret'iakov, who was deputy chief of the Administrative-Penitentiary Department of the GUMZ and a former employee of the GUPR, insisted that NKVD employees exclusively staff the commission. Even though the demand was not overtly directed at former TSITO employees, who belonged to the NKVD by this time, they believed that his proposal, if adopted, would relegate them to permanent outsider status. The head of the Labor Department, one Burlachenko, acted as spokesman for the TSITO people attending the conference.

He declared that the Statutes Commission must include representatives from other People's Commissariats, particularly from the NKIU. Trying to head off a conflict, Shirvindt postponed the decision on the composition of the commission, and the debates continued well after the conference.[9]

In fact, Shirvindt's views were close to those of Burlachenko, and events suddenly began to move in his favor. During the first four years after the Revolution, the Soviet government had viewed the places of confinement as temporary. They were to wither away with other state agencies after the Civil War and the establishment of socialism. In a socialist society, the exploitation of man by man would cease; crime and the need for places of confinement would disappear. When the NEP was introduced in 1921, however, what withered were such dreams. Most bureaucrats in the penitentiary system started to look at their jobs as permanent and rallied around Shirvindt. Hence, there were no serious objections when Shirvindt invited personnel from the People's Commissariat of Justice to participate in the Statutes Commission in the spring of 1923.[10]

Once united, the GUMZ was able to defend its interests better than any other prison agency that had operated after 1917. In May 1923 the GUMZ even received additional moneys for its places of confinement. A month later, when the SNK attempted to introduce some uniformity to government salaries, Shirvindt managed to get raises for nonmanagerial personnel, whose salaries had been scandalously low for years. Now they were to receive 17.40 rubles a month, or about half a ruble more than comparably skilled government workers.[11]

While the uniformity of salaries strengthened the comradery of employees, it also weakened the authority of managers, who could no longer manipulate their salaries. As a result, Shirvindt asked the government to introduce military discipline at the places of confinement. The SNK and the VTSIK complied in a joint decree of 12 June 1924. The staff did not seem to mind; prison workers were receiving the larger rations and other benefits traditionally afforded military personnel and Cheka-GPU operatives. As far as most employees were concerned, the benefits of this decree outweighed the disadvantage of possible military punishment.[12]

Despite these new benefits, some employees at the places of confinement realized that things were not twice as good but only half as bad. Their standard of living was still only half what it had been before 1917. Guards and warders still looked for outside jobs and still ignored their duties. The annual number of escapes during this period significantly exceeded the pre-Revolutionary average.[13] Security problems at NKVD facilities contributed to the expansion of GPU-OGPU places of confinement.

An additional development rallied GUMZ officials. In early 1924, opponents demanded the abolition of the People's Commissariat of Internal Affairs, calling it excessively bureaucratic and expensive. They suggested that major departments of the NKVD should be transferred to other agencies: the militia could be attached to the OGPU, the places of confinement to the NKIU, and some NKVD departments to local soviets. Defenders of the NKVD contended that the transfers of bureaucrats from one jurisdiction to another would not save the government any money. Hence, the critics did not find much support, and the question was tabled until 1929.[14] The fact the question had been raised at all, however, persuaded bureaucrats in the Main Administration of the Places of Confinement that their interests differed from those in the People's Commissariat of Internal Affairs. On the other hand, common interests led to a reconciliation of former GUPR and TSITO employees.

The VTSIK approved the work of the Statutes Commission on 16 October 1924, giving the new Statutes the official title of Corrective Labor Code of the RSFSR (*Ispravitel'no-trudovoĭ kodeks RSFSR*).[15] This document restated and elaborated ideas advanced by Shirvindt in 1922. During the industrialization and collectivization of 1928-32, these ideas would be labeled "liberal" and "petty bourgeois."[16] From 1924 to 1927, however, his cautious policies provoked little, if any, opposition. Shirvindt was unable to abandon those ideas of self-sufficiency and reeducation that he had inherited from the 1918-22 system, but he interpreted them in such a way that everyone understood he did not take them seriously. Moreover, no one forced him to take these ideas seriously.

Still, the corpse would not stay buried. Article 7 of the Statutes of 1924 stated that corrective labor institutions should try to cover all of the expenses of the places of confinement without losing sight of their goal of reeducating inmates. V. Iakubson, a former TSITO official who became a chief of the Statistical Sub-department of the GUMZ and Shirvindt's spokesman, asserted in comments appended to the Statutes that self-sufficiency was desirable but not a major objective. He claimed that efforts of the prison administration to derive income from the labor of inmates had paralyzed the work of educators.[17]

Iakubson freely interpreted Article 7, finding it to mean quite the opposite of what Shirvindt had told the November 1922 conference. Shirvindt had stressed "increasing the material value of inmates' labor"; Iakubson emphasized reeducation and doubted the feasibility of prison self-sufficiency. He was not corrected or reprimanded; in fact, Shirvindt certainly supported him on these issues and may have prodded him to take this position. Shirvindt was known for supporting certain initiatives of his subordinates without telling other members of the GUMZ staff that he approved. Prominent Soviet penologist Boris Samoĭlovish Utevskiĭ, who worked under Shirvindt at the GUMZ, recalled that the chief once allowed him to take juveniles from a Moscow prison for an unguarded trip to the Moscow Zoo but asked him not to tell anybody that his superior had granted permission. In case of an escape, the trip would have been considered a mistake, and somebody would have had to take the blame. Shirvindt's honesty was not tested this time; fortunately for both Shirvindt and Utevskiĭ, all the juveniles returned to the prison.[18]

Juvenile delinquency, which was especially acute at this time, prompted Iakubson to emphasize the contradiction between self-sufficiency and re-education. He wanted both to show the negative side of self-sufficiency and to explain the failure of the GUMZ to reform inmates. The failure had been dramatic. As result of the catastrophe of World War I, the Civil War, and the hunger of 1921, millions of children had lost their parents. A million and half were homeless in 1922, and hundreds of thousands became juvenile delin-quents and recidivists.[19]

Iakubson repeatedly stressed the importance of inmate reeducation but interpreted the matter quite differently from the NKIU Instruction of 1918. The People's Commissariat of Justice was adamant that no properly reformed inmate would commit a crime after his or her release; Iakubson noted that severe budgetary constraints limited reeducation to nothing more than im-proving a released inmate's ability to "adjust to social conditions" on the outside. Liberal penologists of Imperial Russia who stayed in the Soviet Union after the October Revolution of 1917—M.N. Gernet, M.M. Isaev, P.I. Liu-blinskiĭ, and A.N. Traĭnin—supported these objectives. All of them worked at the State Institute for Studies of Crime and Criminals (*Gosudarstvennyĭ institute po izucheniiu prestupnosti i prestupnika*), which had been estab-lished in 1925 and was headed by Shirvindt.[20]

During 1917-22, all places of confinement tried to prevent inmates from escaping. Two of the three prison agencies, however, insisted that they had more pressing tasks: the NKIU had promised to reeducate inmates; the NKVD had claimed it could make the camps and prisons self-sufficient. Only Cheka places of confinement had the single goal of keeping inmates where they were. By refusing either to reeducate inmates or to make the camps and prisons self-sufficient, the GUMZ tacitly acknowledged that its single imme-diate goal, too, was to prevent escapes—but that similarity to the objectives of the Cheka in 1918-22 naturally embarrassed the GUMZ. It took semantic refuge: it introduced the term "social defense" (*sotsial'naia zashchita*) to replace "isolation of people dangerous to the worker's state." In keeping with this new terminology, a prison sentence or term was euphemistically called "a measure of social defense."[21]

Reeducation remained a potent idea, though by 1924 its meaning had little relation to what had been intended by the Instruction of 1918. The concept of prisoner reform nonetheless affected the structure of places of confinement and the segregation of inmates. The Statutes of 1924 classified prisoners by sex, age, personality, class origin, crime, and length of sentence.

It established five basic kinds of facilities: (1) houses of detention for all suspects and inmates sentenced to less than six months; (2) corrective labor houses for inmates sentenced to more than six months; (3) agriculture and industrial labor colonies for inmates convicted for up to five years but disinclined to escape; (4) special-purpose isolators for political prisoners, inmates from the exploitative classes, and recidivists; and (5) transitional corrective labor houses for prisoners who had evidenced reform at other places of confinement. In addition, there were labor houses for juvenile delinquents and for inmates of worker and peasant origin. Each place of confinement had three regimes: preliminary, intermediate, and superior categories each allowed inmates certain privileges. Those who behaved and worked well were usually transferred to more lenient places of confinement or put on a regime with more privileges.[22]

The name and structure of the GUMZ had resulted from Shirvindt's compromises, first, between the pre-Revolutionary tradition and Revolutionary tendencies and, second, among factions within his organization. The pre-Revolutionary tradition had accepted the places of confinement as permanent institutions. Marxists considered them temporary. The name GUMZ was first used by the Provisional Government in May 1918, abolished by the Bolsheviks in July 1918, and reintroduced in November 1922. Its structure of five departments and nine subdepartments remained the same after 1922. Shirvindt did what he could to appease the conflicting interests of former TSITO and GUPR officials. This meant, in effect, changing nothing.[23]

The GUMZ in outlying regions altered only slightly. Provincial offices were renamed "inspections" (*inspektsiia*), and each chief became an "inspector" (*inspektor*). The Provisional Government had used the term "inspections" in May 1917, and it too was changed by the Bolsheviks in July 1918. The provincial offices after 1917 were not semiindependent of local authorities, as they had been in Imperial Russia, but became departments of the provincial soviets.[24]

Each provincial inspection had two subagencies. Neither the Bureau of Forced Labor without Deprivation of Freedom (*Biuro prinuditel'nykh rabot bez sodershaniia pod strazhei*), created in 1919, nor the Distributive Commissions, established in July 1918, had existed before the Revolution. The Bureau was the only truly self-sufficient agency in the penitentiary system. All its expenses were covered by deductions from the salaries of those sentenced to forced labor without deprivation of freedom. The 1924 Statutes set deductions at 25 percent of salary.[25]

The government encouraged courts to sentence more suspects to forced labor without deprivation of freedom in order to decrease the costs of operating the prisons and camps. The number of such sentences increased at a rate of about 5 percent a year. The number of imprisoned criminals grew 15 percent annually, however, so the proportion of those sentenced to forced labor without confinement actually decreased from 38 percent of all those convicted in 1922 to 13.9 percent in 1926. Some authors have concluded from these figures that the system "all but disappeared" after 1926. Nothing could have been further from the truth: its share drastically increased after 1928, and reached more than 50 percent of all those convicted in 1930.[26]

The Distributive Commissions were a legacy of 1917-21. Their major function was to speed the reeducation of prisoners. As long as Lenin supported their activities in 1920-21, they were influential.[27] They lost power when Lenin became ill in 1922, and after 1924—when Shirvindt viewed the reform of inmates as a long-term project—questions were raised about disbanding them. Nevertheless, they lasted until October 1929. Their successors were the Observation Commissions (Nablíudatel'naíà kommissíià). Established in 1922, these organizations were controlled by the individual places of confinement, whereas the Distributive Commissions had been under the GUMZ. The Observation Commissions had been named after similar organs in Petrograd which had functioned under both the Imperial regime and the Provisional Government but were abolished by the Bolsheviks after October 1917.[28]

Each Observation Commission had three members: a chief of the place of confinement, a judge from the local people's court, and a representative of the local trade unions. The prison chief chaired the commission, which was supposed to supervise the activities of the place of confinement. Critics of the commissions pointed out that their composition conflicted with their very reason for existence, since chiefs of the prisons and camps were in effect supervising their own activities.[29] Undeniably, the mere existence of the Commissions somewhat limited the power of the chiefs. Similar restrictions had been imposed on the directors of the NKÍU places of confinement during 1918-22. No such limits had been put on the commandants of the Cheka institutions and NKVD forced labor camps during this period.[30]

The traditional rule of the Soviet government was that all inmates had to work. This rule had been established by the People's Commissariat of Justice in January 1918 and was affirmed by the Statutes of October 1924. The NKÍU Instruction had fixed prison wages at the levels of free workers. The Statutes had said, however, that inmates were to receive 25-75 percent of the salaries of free workers. After 1924, inmate salaries were always a fraction of what free workers were paid. Íakubson had argued that the wages of prisoners should be lower because they did not work as hard as free laborers. He believed that prisoners thought more about escaping than about working; in any case, they could always count on getting a meal, whereas most free workers had to survive entirely on their salaries.[31]

In Imperial Russia, inmates who were cooks, janitors, and other service personnel were not paid; rather, their terms were reduced by one day for every two work days. The NKĨU instruction of 1918 provided them with salaries equal to the pay of free workers. The Statutes of 1924 restored the rule of Imperial Russia regarding the service personnel and took away their salaries. A GUMZ decree of 10 October 1925 introduced a provision giving inmates who were not paid for work an additional half-pound of bread. This was not a trend toward improving the lot of prisoners; it merely reflected the desperate hunger in the system.[32]

The GUMZ changed the rule about reducing terms in May 1925. Those who labored more efficiently had their sentences reduced by greater amounts. It was hoped that this change would provide inmates with additional incentives to work without having to restore their salaries. This rule, which lasted until December 1958, applied only to common criminals; politicals had to serve their full sentences.[33]

The Statutes of 18 October 1924 tried to interest both prisoners and staff in increasing inmate productivity at the places of confinement by specifying that 25 percent of the increased profits would be split evenly between expenditures on food for the prisoners and bonuses to free workers (administrators, guards, technical managers, warders, and clerks). Of the rest, 40 percent would be devoted to industrial development at the facility, 15 percent to the Aid Committee for Released Prisoners, and 20 percent to the GUMZ. Despite these financial incentives, the productivity of inmates remained about half that of free workers. Free laborers feared growing unemployment during this period, and worked harder to save their jobs. Punishment for sloppy work at the places of confinement had little effect; food was guaranteed regardless of the quantity or quality of the work. The government, which provided some funds for the maintenance of inmates, initially did not allot moneys for industrial development. Hence, most places of confinement had neither facilities nor tools, and many officials believed that forced labor could never be as productive as free labor. By the 1930s, however, opinions had changed; the government did provide some very limited funds for industrial development, and inmates had to choose between working harder than free workers and starving. Many worked harder.[34]

Unemployment in Soviet Russia created additional problems at the places of confinement. Trade union representatives on the Distribution and Observation Commissions were supposed to assist industrial development. In fact, they did everything possible to obstruct development; trade unions did not want competition from the prisons. The government, of course, was more interested in employing productive free workers than prisoners, and naturally supported the unions. It prohibited inmates and persons sentenced to forced labor without deprivation of freedom from working in the industries that attracted free workers.[35]

The GUMZ encountered the same old problem. In 1926 its places of confinement in the RSFSR housed 112,000 prisoners; the NKVDs in other socialist republics and the OGPU had 76,000. This totaled a prison population of 188,000. Between 1924 and 1926, the GUMZ managed to increase the number of working inmates by 4 percent a year, but the number of inmates in the system grew 15 percent annually. Consequently, the share of working inmates decreased from 55 to 40 percent—approximately the proportion of inmates who had worked in Imperial Russia.[36]

The places of confinement swelled beyond their capacities. There were 1.5 inmates for each accommodation in 1926, and in some places the number of inmates was 300 percent above the norm. Prisoners slept on the cold floor, often without mattresses. When Shirvindt requested funds to build new facilities, the government refused on ideological grounds. Some Bolsheviks continued to believe that crime resulted from the injustices of capitalism and that the upsurge in criminality was only temporary; with the end of both the Revolution and the Civil War, crime would start falling, and new facilities would be necessary. Lacking additional funds, Shirvindt then asked the NKIU courts to sentence prisoners to shorter terms. Justice reduced sentences from an average of 1.24 years in 1924 to 0.98 years in 1925, then to 0.72 years in 1926. The NKIU and NKVD both offered paroles and amnesties to ease the congestion; most convicts served less than 75 percent of their terms. Peasants, who made up half of all inmates, were allowed to work in their fields during the summer, and this was counted as time served.[37]

Prisons still filled more rapidly than inmates could be released. Never in the history of the country had so many crimes been committed and so many criminals gone unpunished. Some NKIU officials admitted defeat. Critics of the system pointed out, quite correctly, that the short sentences and an abundance of privileges stopped deterring criminals; they simply no longer feared jail. In a conversation with Utevskiĭ, a professional thief named Mundshtukmakher favorably compared the Soviet judicial and penal systems with those of other countries. How much he knew about prisons outside Russia is open to question, but Mundshtukmakher especially praised Soviet short sentences and paroles. He was confident that within two years after his release he would make enough money to retire in comfort.[38] Of course, Mundshtukmakher and other professional thieves had money to bribe the guards and to live comfortably in prison. Most prisoners did not.

Shirvindt insisted that prison conditions were harsh. He fell in with those who thought that the upsurge in crime was only a temporary phenomenon resulting from the atrocities of the Civil War. Neither he nor they had any quick solutions, however, and all relied on the clichés of patience, better living conditions for children, reeducation of criminals, and, ultimately, more prisons.[39] At the beginning of 1928, Shirvindt was apparently supported by

Nikolai Bukharin, head of the Comintern; Aleksei Rykov, chairman of the Council of People's Commissariats; and Mikhail Tomskiĭ, chairman of the Council of All-Russian Trade Unions.[40] Ordinarily, the backing of such powerful people would have been decisive. Contrary to expectations, it proved to be a kiss of death. Stalin's men insisted on the rapid collectivization of agriculture and crash industrialization. Bukharin's people wished to move in these same directions, but more slowly. Stalin's final victory affected at least 130 million people, or 80 percent of the Soviet population. It drastically changed the structures and functions of most government agencies and, with them, disastrously altered life at the places of confinement.

COLLECTIVIZATION AND INDUSTRIALIZATION, 1928-1930

The fifteenth Party Congress, which met 2-19 December 1927, decided to collectivize agriculture and to draft the First Five-Year Plan of economic development. In order to fund its new projects, the government planned to cut most other programs that did not contribute directly to realizing the Five-Year Plan.

One logical choice was the GUMZ budget. The GUMZ of the RSFSR alone was supposed to receive 14 million in 1928, or about 0.25 percent of the entire state budget. Accordingly, the subsidies to the GUMZs of other republics constituted at least 0.1 percent and that to the OGPU prison agency probably 0.05 percent. Thus all Soviet prisons and camps were expected to receive 0.4 percent of the state budget. Although this percentage seemed high to people who thought the places of confinement could and should be self-sufficient, it was lower than previous expenditures. The Imperial government had devoted 1 percent of its budget to the penal system between 1912 and 1916. By the end of 1927, the Soviet penal system housed at least 200,000 inmates; Russian places of confinement had held 142,000 in 1916. This meant that the Soviet government was actually spending considerably less per inmate than had the Imperial government.[41] Under such circumstances, any cuts would be painful. It was decided to alter the penitentiary system before making any budgetary reductions.

The VTSIK and the Council of People's Commissars of the RSFSR issued the law "On the Punitive Policies and the Conditions of the Places of Confinement" (*O karatel'noĭ politike i sostoĭanii mest zakliucheniĭa*) on 26 March 1928. The idea behind this new document was simple: in order to reduce expenses, the number of inmates had to be cut.[42] The decrease was unspecified, and the goal and measures to implement the decree were debated for more than two years, until the places of confinement were transferred from the NKVD back to the NKIU.

The purpose of this law contradicted the views of some authors who had believed that the Soviets planned to expand the places of confinement in 1928. In March 1928 the government had flatly refused to build new facilities. It reversed this decision in April 1930 by establishing corrective labor camps under OGPU supervision in order to absorb an increasing number of peasants arrested for resistance to collectivization.[43] When this law was enacted in March 1928, collectivization was just beginning, and the government simply did not foresee that its policy toward the peasants would lead to so many arrests.

The law had two sections. The first and shorter part praised both the NKIU and the NKVD for supporting government policies. The NKVD was singled out for "generally correct applications of corrective labor measures, . . . the growth of cultural work among inmates, and also scientific studies of criminals and criminality." In its second, analytical part the law bluntly stated that there were too many inmates in the GUMZ facilities, and conditions there were too soft to deter criminals. The NKIU's courts were blamed for sentencing an excessive number of defendants to prison terms and, therefore, making insufficient use of the "measures of social defense" not connected with "deprivation of freedom." They were also criticized for finding guilty certain people whose guilt was not conclusively demonstrated, and for not ensuring that prison sentences were properly served. The NKVD got its share of criticism as well, for failing "to apply consistently the class policy in places of confinement," for granting undeserved privileges to inmates who belonged to the "exploiting classes and/or were socially dangerous," and for showing "little interest in the reeducation of young inmates of worker and peasant origin." It was also blamed for failing to enforce discipline among inmates and warders and for poor work by the Observation and Distributive Commissions.[44]

The law of 26 March 1928 proposed four remedies. It was necessary to punish severely "class enemies, professional criminals and recidivists (bandits, arsonists, horse thieves, embezzlers, bribetakers, and thieves)." Short sentences had to be replaced by "other measures of social defense," such as forced labor without deprivation of freedom, demotions at work, dismissals, reprimands, fines, and the partial confiscation of properties. The courts needed the power to extend the sentences of inmates who did not respond to corrective labor. Privileges, such as paroles, leaves, and transfers to better regimes, had to be limited in dealing with "class enemies, socially dangerous elements and recidivists."[45]

Three reform measures were specified. Those sentenced to forced labor should 1) work without pay 2) at projects beneficial to the economy 3) under harsher conditions than those found in jobs created for the unemployed by the People's Commissariat of Labor. The new law stated that working conditions for persons sentenced to forced labor without deprivation of freedom should be looked upon as "a real measure of punishment." Those sentenced to exile were to be transported to remote areas where living conditions were more severe than in the central regions. The law characterized the current system of exile as a matter of central provinces merely passing their "socially dangerous elements" back and forth.[46]

The two agencies affected by the decree, the NKIU and the NKVD, reacted differently. The People's Commissariat of Justice willingly adjusted its policy to the government demands; Internal Affairs did not. Contrary to the dreadful image it had acquired while running the forced labor camps during 1919-22 and all the places of confinement from 1934 on, the NKVD in this case backed the more liberal policy. It was even accused of supporting Bukharin.[47]

The 26 March 1928 law sought to ease crowding at the camps. In August, the Supreme Court of the RSFSR instructed local courts to sentence persons who had committed petty thefts or assault without bodily harm to forced labor without deprivation of freedom. Recidivists, socially dangerous individuals convicted of rape, robbery, or murder, habitual criminals guilty of bribery or fraud, and class enemies were to get terms lasting not less than one year. The local courts by and large followed these instructions, but prison populations still grew. During 1928, 300,000 people were sentenced to prison terms.[48]

The NKIU issued several directives to local courts strengthening the Instruction of August 1928 and demanding fewer sentences involving confinement. The NKIU *Ezhenedel'nik sovetskoĭ iustitsii* (Weekly of Soviet Justice) published reports on the percentage of defendants sentenced to forced labor without deprivation of freedom.[49] The intensity of these reports resembled communiqués from a battlefront. The NKIU courts reacted with uncharacteristic vigor by sentencing more and more defendants in this way (see Table 5).[50] One otherwise reputable source has stated that the number of people sentenced to forced labor without deprivation of freedom actually decreased during 1928-29.[51] This was clearly not the case.

In contrast to the NKIU, the NKVD reacted to the March 1928 law with caution and reluctance. Iakubson insisted that the Main Administration of the Places of Confinement (GUMZ) had already applied the class policy at its camps and prisons: for instance, the GUMZ had given peasants and workers twice as much chance of parole as representatives of the nontoiling classes. Iakubson maintained that the NKVD policy was fundamentally correct and that the agency had strictly followed the laws and regulations established by the Statutes of 1924.[52]

To suppress NKVD resistance to the new policies, Mikhail Ivanovich Kalinin, chairman of the VTSIK and a Politburo member, dismissed the Commissar of Internal Affairs. The newly appointed man named Tolmachev had strongly supported the law of 26 March 1928 at the Second Congress of

Table 5. Persons Sentenced to Forced Labor without Deprivation of Freedom

	Convictions	Sentences without Confinement	Percentage
First half 1928	466,000	71,335	15.3
Second half 1928	489,552	137,564	28.1
First half 1929	578,136	283,866	49.1
Second half 1929	666,426	344,542	51.7

Officials of the Administrative Department of the NKVD of the RSFSR, held in June. He had spoken about privileges at the camps and prisons:

> Our problem is that we do not want to return to old [pre-Revolutionary] conditions and therefore try to follow certain labor, professional, and other norms regarding the inmates. . . . [We are] too loyal to these principles, [we are] too liberal. . . . We have already given the inmates the major privilege—the right to work. . . . Work is, indeed, a privilege. . . . [and because it is a privilege,] we do not have to give inmates other privileges. The convicts are the people who have harmed our state and who have to pay a price for that. . . . We have to pay them [for their work] only enough to maintain their productivity. . . . The prisons should not be a desirable place to live. Imprisonment should be a frightening experience. . . . Our class enemies should be put in especially difficult conditions.[53]

Soviet propaganda had portrayed the living conditions in pre-Revolutionary Russia as extremely severe. The greater the difficulties under the Soviet regime, the more negative became descriptions of life under the Tsars; hence, prison conditions before the Revolution were depicted as appalling. Most Bolsheviks, including Tolmachev, had been political prisoners, and the severity of their ordeals enhanced their revolutionary credentials.

Tolmachev supported the self-sufficiency of the places of confinement. After so many years of debate, for reasons unknown, the law of 26 March 1928 had said nothing about self-sufficiency. Tolmachev, acknowledging that financial difficulties would prevent the GUMZ from becoming independent quickly, felt that places of confinement should, like factories, borrow money from the government for their immediate needs and pledge to achieve financial independence at a specific time in the future. Without providing names and places, he said that some places of confinement were already self-sufficient and even profitable. He insisted that the major obstacle to reform was prison congestion. To relieve overcrowding, courts must sentence defendants to realistic terms; ten times more inmates had been sentenced to strict isolation than there were isolation cells. Tolmachev did exactly what NKVD officials had always done: he blamed his problems on the NKIU.[54]

Ironically, NKIU officials applauded his comments; they had used

Tolmachev's arguments on the necessity of applying class policy at the places of confinement in order to attack the GUMZ and Shirvindt. Shirvindt had maintained that "class policy should be applied to a class as a whole, but not against individual representatives of the class." The NKĨU retorted sarcastically, "We cannot arrest a class as a whole, but only individual representatives of the class."[55] It was a clever response, but it distorted Shirvindt's argument that the punishment should fit the crime. Soon, in fact, the NKĨU, along with the OGPU, would attempt to arrest a class as a whole!

In responding to Tolmachev's ideas about prison congestion, the People's Commissariat of Justice admitted that the courts had made mistakes, which, in turn, contributed to overcrowding. But at the same time, it claimed that such mistakes were inevitable because the NKĨU had to communicate with the prisons indirectly through the NKVD board. It would therefore be better to remove the places of confinement from the jurisdiction of the NKVD and put them under the NKĨU, which already controlled the courts.[56]

The NKĨU strengthened its case with an avalanche of criticism against the GUMZ. The Main Administration of Places of Confinement had permitted engineers convicted of taking bribes to work as engineers at the camps and prisons. NKĨU officials mocked the GUMZ for trying to reeducate a convicted priest by letting him read Marxist literature, and for using White Army officers as prison librarians and teachers. "What would these people teach peasants and workers?" they queried.[57]

Shirvindt responded in December 1928. He said that no former White officer had ever worked as a teacher in the GUMZ places of confinement, but acknowledged that both priests and White Army officers had been encouraged to read Marxist tracts. "Does reading Marxist literature contradict Marxist principles?" he asked rhetorically. "No. It does not contradict any principle!" Shirvindt also had an answer to the criticism about the engineer. It was unreasonable to hire a free engineer, he argued, while making an inmate-engineer "peel potatoes." Shirvindt quoted Nikolai V. Krylenko, a Deputy People's Commissar of Justice who, as state prosecutor at the Shakhty trial of engineers in 1928, had demanded severe punishment for the accused but at the same time insisted that places of confinement put convicted engineers to work for the good of the country.[58]

In response to NKĨU demands for stricter punishment, Shirvindt asserted that prison conditions should be no more harsh than those of 1928. They had been severe enough throughout the year to make people avoid prison; why should they change? Shirvindt continued:

> The goal of the measure of social defense [the prison term] should not be to inflict physical punishment on the inmates or to take revenge on the inmates for their crimes. . . . The ideas of punishment and revenge are undoubtedly a result of an

ideology which is completely alien to [Marxism]. . . . If one starts speaking about keeping embezzlers and bribetakers in harsher conditions, as incorrigible enemies of Soviet construction, then the same things may be said about recidivists. Then comes the turn of inmates who, though they belong to the toiling classes, have nevertheless committed crimes that are especially dangerous to the Soviet state (bandits, murderers, hooligans, et al). And then there will be no one left to whom one will be allowed to apply the Soviet Corrective Labor Code.[59]

Shirvindt's reference to the code gave the debates a new direction. Prominent officials of the NKIU—Konovalov, Krylenko, and Traskovich, all supporters of Stalin's collectivization—claimed that every judicial statute (the Civil Code, the Code of Civil Procedure, the Criminal Code, the Code of Criminal Procedure, and the Corrective Labor Code) should conform to the new government policy. In the words of Traskovich, one needed to remove "all the elements which represented bourgeois juridicial thought." Krylenko insisted that the Criminal Code be changed to allow judges more freedom to determine individual punishment. Konovalov proposed that all offenders be divided into three groups: most dangerous, moderately dangerous, and least dangerous. This division should be made on the basis of the crimes for which they had been convicted and on their personalities, which, Konovalov stressed, had mainly been determined by class origins. The most dangerous offenders should receive up to ten years' deprivation of freedom, or even death. Moderately dangerous criminals should remain at the places of confinement until they were reeducated but no longer than the maximum term fixed by the court. The least dangerous should not be sentenced to deprivation of freedom at all.[60]

Traskovich demanded that the places of confinement be transferred to the NKIU. He drafted a reform suggesting five kinds of places of confinement instead of three. The major change was less in the number of places than in the distribution of inmates. Under the existing system, inmates who improved were moved to facilities giving them more privileges. Traskovich wanted inmates to stay where they were sent. The most dangerous should be put in isolators on strict-regime; they were to be considered incorrigible, and no attempt would be made to reform them. Moderately dangerous inmates were to be placed in concentration camps, and the least dangerous sent to labor colonies and local forced labor camps. Krylenko and Konovalov obviously wanted to restore the judicial system to what it had been during 1917-21; Traskovich wanted to do the same with the places of confinement. He even hoped to revive the old terminology: concentration camps, forced labor camps, and so on. The big difference, however, was that during 1917-21, all inmates were deemed reeducable; by 1929, many were not.[61]

Responding to the NKIU challenge, Shirvindt characterized its criticisms as superficial. Unless it elaborated a plan for prison self-sufficiency, no reforms should commence. He emphasized that the NKVD must control the places of confinement; it had had much more experience with them than the NKĨU.[62] The government was usually responsive to Shirvindt's reasoning, but this time political considerations outweighed economics. The government planned to disband the NKVD, which had had been accused of supporting Bukharin, and the transfer of its places of confinement to the NKĨU was part of the plan. After camps and prisons were turned over to the People's Commissariat of Justice in Turkmenistan in September 1928, however, they were unexpectedly returned to the NKVD four months later: the Turkmen NKĨU had no resources to run the facilities without help from the NKVD. The failure of that transfer caused the Sixth All-Union Congress of the NKĨU in February 1929 to reconsider its role. A resolution of the congress called for the transfer only when the NKĨU was prepared to accept the places of confinement. The NKĨU was also un-happy about the First Five-Year Plan, which envisaged self-sufficiency for the camps and prisons by 1934. NKĨU officials believed this to be infeasible.[63]

The First Five-Year Plan created economic and political opportunities unforeseen by the NKĨU. For one thing, the proportion of working inmates drastically increased. In 1927, only 40 percent of all prisoners worked. In 1929, this share reached 65-70 percent, and in remote areas where it was difficult to find free workers, some places of confinement enjoyed full employment and demanded more inmates. In response, the First All-Union GUMZ Con-ference, which was held 24-25 October 1929, resolved that all convicts sen-tenced to more than three years and not employed at local camps or prisons should be sent to these remote areas. Correspondingly, government subsidies to the places of confinement in 1929 decreased for the first time since 1922.[64]

While NKĨU officials missed these opportunities, Shirvindt, with his political acumen, was quick to see them. Bukharin was removed from the Politburo in November 1929, and Stalin's victory appeared certain. Shirvindt, who had abstained from supporting Stalin's position of rapid collectivization while Bukharin was in the Politburo, published an article entitled "To the 12th Anniversary of the Soviet Corrective Labor Policy" (*K dvenadtsatiletiiu so-vetskoĭ ispravitel'no-trudovoĭ politiki*).[65] In it, he not only embraced collec-tivization and the Five-Year Plan but, in an attempt to make the places of confinement part and parcel of these policies, theoretically justified the most ruthless exploitation of their inmates in the history of the country. This reversal of position probably saved Shirvindt's life. He was later arrested but not executed whereas most high officials accused of supporting Bukharin perished in the purges.

Shirvindt's article outlined the history of the places of confinement from 1917 until 1929, identifying four periods: the Revolutionary period, 1917-21; the NEP, 1922-24; the Restoration, 1925-28; and the current period of the First Five-Year Plan, 1929. (Shirvindt's periodization is unusual for a modern reader. According to the present view, the NEP included the Restoration, started in 1921, and ended in 1928; industrialization started in 1928; and "complete"—according to Stalinist terminology—or, more accurately, "forced" collectivization began in 1929.) Shirvindt maintained that self-sufficiency and reeducation were the major ideas to emerge during the first period but that the conditions necessary for their realization did not exist. The Civil War had forced the government to use the places of confinement for another purpose: namely, to isolate the "enemies of the toiling people." Then, during the second period, administrative and legal problems dominated the agenda; self-sufficiency and reeducation were again ignored. Although the government had emphasized the economy during the Restoration period, no economic successes were achieved in the penitentiary system. The places of confinement had merely established "a base for a slow transition to self-sufficiency" and made no significant progress in reeducating inmates. Shirvindt argued that the general unemployment in the country had pitted the inmates against free workers. The competition had prevented the places of confinement from finding jobs for most inmates, and alienated free workers from prisoners.[66]

Shirvindt made sure to stress that the Five-Year Plan had eliminated this competition by ending unemployment. Free workers no longer considered convict labor a threat. He urged the government to include the inmate production in the All-Union plan as soon as possible. Some provinces were already doing so. In this way, the All-Union Five-Year Plan would unite inmates with the rest of the country. Soviet citizens would appreciate the contribution of inmate labor, and prisoners would find honor and dignity in fulfilling the plan. Labor within the prison system would finally achieve its potential for reform. By helping to build socialism, inmates would move the country toward "the time when no places of confinement would be needed." On the practical tasks of the places of confinement under the new conditions, Shirvindt quoted the resolution of the First All-Union GUMZ Conference of 24-25 October 1929:

> The Five-Year Plan of industrial development and the collectivization of agriculture established [economic] tasks involving great demand on unskilled labor. Local conditions [bad climate and shortages of food and housing] sometimes present serious obstacles to the recruitment of labor. It is here that the places of confinement, having at their disposal excess labor in great quantities which is not engaged in production near the places of confinement, can assist those economic enterprises which experience a labor shortage.

Citing other sections of the resolution, Shirvindt urged: "Chiefs of the Administrative Departments of the Ural and Northern regions and the NKVD of Karelia must opportunely organize lumber-cutting colonies and furnish them with quarters, tools, clothing, etc."[67]

The inclusion of inmate production in the Five-Year Plan would drastically revise the NKIU interpretation of a major point in the VTSIK-SNK law of 26 March on class policy in the prison system. The NKIU had demanded that inmates work only as laborers at the places of confinement, not as specialists. Shirvindt argued that regardless of their class origins, inmates should contribute to the fulfillment of the plan in accordance with their abilities. Thus, a convicted engineer ought to work as an engineer, not as a janitor.[68] The Soviets had always debated what to do with intellectuals at the places of confinement. Should they serve as professionals or as ordinary laborers? More often than not, Shirvindt's view prevailed, particularly when it came to engineers. Other points of Shirvindt's article became cornerstones of Soviet policy. OGPU writers especially liked to use his ideas to compare their places of confinement with prisons in capitalist countries.[69]

The article was a smashing propaganda success, but it failed to achieve Shirvindt's goal of retaining the places of confinement under the NKVD. Stalin apparently wanted to get rid of the organization for political reasons, and the NKIU had become his instrument. Near the end of November 1929, two weeks after Shirvindt's article had appeared, a pamphlet was published by Evgeniĭ B. Pashukanis, a leading theoretician of the Soviet legal system. Like Krylenko, he had strongly opposed Shirvindt and his people. Pashukanis claimed that inmates from the privileged classes had been purposely granted special treatment by sympathetic GUMZ officials—and not because they possessed professional skills, as Shirvindt had insisted. The GUMZ, Pashukanis argued, consisted to a great extent of former "warders and merchants," who naturally gave preferential treatment to their own kind. Other NKIU spokesmen and writers joined the chorus, and accused the NKVD of supporting Bukharin.[70]

On 30 December 1929, *Pravda* published an article titled "Is the NKVD Needed?" The article urged disbanding the Commissariats of Internal Affairs in all Soviet republics and outlined a plan to distribute NKVD functions among various other agencies. It was actually a revival of the 1924 plan to transfer the places of confinement to the NKIU.[71] Then an All-Union conference of various agencies, meeting 3 January 1930, decided that the NKVD had no future and recommended its abolition. Apparently, the Internal Affairs representatives at the conference were carefully selected, for the resolution passed unanimously. The OGPU also favored the resolution.[72]

The NKVD lasted for one more year. The Council of People's Commissars under Rykov apparently created major obstacles to its dismemberment. Rykov lost his seat on the Politburo, however, and was replaced as chairman of the SNK by Viacheslav Molotov in December 1930. At the same time, the SNK and the VTSIK issued a joint decree, "On the Liquidation of the People's Commissariats of Internal Affairs of the Union and Autonomous Republics" [*O likvidaĩsii narodnykh kommissariatov vnutrennikh del soĩuznykh i avtonom-nykh respublik*]. The enactment stated that the NKVDs at the All-Union and Autonomous Republic levels had played an important role in organizing communal services, in struggling against criminals, and in running state security agencies and places of confinement; nevertheless, during the period of the "all-around attack on the capitalist elements of the city and the village and the socialist reconstruction of the national economy," the NKVD had been unable to execute its functions with the necessary efficiency. The law announced that communal services needed to be included in the Five-Year Plan, and that law enforcement agencies required more "self-discipline and self-reliance."[73]

The decree did not explain why the NKVD had failed to achieve these goals or why it could not achieve them. It did not even mention any deficiencies at the prisons and camps. It simply put all of the NKVD places of confinement, and the agencies that had supervised exiles and persons sentenced to forced labor without deprivation of freedom, under the jurisdiction of the People's Commissariats of Justice in the Union and Autonomous Republics.[74] In fact, Shirvindt's efforts to change the places of confinement to conform to Stalin's policy were very much appreciated by the government. This transfer and presumably his life were his rewards.

6 THE NKIU'S LAST CHANCE
1930-1932

During the early 1930s, the main efforts of officials of the People's Commissariat of Justice (NKIU), like those of officials everywhere in the Soviet Union, went toward fulfilling the Five-Year Plans. Most NKIU places of confinement failed to meet their targets, whereas the Unified State Political Administration (OGPU)—whose share of prison facilities gradually increased—created the impression that it was doing better than other prison agencies. The government decided in October 1934 to transfer the NKIU camps and prisons to the new All-Union People's Commissariat of International Affairs (NKVD), which was set up in July 1934 and had absorbed the OGPU.

The desperate need to fulfill Five-Year Plans changed NKIU ideas about reeducation. Justice began to measure the success of its reeducation efforts by a prisoner's productivity. Inmates who exceeded production norms by 20 percent were considered more successfully reformed than those who surpassed norms by only 10 percent. The NKIU announced in 1931 that it had finally achieved its thirteen-year goal of making its places of confinement self-sufficient. Its budget proposal for 1931 (the last year for which reliable figures are available), even stated that the places of confinement should become not merely self-supporting but profitable. Despite these claims, profits from inmate production did not meet the costs of the prison system; persons who had been sentenced to forced labor without deprivation of freedom still subsidized the Main Administration of Places of Confinement (GUMZ) by turning over 25-50 percent of their salaries to the prison agency. Other organizations did not question the NKIU announcement because they were absorbed in fulfilling their own plans. Energies were directed toward plan fulfillment; challenging bureaucratic boasts was not important at the time.

The NKIU role in economic development led to a far more sinister practice. Beginning in 1931, free workers who were considered unproductive were often arrested and sentenced to prison. The government used fear to persuade the population to work harder. It was no coincidence that in 1930 unemployment was eliminated and the government became the only employer in the USSR. In capitalist countries, employers fire inefficient or disobedient employees. In the Soviet Union, the sole employer imprisoned them. The fear of being fired was replaced by the fear of being arrested.

For the fifteen months from December 1930 through February 1932, the Main Administration of Places of Confinement, under the jurisdiction of the NKIU, tried to compete with the Unified State Political Administration. Both wanted healthy, young inmates. Most of them had been given to the OGPU. The GUMZ lobbied to change this policy, the OGPU to preserve it. The government sided with the latter agency in February 1932 and passed several decrees the following summer which increased OGPU advantages. From then until October 1934, when it lost all its places of confinement, the NKIU was decidedly passive in competing for control of the camps and prisons.

THE NKIU AS A COMPETITOR, 1931

During the early years of the struggle for the places of confinement (1928-30), the NKIU received considerable help from the bureaucracy. People's Commissar of Justice Nikolaĭ Mikhaĭlovich Ianson planned to disband the GUMZ, the prison agency of the NKVD, and to put all the camps and prisons under the jurisdiction of NKIU judges. The NKIU was all for it, particularly the judges and procurators of its two subdivisions. The chief judge was the chairman of the RSFSR Supreme Court, Alekseĭ Nikolaevich Vinokurov, who was to be given the responsibility for the places of confinement if the NKIU won. Nikolai V. Krylenko was chief procurator of the RSFSR and Deputy People's Commissar of Justice. Another deputy commissar, Pëtr Stuchka, was the only high-ranking NKIU official who opposed disbanding the GUMZ. Stuchka was friendlier toward Shirvindt, who headed the agency from 1922 to 1930.[1]

To Ianson's surprise and dismay, the government decided to preserve the GUMZ. On 15 December 1930 it transferred the agency to the NKIU and replaced Shirvindt with P. Apeter. Shirvindt had repeatedly been accused of supporting Bukharin during 1928-29; Apeter did not belong to Shirvindt's group.[2] Shirvindt was also dismissed from his position as director of the State Institute for the Studies of Crime and Criminals, a GUMZ subagency. However, his former colleagues and supporters—M. N. Gernet, M. M. Isacv, P. I. Liublinskiĭ, A. N. Traĭnin, and B. S. Utevskiĭ—remained at the Institute. Shirvindt was a smart and experienced politician, and he had been more influential in the GUMZ than Apeter.[3]

To enhance Apeter's status, Ianson persuaded the USSR Council of People's Commissars (SNK) to appoint Apeter a Deputy People's Commissar of Justice. This made an unknown bureaucrat equal in rank to Stuchka and

Figure 8

The Prison System of the People's Commissariat of Justice of the RSFSR
December 1930 – October 1934

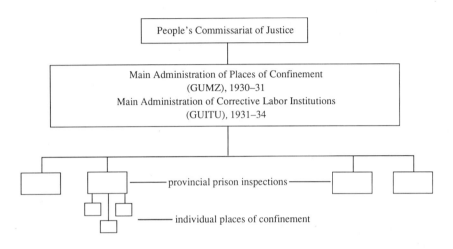

Note the penal agency's name change in 1931

Krylenko.[4] No chief of a prison agency had ever been a Deputy People's Commissar; as head of the GUMZ, Shirvindt had been merely a chief of one of the NKVD departments. Krylenko replaced Ianson as People's Commissar of Justice at the end of 1931, and Andreĭ Ianuar'evich Vyshinskiĭ became the procurator of the RSFSR. Nevertheless, NKIU officials initially welcomed Apeter's promotion, believing that he would allow them to advance rapidly within the GUMZ. This did not occur. One bureaucrat commented bitterly that "nothing had changed except for [the appointment and promotion of] Comrade Apeter."[5] Even Shirvindt had been unable to reconcile rival groups in 1922, and Apeter certainly lacked his political skills.

The growing antipathy toward Apeter could not have come at a worse time. The GUMZ was struggling with the OGPU for its very survival. Whichever agency would more successfully fulfill the First Five-Year Plan would continue to function. In the competition for strong inmates, the OGPU clearly had the edge: it received political prisoners, counterrevolutionaries, and so-called "socially dangerous" elements. Political prisoners included the socialist Mensheviks, Esers, Left Esers, and Anarchists. Members of all other political parties in pre-Revolutionary Russia and former White Army officers and soldiers were deemed counterrevolutionaries. The category of "socially dangerous elements" continually expanded. It included several thousand people in 1921; by 1930 it comprised everyone who had been sentenced to three years or more, which amounted to several *hundred* thousand people. The category of political prisoners was broadened to encompass Communist oppositionists in 1925.[6]

At the beginning of 1930, the OGPU flatly refused to accept disabled and elderly inmates as socially dangerous elements and counterrevolutionaries (it did continue to take all political prisoners, but they amounted to less than 1 percent of OGPU inmate population), and the Main Administration of Forced Labor had to accept inmates rejected by the OGPU. It vigorously protested, but the Stalinist majority obviously backed the OGPU decision. The GUMZ had frequently been accused of siding with Bukharin. Stalin had no trouble deciding whom to support.[7]

Ianson and other NKIU officials also backed the OGPU. Ianson had insisted on the restoration of the original rule of inmate distribution when the places of confinement were transferred to the NKIU. The OGPU would house only political prisoners, counterrevolutionaries, and (in exceptional cases) common criminals. When the government decided to preserve the Main Administration of the Places of Confinement, however, Ianson changed his mind; at the Fourth All-Russian NKIU Conference on 20-24 January 1931, a little more than a month after the GUMZ was transferred to the NKIU, he switched his position on inmate distribution. He noted that the NKIU had demanded control of the NKVD places of confinement because the NKVD had been too soft on prisoners. Ianson said he had not heard any other criticisms of NKIU officials, and suggested they could be satisfied if "harshness were guaranteed."[8] He did not explicitly say that the GUMZ had no reason to revise the current system of distributing inmates, but he certainly implied it. As a result, the GUMZ had to compete with the OGPU without Ianson's support.

Its only advocate in the People's Commissariat of Justice was Stuchka. On 17 March 1931, at a session of the Institute of Soviet Construction and Law of the Communist Academy, the highest educational and research organization in the Soviet Union, Stuchka announced that the places of confinement were indeed becoming financially independent, though the reeducation of inmates, a favorite NKIU thesis, had yet to be addressed. Stuchka proposed segregating inmates according to toiling and nontoiling classes. The most natural segregation along class lines was to put all prisoners from nontoiling classes in OGPU places of confinement and all common criminals in GUMZ facilities.[9] In other words, he would restore the original rule of inmate distribution.

The theory of reeducation formulated by Shirvindt in 1929 had said nothing about inmate segregation. This problem was not as important in 1929 as it became in 1931. Shirvindt believed that the efforts of prisoners toward fulfilling the Five-Year Plan would lead to their reform. This idea was exceed-

ingly popular, and Stuchka was forced to explain in some detail why segregation was essential for reeducation. Stressing that the major step toward
reeducating inmates from the toiling classes was the development of class
consciousness, he quoted Marxist theory which claimed that individuals
developed class consciousness only in struggling against the opposing class.
He asserted that the conditions at the places of confinement did not contribute
to developing class consciousness; in fact, the opposite was true. With inmates
from toiling and nontoiling classes living together, Stuchka noted, they had
united in their hatred of the Soviet state. To break this solidarity, inmates had
to be segregated along class lines. Trade unions must then help inmates from
the toiling classes, both while they were in prison and after their release. In
his explanation, Stuchka simply ignored the inmates from the nontoiling
classes who made up 35 percent of the GUMZ prison population.[10]

Apeter, in his report right after Stuchka's, supported segregation along
class lines but challenged the idea that segregation was necessary for reeducation. In describing the reeducational efforts of the GUMZ, he reverted to
Shirvindt's notion that inmate participation in the Five-Year Plan was a reform
measure in itself. Inmate involvement in "socialist competition" and in the
"shock workers' movement" would bridge the gap between forced and free
labor.[11] These concepts had been introduced in 1929 when Soviet managers
attempted to make free laborers work harder: Socialist competition pitted one
work team against another in performing their jobs; those teams that con-
stantly fulfilled their targets were denoted shock workers.[12] The whole idea
was much despised, but people did not have much choice. Shirvindt had
introduced these notions at the places of confinement in 1930. Apeter was first
to say that the difference between free and forced labor was disappearing
because both had joined the same movement and competed with each other as
equals. Some wits agreed that the difference between forced and free labor
was disappearing, but only because free workers were being forced to work
like inmates.

Apeter was also the first to measure an inmate's reeducation by his productivity. This idea became instantly popular and overshadowed Stuchka's
formulation of the issue. Apeter did not ask that the current distribution of
inmates be altered. He merely suggested that the OGPU could more successfully reeducate the same classes than the GUMZ. Apeter identified an
OGPU agricultural colony near Moscow as the most successful place of confinement in the reeducational effort.[13]

The differences between Apeter and Stuchka over inmate reeducation
may have resulted from the fact that Stuchka had not told anyone he planned
to talk about the issue at the 17 March session of the Institute of Soviet
Construction and Law. All the delegates, especially Apeter, were surprised by
his speech. Apeter was not prepared to alter his remarks at a moment's notice,

and anyway, he believed that Stuchka unfortunately had divorced reeducation from the struggle to fulfill the Five-Year Plan. Months later, Boris Utevskiĭ would try to combine their ideas.[14] For the moment, however, the theoretical split was real and divisive.

Apeter apparently did not fully realize the seriousness of the competition between the GUMZ and the OGPU. Otherwise, he would not have praised the OGPU agricultural colony. In the struggle of the People's Commissariat of Justice against the People's Commissariat of Internal Affairs during 1929-30, Apeter and other NKIU officials had praised the OGPU in order to accentuate the GUMZ's mistakes.[15] Apeter seemed to feel this praise must continue for the sake of consistency. Obviously, he was told about this mistake, for he never again had a kind word for the OGPU places of confinement.

Other NKIU officials were also slow to get the message. In April 1931, V. Men'shatin, an NKIU career officer, reviewed a book by Shirvindt and Utevskiĭ on the Soviet penitentiary system. Men'shatin reproached the authors for failing to portray the achievements of the OGPU in reforming inmates. He regretted not finding a "balanced and . . . nonpartisan" approach in the book and insisted that the OGPU had been more successful than the GUMZ in its program, especially in reeducating juveniles.[16] Several NKIU officials continued their hostility toward the GUMZ throughout the period, undermining its efforts to compete with the OGPU.[17]

Utevskiĭ attempted to seize the day in July 1931. He combined Stuchka's idea that segregation along class lines was necessary for reeducation with Apeter's notion that socialist competition and the shock workers' movement had a reform effect that could be measured by work performance. Utevskiĭ argued that an individual approach to inmates had often created an "individualistic psychology" of capitalist society contrary to the "collective psychology" of socialist society. Any attempt to evaluate an inmate on the basis of his or her work efficiency, a practice introduced at the places of confinement after Apeter's speech of 17 March 1931, had elements of this individual approach. Such elements surely were not strong enough to affect inmates from the toiling classes, who had already acquired a "collective psychology" from their class origin; the concern was that such a practice might strengthen the "individualistic psychology" of inmates from the nontoiling classes. Utevskiĭ proposed evaluating, rewarding, and paroling productive inmates from the nontoiling classes in teams rather than as individuals, thus helping them to develop a "collective psychology." Utevskiĭ suggested inmates be segregated along class lines: that is, exactly what Stuchka had proposed.[18]

The Main Administration of the Places of Confinement (GUMZ) gave these ideas mixed reviews. The organization had splintered in 1929 when Shirvindt gave his support to Stalin's idea of rapid industrialization and collectivization. Iakubson had advocated an individual approach to all inmates, regardless of the class origins, ever since 1922. Curiously, Utevskiĭ had been a proponent of this idea until 1931. Ĭakubson reproached Utevskiĭ for betraying his previous views, calling his proposal a "simplification" of the problem of reform. Ĭakubson found an ally in another GUMZ veteran, Ĭu. Bekhterev, who stressed that anitreligious propaganda, presented individually to religious people, provided a good example of adult reeducation in the Soviet Union. Bekhterev wanted to continue the individual approach to inmate reeducation.[19]

This was not the end of Utevskiĭ's idea on releasing prisoners in teams. Things took an unpredictable turn: the OGPU adopted the proposal—though not for inmates from the nontoiling classes, as Utevskiĭ had suggested. Instead, it mainly paroled common criminals, and on a scale Utevskiĭ had not imagined. After completion of the Baltic Sea–White Sea Canal in 1933, the OGPU released a "team" of 12,484 prisoners all at once.[20]

Perhaps Utevskiĭ's article of July 1931 also saved his own life. In 1929-30, like his boss Shirvindt, Utevskiĭ had been accused of supporting Bukharin. In his memoirs he writes that during the late 1930s he experienced a torture that "even [the Marquis de Sade] had failed to imagine." Utevskiĭ called it "the torture by fear [of arrest]." "When we came [to work] in the morning," he recalls, "we anxiously checked whether all had come, and if somebody was not there, we knew [what had happened]—it was not a sick leave." Utevskiĭ was not arrested; he became convinced that "his turn just did not come."[21] But his article had provided a rationalization for repudiating the individual approach to prisoners. Perhaps somebody remembered this and just put his file at the bottom of a drawer.

The GUMZ made another attempt to enter the field. Its name was changed to the Main Administration of Corrective Labor Institutions (*Glavnoe upravlenie ispravitel'no-trudovykh uchrezhedenii*, or GUITU), and the Bureau of Forced Labor without Deprivation of Freedom, a GUMZ agency, was renamed the Bureau of Corrective Labor without Deprivation of Freedom. These titles recalled the NKIU's Central Corrective Labor Department (TSITO) of 1921-22, which also stressed that the major goal was corrective labor. The interest in reeducation was reflected as well in the title of the OGPU prison agency: the Main Administration of Corrective Labor Camps.[22]

Although the name GUITU emphasized that the agency's major goal was corrective labor, the real purpose of its subagency was to help fulfill the Five-Year Plans. Shirvindt had given a major role to reeducate in his plan for 1929. The Stuchka declaration of 17 March 1931 had also afforded top priority to the reform of inmates, assuming that self-sufficiency would result from the reeducation of prisoners. Stuchka maintained that self-sufficiency was possible in 1931; the proposed GUMZ budget was supposed to prove that assertion (see Table 6).[23]

Table 6. Proposed GUMZ Budget, 1931

Revenue (million rubles)	
From enterprises employing those sentenced to forced labor without deprivation of freedom	32.2
Deductions from wages of such persons who continue to work where they were employed before conviction	17.7
Other [unspecified] sources	1.0
Total	50.9
Expenditures (million rubles)	
Maintenance of places of confinement for adults	15.4
Maintenance of Bureau of Forced Labor without Deprivation of Freedom	6.0
Maintenance of local GUMZ agencies	1.0
Rewards for hard-working prison inmates and personnel	9.8
Maintenance of places of confinement for juveniles	5.0
Construction of new places of confinement	9.8
Total	47.0
[Profit	3.9]

It was easy to challenge Stuchka's claim of self-sufficiency. Indeed, the places of confinement needed 41.0 million rubles in subsidies in 1931. Revenue was supposed to come exclusively from persons sentenced to forced labor without deprivation of freedom—a form of punishment Utevskiĭ had called a "reduction" in worker salaries. Since the reduction varied from 25 to 50 percent, it was profitable to sentence as many people as possible in this way: the innocent were sentenced with the guilty; petty criminals with murderers, rapists, robbers, and thieves. In fact, in 1930, 20 percent of all murderers, 31 percent of rapists, 46.2 percent of robbers, and 69.7 percent of all thieves were put on forced labor without deprivation of freedom. They were profitable, but they were also loose! The proposed budget assumed that those sentenced to forced labor without deprivation of freedom would actually do what they were told to do. Yet even the NKVD, whose system of local offices was much improved by 1931, failed to enforce these sentences in 34 percent of the cases.[24]

Nevertheless, Stuchka continued to insist that the facilities would become self-supporting, though he acknowledged "a danger that this goal, having been achieved, would become a goal in itself. . . . Indeed, if it is so profitable to have inmates, why should we try to reduce their number?"[25] Stuchka asked the question, but he did not answer it. It was a question asked also by millions of innocent people on their plank beds in Soviet places of confinement, and many would decide that the government had arrested them because the places of confinement were profitable and needed more workers. Some Western scholars have shared this opinion, insisting that the Soviet prison system expanded so rapidly simply because it was profitable.[26] Yet there is no proof that places of confinement were either profitable or even self-sufficient at any time from 1917 through 1931, when reliable figures were last available (by then, the system accommodated two million people, and the GULAG Arkhipelago had been established).[27] The GUMZ expected to receive all of its revenue in 1931 from persons sentenced to forced labor without deprivation of freedom—that is, from people *not* in the places of confinement—and NKIU courts sentenced more than 50 percent of the people it convicted to this form of punishment during 1930-34.[28] Astonishingly, most authoritative Western studies on the penal system have simply ignored or even denied the existence of this form of punishment.[29] Western writers determined that the places of confinement were profitable without any knowledge of the real source of GUMZ-GUITU revenue.

The GUMZ-GUITU knew very well that expenditures exceeded revenues. When Stuchka spoke about profitability on 17 March 1931, he was intentionally misleading the government. Under pressure from the OGPU, his agency tried to reduce expenses and increase the number of employed inmates. Apeter was particularly concerned about finances. Immediately after the GUMZ was put under the jurisdiction of the NKIU in December 1930, he had encouraged local places of confinement to employ inmates as warders and military guards, a measure which, he reported in March 1931, reduced the number of non-inmate employees and saved money on salaries. It was true that more people were escaping, especially from remote areas where living and working were harshest, but Apeter assured NKIU authorities that the increased number of escapes was not sufficient to terminate the practice.[30] The use of inmates as warders did not end until the late 1930s, and prisoners stopped serving as guards in the early 1960s.

In order to employ more inmates. Stuchka had the GUMZ-GUITU initiate two actions in March 1931. The first was to separate the elderly and disabled from young and healthy inmates and to employ the former in special factories. Segregation of inmates on the basis of health and age continued thereafter. The second measure involved employing suspects traditionally confined to prison.[31] This idea had been formulated in January 1918 in the NKIU enactment on work teams but had never been implemented.[32] At the 17 March 1931 session of the Institute of Soviet Construction and Law, Stuchka had demanded that suspects work under any conditions, even if it created problems for their interrogators and increased their chances of escape. An NKIU Instruction of 3 April 1931 established the rules for employing suspects at the GUMZ places of confinement, but the percentage of working suspects remained low. Fewer than 15 percent were employed in 1931—apparently a record—whereas about 75 percent of all NKIU inmates worked.[33]

Apeter made another attempt to save money for the GUMZ. The pre-Revolutionary tradition had provided all freed prisoners, regardless of their class origins, with tickets to travel home or to their chosen destinations and with food rations for the trip. On 16 April 1931, Apeter ruled that such inmate privileges should be reserved exclusively for the toiling classes, except in cases of "extreme necessity."[34]

THE TRIUMPH OF THE OGPU

The OGPU implemented some of these NKIU innovations at its facilities. Primarily, it too attempted to employ suspects and to reduce the allowances for released inmates.[35] The competition between these agencies expanded their prerogatives into new areas. In May 1931 a procurator named Galkin, working in the small town of Sereda, reported that local NKIU agencies had convicted both industrial and agricultural workers of nothing more than inefficient work. Only 8 percent were punished with imprisonment or exile; 55 percent were sentenced to forced labor without deprivation of freedom; 24 percent were fined; 13 percent were fired and reprimanded. Galkin was not objecting to conviction for minor infractions; he was insisting that sentences for inefficiency should be more severe, that more inmates should be deprived of their freedom. Similar reports from the provinces were published in the NKIU periodical *Sovetskaia iustitsiia* [Soviet Justice]. The OGPU actually had started to punish unproductive workers several months sooner than the NKIU.[36]

Requests by local NKIU officials to sentence more people to deprivation of freedom contradicted the policy of the central government, which wanted a greater number of sentences to forced labor without confinement. Since the revenue of the GUMZ-GUITU came exclusively from those who worked without losing their freedom, there was no profit in sending more people to the camps. There was, in fact, no profit at all at most camps. Even more amazingly, it really didn't matter. During the First Five-Year Plan, as places of confinement were awarded major construction projects such as dams, hydroelectric power plants, and canals, economic self-sufficiency became meaningless. The government entirely subsidized these projects.

This fact had serious implications for prisoners. Construction needed workers. In provinces where prison camps were entrusted with these massive projects, judges tended to increase the proportion of inmates at the expense of those sentenced to forced labor without deprivation of freedom. Some inmates had been guilty of nothing more than being inefficient, and many of these people went to work on major construction projects. The threat of such a fate helped to maintain high labor productivity elsewhere in the USSR.[37] It was a useful and timely practice, since the fear of unemployment, which had stimulated productivity in the 1920s, had disappeared with the Five-Year Plans.

The GUMZ-GUITU remained at a disadvantage because its inmate population included more elderly and disabled prisoners than that of the OGPU; its personnel were less educated and its warders and guards lower paid. The OGPU, of course, considered this entirely reasonable: its charges were better educated and more hostile to the Soviet state; therefore, its personnel had to be better educated and more qualified. Only 3-4 percent of all GUMZ-GUITU inmates belonged to the nontoiling classes in the 1920s; such inmates made up more than 50 percent of the population at OGPU places of confinement. After the OGPU had refused to accept "socially dangerous" elements who were disabled and old, however, the share of inmates from the nontoiling classes reached 35 percent at GUMZ-GUITU places of confinement in 1931. Apeter was quick to use this development to his advantage. He noted in June 1931 that changes in the GUMZ-GUITU contingent of prisoners required changes in staff. He pointed out that 71 percent of all GUMZ-GUITU employees had only graduated from primary school; just 1.9 percent had some professional training. Apeter complained that his organization had difficulty attracting competent professionals, and the difficulty could be solved only by increasing salaries to the wage levels of military personnel.[38] The government was not persuaded, and salaries remained the same until the NKIU lost its places of confinement in 1934.

The Smolensk Archive contains a document vividly portraying one GUITU prison colony at the beginning of 1934. The living conditions of the colony warders and guards was not much better than housing for the inmates: "There were no separate living quarters for the guards; the chief of one of the guard units with a family which included children of school age shared the prisoners' barracks and ate the prisoners' food. Some of the guards had no shoes and walked around in *lapti*, or bast sandals."[39] Warders, guards, and other low-paid employees of the GUITU knew they would personally benefit if their places of confinement were transferred to the OGPU.

The low standard of living tempted many guards to search for additional income. It was the old story of conducting illegal activities with inmates and ignoring their duties. About 40 percent of the inmates at one GUITU place of detention managed to escape. The GUITU policy of hiring inmates as guards certainly contributed to the inadequate and inept security. Worst hit were the lumber and peat industries. Conditions were horrible, and escapes represented acts of survival rather than any real hope of freedom. Some escapees surrendered at the nearest militia station and begged to be transferred to another place of confinement where jobs were less difficult.[40]

The OGPU had one more advantage over the GUITU by being an All-Union agency, whereas the NKIU, which controlled the GUITU, was merely a republican agency: each Soviet republic had its own NKIU and GUITU. Although the People's Commissariat of Justice of the RSFSR was the head office, it often had difficulty enforcing decrees in the subordinate Autonomous Republics. Apeter tried but failed to centralize the system in December 1930; the central organization simply lacked enough competent personnel to enforce its orders. In June 1931 a provincial GUMZ official characterized communication between the central and local offices: "There was no supervision over our work. Only in very rare cases, a [GUMZ-GUITU] inspector visited us, but when he came, he just boasted that in Moscow everything was much better than here. He did not give any directives and did not provide any assistance."[41]

GUMZ-GUITU setbacks were not over. Stuchka, a long-time GUITU backer who probably had the most original mind of all Soviet penologists died in January 1932. Stuchka was an Old Bolshevik with strong connections. No other person in the People's Commissariat of Justice could have provided the Main Administration of Corrective Labor Institutions (GUITU) with stronger support.

The government finally ruled on the distribution of inmates on 13 February 1932. At the Sixth NKIÛ Conference, a secretary of the Central Committee of the VKP (b), Pavel Petrovich Postyshev, restated the ideas advanced by Shirvindt and Apeter and omitted those promoted by Stuchka and Utevskiĭ.[42] Stuchka and Utevskiĭ had wanted to change the distribution of inmates between the GUMZ-GUITU and the OGPU; Shirvindt and Apeter accepted things the way they were. The government supported the OGPU, and that agency would continue to get the young and healthy inmates. From 1932 until 1934, every government decision on the places of confinement favored the OGPU, whose camps and prisons were expanding at incredible rates. The GUITU population also increased, but its share of inmates in the USSR dropped sharply. The OGPU had won. The GUITU would pay.

7 THE GUITU UNDER SIEGE 1932-1934

Soviet penologists, including Petr Stuchka and Boris Utevskiĭ, accepted the Marxist theory that the number of crimes increased under the influence of capitalism. Conversely, as capitalism waned in the Soviet Union, crime should have decreased. Yet at the beginning of 1932 the number of inmates had probably reached a record two million.[1] The maximum number of prisoners before the Revolution had totaled less than 184,000. Now there were ten times as many. To shift the blame, the Soviets argued that crime increased under the "remnants of capitalism" from habits acquired before the October Revolution.[2] This was face-shaving, if not convincing. It meant that more people committed crimes under the "remnants of capitalism" than under capitalism itself.

The government eventually found a better explanation based on an idea proposed by Stalin in 1930. During the "socialist offensive" against capitalist elements in the country, Stalin had claimed, "the class struggle intensified."[3] Central Committee Secretary Pavel Postyshev restated this notion at the Sixth NKĨU Conference on 13 February 1932. He added that during the current period of collectivization and industrialization, the class struggle took new forms, such as "sabotage" and "careless work." The latter included inefficient work as well.[4]

Postyshev's statement unleashed attacks by officials of the People's Commissariat of Justice (NKĨU) against the cadre of the Main Administration of Places of Confinement-Main Administration of Corrective Labor Institutions (GUMZ-GUITU). At the end of February 1932 an NKĨU official named I. Aminov reviewed P. Shepilov's *Alkogolizm i prestupnost'* [Alcoholism and Criminality]. The volume had been published by a GUITU subagency, the State Institute for the Study of Crime and Criminals, which was headed by Shirvindt until 1931. Shepilov had said that in a socialist economy "both alcoholism and crimes were anomalies; they occurred under the influence of the remnants of the past and the economic and social difficulties connected with the construction of socialism in a backward country." Shepilov claimed

that the USSR already had a socialist economy by 1932.[5] Aminov said quite
bluntly that Shepilov was wrong. Crime was not an anomaly in the Soviet
Union but a natural phenomenon. In the USSR it reflected economic, political, and social conditions that had emerged as a result of the intensification
of the class struggle. Class struggle had been and always would be merciless.
The only correct response to crime was the merciless repression of the
criminal.[6]

Aminov's suggestion to intensify repression, which meant increasing
prison terms, was favored by the Unified State Political Administration
(OGPU). The current rule of prisoner distribution between the GUITU and
the OGPU sent all persons sentenced to three or more years to the OGPU
places of confinement. An increase in the prison terms for crimes would bring
more inmates into the OGPU system.[7]

The government issued several decrees, significantly lengthening the
punishments for various crimes, during the summer of 1932. A joint council of
People's Commissars and the Central Executive Committee (SNK/TSIK),
produced "On the Defense of the Properties of State Enterprises, Collective
Farms, and Cooperative Enterprises and on Strengthening Public Property,"
popularly known as the "Seven-Eight Decree" (issued 7 August 1932). It set
the punishment for anyone caught stealing state or public property at ten
years' deprivation of freedom or even execution. It protected persons loyal
to the government by stipulating that anyone who assaulted or threatened
to assault collective farmers would be sentenced to five to ten years in
prison.[8]

People's Commissar of Justice Nikolaĭ Krylenko justified the harshness of
the law by dividing thieves and embezzlers of state and public property into
five groups: (1) knowing enemies, such as counterrevolutionaries, who organized arson, destruction of imported equipment, and terrorist acts on the
instruction of foreign powers; (2) former private entrepreneurs who tried to
enrich themselves by stealing government and public property; (3) rich and
middle-income peasants who stole from collective farms (Krylenko omitted
poor peasants because those who stole something were usually identified as
middle-income—a paradox from a Marxist point of view: poor peasants appeared to have a greater sense of socialist consciousness than workers who,
unlike poor peasants, stole state and public property); (4) professional thieves;
and (5) simple workers who used government and public property for their
own needs. Krylenko stressed that those who belonged to the first four groups
should be punished without mercy. Leniency might be shown to simple
workers in special cases. Krylenko insisted the times demanded repression.[9]

In September 1932 the Institute of Soviet Construction and Law, now
headed by Krylenko, issued an Instruction on applying the decree of 7 August
1932: those who committed any theft of government or public property,

including simple workers, should be treated as "enemies of the people." A theft of fifty rubles or less, previously considered a petty crime punishable by a reprimand, was now to be thought a "political act" and punished accordingly.[10]

Judges were divided in their reactions. Some tried to apply the decree in each case of theft of state or public property; others refused to apply it at all. *Sovetskaia iustitsiia* reported some extreme cases with disapproval. One peasant was executed for stealing a pig; another received ten years because his dog barked at the chairman of a collective farm. Five persons were sentenced to terms ranging from five to ten years for breaking the branches of a peach tree in a forest. Many judges chose instead to apply the pertinent articles of the old Criminal Code. Those in the Volga German Republic successfully resisted government pressure to apply the decree during the first five months of its publication.[11]

Debates about its provisions apparently embarrassed the government. Stalin lent his strong support to the 1932 decree at the joint plenum of the Central Committee and the Central Control Committee of the VKP(b) in January 1933: "The basis of our system is public property, just as private property is the basis of capitalism. If the capitalists proclaimed private property sacred and inviolable when they were consolidating the capitalist system, all the more reason why we the Communists should proclaim public property sacred and inviolable in order to consolidate the new socialist forms of economy in all spheres of production and trade."[12] Stalin's support encouraged the NKIU to force recalcitrant judges to apply the decree. In February 1933 the NKIU declared that judges who refused were undermining the Soviet state and thenceforth enemies of the people. Newspapers printed similar accusations directed against so-called lenient government, soviet, and Party officials who failed to unmask those who stole state and public property.[13] Just as during the first years of the Revolution, the turmoil and extreme threat to the Soviet state dictated that those with authority must arrest and even kill others in order to survive, so now those who were not in authority could be taken into custody and killed by anyone who wielded power. Some 54,000 were arrested in the first five months after the decree was published. Some 300,000 were incarcerated during the first year.[14]

The increasing number of inmates worried the government. A letter from Stalin and Molotov dated 8 May 1933 was addressed to all Party and soviet workers and to all organs of the OGPU, the courts, and the Procuracy:

> The Central Committee and the Sovnarkom [Council of People's Commissars] are informed that disorderly mass arrests in the countryside are still a part of the practice of our officials. Such arrests are made by chairmen of collective farms and members of collective farms, administrators, by chairmen of village soviets and

secretaries of Party cells, by regional and provincial officials; arrests are made by all who desire to, and who, strictly speaking, have no right to make arrests. . . . It is not surprising that in such a saturnalia of arrests, organs which do have the right to arrest, including the organs of the OGPU and especially the militia, lose all feeling of moderation and often perpetrate arrests without any basis, acting according to the rule, "First arrest, then we'll see whom we have arrested."[15]

The letter went on to prohibited arrests by anyone except the officials of the Procuracy, the OGPU, and the militia. In order to ease prison overcrowding, the letter ordered that the number of inmates at the places of detention of the NKĬU, the OGPU, and the militia, then housing 800,000 prisoners, be reduced by half. Inmates at NKĬU colonies and OGPU corrective labor camps, which held 70-80 percent of all the prisoners in the country (at least 1.8 million people), were not included in this number, but the OGPU and the Procurator of the USSR were told to establish quotas for prisoners in each province and republic. Among the 400,000 persons expelled from prisons, those sentenced to five or more years or considered especially dangerous regardless of their terms were dispatched to OGPU corrective labor camps. Those sentenced to three to five years were sent to OGPU labor settlements.[16]

The Stalin-Molotov letter did not allocate any inmates to the places of confinement of the Main Administration of Corrective Labor Institutions (GUITU). People who received terms of less than three years had been customarily interned in GUITU camps and prisons; now their terms were commuted to one year of forced labor without deprivation of freedom.[17] The decree of 7 August 1932 had put the GUITU in financial straits, and this decision was intended to get it out. About 50 percent of those convicted by NKĬU courts had been sentenced to forced labor without deprivation of freedom in 1929. The proportion increased to 56 percent during 1930-31 and reached a record 58 percent during the first half of 1932. At that time, the GUITU proclaimed itself profitable as a result of deductions taken from the wages of persons sentenced in this way.[18] With the drastic increase in punishments for petty crimes, however, the share of persons sentenced to forced labor without deprivation of freedom compared to those deprived of their freedom had dropped to 49 percent—the lowest figure since 1928—and then to 37 percent during the first quarter of 1933. The Stalin-Molotov letter turned everything around: during the second quarter of 1933 the proportion increased to 45 percent and reached 53 percent in the third quarter, just 5 percent below the record level of the first half of 1932.[19]

During the 1920s, output at places of confinement had not been included in the government production totals. The state was satisfied if the prison agencies were self-sufficient. This lenient attitude changed during the First Five-Year Plan. Although the draft plan of 1929 ignored production at the GUMZ-GUITU places of confinement, more and more provinces were including prison output in their local plans. The Second Five-Year Plan (1933-37) included the production of all GUITU facilities right from the beginning of the planning period, and stressed that fulfillment of quotas was the most important goal of the agency.[20]

The places of confinement met these goals as best as they could. The usual method, the only method available, was to exploit the inmates. In Leningrad and the western provinces, inmates were made to work for months without any time off. In another province, prisoners were not allowed to leave their places of work until they had fulfilled daily quotas. Although the NKIU reprimanded the camps and prisons for such practices, it criticized them more severely if they failed to meet their quotas; hence, administrations at these places felt justified in employing whatever means were necessary to make the inmates work harder. Still, the GUITU was not entirely successful: Only about 70 percent of the target goals were met, and the textile industry at the places of confinement never attained as much as 20 percent of its planned output.[21]

These failures were reported by the NKIU in every issue of *Sovetskaia iustitsiia;* career officials of the People's Commissariat of Justice had disliked the GUMZ-GUITU ever since 1922. The OGPU, on the other hand, never reported its failures, only its successes.[22] The government and the public were persuaded by this deception that the OGPU was running things more efficiently than the NKIU. In October 1934 the government united all the places of confinement under the All-Union NKVD—which had been established in July 1934—including the OGPU prison agency and its subagencies.

The GUITU failure to meet its targets did not mean it was unproductive; on the contrary, GUITU output grew very rapidly. If we take 1930 production as 100, the index of production was 220 in 1931, 335 in 1932, and planned to reach 552 in 1933. Labor productivity at the GUITU facilities increased slightly during this period, from 10 to 20 percent. In some areas such as agriculture, it did not increase at all, and it exceeded 20 percent only in the timber industry.[23]

This increase in production must be attributed to the larger number of prisoners entering GUITU places of confinement. Assuming that the GUITU production statistics were not inflated, one may infer that the number of its inmates increased two to three times between 1930 and 1933 and reached at least 600,000. In 1933, the OGPU may have housed at least 2 million inmates. As has been mentioned, the number of prisoners in the country in May 1933 was at least 2.6 million.[24]

Agriculture, the biggest GUITU failure, and timber, its biggest success, were considered the most important industries. The agricultural places of confinement had been established in Imperial Russia, but not until after the October Revolution were they supposed to feed all the inmates in the country. This goal, never realized, was ignored during the 1920s but attracted renewed

interest in 1929 when the government began to collectivize agriculture. Some
GUITU officials even proclaimed enthusiastically that their agricultural
camps should become exemplary collective farms. The reality was something
else. The productivity of the agricultural colonies in 1933 reached only 60
percent of the average yield of Soviet collective farms, which was itself not very
high.[25] Chief Agronomist Iashkov, of the GUITU Agricultural Division attributed the low production to a shortage of permanent workers: the GUITU
got only those convicts whose terms were less than three years.[26] The agency
complained further, quite correctly, that the central and local government did
not adequately provision its colonies. According to the rule of the central state
planning agency, USSR Gosplan, collective farms had to receive one horse for
every eight hectares of cultivated land. GUITU agricultural colonies got one
for every thirteen hectares.[27]

The success of the GUITU lumber industry certainly resulted from the
fact that the inmates were actually the first full-time lumberjacks in the
country. The majority of lumberjacks had been local peasants who worked at
these jobs during the winter and used their own primitive tools and draft
animals. The Finnish lumberjacks produced three to four times as much
lumber as the peasants had. The GUITU success in increasing the productivity of its workers by 20-25 percent must be seen in this perspective.[28]

The Statutes of the GUITU Places of Confinement were approved jointly
by the SNK and the VTSIK on 1 August 1933. They had been compiled by the
State Institute for the Study of Crime and Criminals, a GUITU subagency,
and by the Institute of Soviet Construction and Law, directed by Krylenko.
Work had begun in April 1932, some two months after the government had
taken the side of the OGPU against the GUITU in the competition for young
and healthy prisoners.[29] For about a year and a half, the GUITU published
nothing new.

The Statutes replaced those issued in 1924. Ever since the beginning of
collectivization in 1929, the Soviet press had continually criticized the 1924
document for being bourgeois in outlook. The 1933 Statutes stated outright:
"The goal of the criminal policy of the proletariat during the transitional period
from capitalism to Communism is the defense of the dictatorship of the
proletariat and the process of socialist construction from hostile attacks by class
enemies and from transgressions by both the declassed and the unstable elements of the toiling classes." The goal of criminal policy so tortuously described in this decree differed from that formulated by the Institution of Soviet
Construction and Law in September 1932. Everyone who stole state property
was an enemy of the people, regardless of his or her class origin. This more
temperate goal nonetheless fully corresponded to government policy following the Stalin-Molotov letter of May 1933. These new Statutes also confirmed
the policy in effect since 1929 which stipulated that the main punishment for

crimes should be forced labor without deprivation of freedom. The GUITU quite simply needed the revenues generated by such sentencing.[30]

The Statutes recognized four types of prison colonies. There were, of course, isolators for suspects, transit prisons, and labor houses for juvenile offenders, but the main types were industrial, agricultural, mass labor, and penal colonies. Industrial and agricultural colonies were to house petty criminals predominantly from the toiling classes. The mass labor colonies held inmates from the nontoiling classes and all inmates who had committed dangerous crimes. (One should add that while the definition of dangerous crimes changed, it never included the theft of personal property or assault without bodily harm.) Penal colonies incarcerated those who had broken rules and regulations while they were being held in other types of colonies.[31]

All Soviet statutes on the places of confinement have been notable for their lack of detail, compared with those issued before the Revolution. The Statutes of 1933 provided even fewer details than earlier ones. Apeter pointed out that they had been drafted to give only "general directives" and to define "general policy"; the particulars would be revealed later in special instructions.[32] The lack of details reflected the social and bureaucratic turmoil. Legal interpretations of various penal measures were revised several times a year. The only thing of any permanence, as the saying goes, was change.

The GUITU did not escape such change. When the government decided in April 1934 to establish the All-Union People's Commissariat of Internal Affairs (NKVD), the GUITU rightly perceived this new agency as a threat to its very existence. Even People's Commissar of Justice Krylenko, never a friend of the GUITU, decided that it was time to defend the old agency and initiated a publicity campaign for the places of confinement. In May 1934 he invited delegations of Greek and Italian workers already in Moscow to visit a GUITU mass labor colony that was engaged in constructing an industrial complex at Magnitogorsk. The newspaper *Magnitogorskii rabochii* (The Magnitogorsk Worker) of 19 May 1934 reported that the foreign workers had been impressed by the achievements of the colony, especially by the fact the inmates labored only eight hours a day, received salaries, and attended theater and circus performances. On 23 May another local paper, *Bor'ba za metall* (The Struggle for Metal) quoted a member of the Italian delegation who remarked that while Soviet inmates had jobs and could hope for a happy future, many workers in capitalist countries were doomed to unemployment. According to the article, the worker declared that inmates in the West were physically tortured because it was the only method of reeducation under capitalism. These same reports appeared in *Sovetskaia iustitsiia*.[33]

Krylenko delivered a radio address called "The Major Principles of the Corrective Labor Policy" on 24 May 1934.[34] He identified two categories of inmates. The first included class enemies, who had to be taught not to interfere with socialist construction. Inmates in this category had been and should be confined in OGPU facilities. The second category included inmates from the toiling classes, "unwillingly" involved in the criminal world by class enemies. These inmates must be treated differently from class enemies, even if they had committed serious crimes. They must be kept in GUITU places of confinement. Hoping to save the GUITU places of confinement, Krylenko asked for the restoration of the original rule of inmate distribution, under which political prisoners, counterrevolutionaries, and the most dangerous criminals had been sent to OGPU places of confinement, while the rest of the convicts were put in GUMZ-GUITU detention centers. This rule had been altered in 1929-1930 to favor the OGPU by giving it all healthy and young inmates with terms of three or more years. The GUMZ-GUITU had tried to restore the original rule, but failed. Now Krylenko was trying again. He had once insisted that anyone who stole any state or public property should be regarded as an enemy of the people; he had moderated this position after the Stalin-Molotov letter of 1933 expressed the concern that too many people were being arrested. He stated that petty theft of state or public property was no longer a political act. On 24 May 1934, Krylenko affirmed in his radio address that petty theft was not an act against the people and asserted that the perpetrators deserved special treatment in a GUITU facility.

If all of this looked desperate, it was. Stalin had apparently promised Krylenko that he would not disband the GUITU after setting up the All-Union NKVD on 10 July 1934. Despite this reassurance, the GUITU was abolished on 27 October 1934. In the interval, Krylenko and other NKIU officials acted as if the subagency would operate for at least another year. *Sovetskaia iusti-tsiia* suggested in June that all GUITU places of confinement should partici-pate in socialist competition by the end of the year. At the beginning of October the periodical stressed that the mass labor colonies of the GUITU had played and would continue to play an increasingly important role during the coming year.[35] Within days, the GUITU was out of business.

On 27 October 1934, a joint SNK and TSIK decree ordered all GUITU places of confinement to be transferred to the All-Union NKVD. All GUITU agencies and their local offices were told to disband, and a Department of Places of Confinement (*Otdel mest zakliucheniia*) was established within the NKVD prison agency. The Main Administration of Corrective Labor Camps and Labor Settlements (*Glavnoe upravlenie ispravitel'no-trudovukh lagereii trudovykh poselenii*) replaced the GUITU.[36]

The Main Administration originated in the 1920s as a subagency of the OGPU, responsible for only a small number of camps and prisons. Under various titles, it has run all of the places of confinement in the Soviet Union since 1934.

8 GPU-OGPU
PLACES OF CONFINEMENT
1922-1928

In 1922 the government tried to reduce the powers of the secret police. The Cheka, which had been directly subordinate to the RSFSR Council of People's Commissars (SNK), was disbanded in February. Its successor, the State Political Administration (GPU), was put under the supervision of the People's Commissariat of Internal Affairs (NKVD). An enactment of the All-Russian Central Executive Committee (VTSIK), passed between February and 2 May 1922, allowed the GPU to retain only two places of confinement—one in Moscow, the other in Petrograd—and transferred some 300 Cheka camps and prisons to the People's Commissariat of Justice (NKIU). This transfer to be completed by 1 July.[1]

The GPU actually was able to retain more places of confinement than the VTSIK had envisaged. The transfer was not completed by the 1 July deadline because the NKIU lacked the manpower to replace Cheka-GPU personnel.[2] In October 1922, apparently because of this problem, the SNK subordinated all the NKIU places of confinement to the NKVD, including those prisons and camps that the NKIU was to take over from the Cheka. The State Political Administration (GPU) retained its two prisons, but the rest were to be directed by a subagency of the NKVD called the Main Administration of Places of Confinement (GUMZ).[3]

The NKVD effectively controlled the Soviet prison system. All three agencies charged with its operation—the GUMZ, the people's militia, and the GPU—were under the NKVD, and the distribution of prisoners among the places of confinement was now considered an internal matter of this commissariat. Power was further concentrated in the person of Feliks Dzerzhinskii, who directed the GPU. He had headed the Cheka during its entire existence (December 1917-February 1922) and during 1921-22 had resisted the idea of reducing the authority of the Cheka and the number of its prisons and camps.

Lenin was the major force behind the initiative to limit the power of the secret police. It was Lenin who had urged disbanding the Cheka and establishing the GPU with restricted authority; to accomplish this end, he sent

Dzerzhinskiĭ on a business trip to Siberia for four months, from December 1921 to March 1922.[4] The plan probably would have worked had not Lenin suffered a stroke in May 1922, which prevented him from participating actively in governmental affairs. Dzerzhinskiĭ returned and managed to undermine the VTSIK decree of 2 May 1922, which had left GPU with just the two places of confinement.

Prior to February 1922 the Cheka-controlled prisons and concentration camps included the Northern Special Purposes Camps (*Severnye lageriа osobogo naznacheniiа,* or SLON) in Arkhangel'sk province. The SLON also encompassed camps in the former monastery and hermitages on the islands of the Solovetskiĭ Archipelago in the White Sea, known as the Solovki. Dzerzhinskiĭ allowed the GPU to retain the Northern Special Purpose Camps, which were apparently renamed the Solovetskiĭ Special Purpose Camps. The SLON administration remained in Arkhangel'sk. The GPU had other facilities throughout the country as well. Besides the SLON camps and its prisons in Moscow and Petrograd, the GPU controlled prisons in other cities, such as Viatka and Suzdal' (from 1923), and about ten small, scattered camps.[5] GPU prisons were termed "isolators"; the official title of the ten camps is unknown. One Soviet writer called all the Cheka-GPU facilities of the 1920s "corrective labor camps," but this is certainly wrong, because that term was not introduced until April 1930.[6]

Shirvindt, chief of the GUMZ, did not publicly object to the establishment of the rival NKVD prison agency under Dzerzhinskiĭ. One compelling reason was that Dzerzhinskiĭ was his boss. Another was that Shirvindt did not immediately perceive a threat from the State Political Administration. At the end of 1923 the GPU's places of confinement housed no more than 7,000 inmates—just 6.5 percent of the total 110,000 prisoners in the country. Additionally, the distribution of inmates between the two agencies seemed likely to prevent the expansion of GPU powers. Its facilities held political prisoners, counterrevolutionaries, and common criminals who were considered "incorrigible." The politicals included only members of the socialist parties (Mensheviks, Esers, and Left Esers) and anarchists. They had hounded by the Cheka, and their numbers had steadily decreased after the October Revolution. The counterrevolutionaries were mainly members of all the other pre-Revolutionary parties and former members of the White Army. They had been persecuted even more harshly than the socialists and the anarchists, and their numbers had also fallen since the Civil War in 1920.[7] The only category of inmates that had remained unchanged or even slightly increased since the Civil War was the common criminal. Of the record total of 200,000 prisoners in 1922, half were common criminals. By the end of 1923, the total number of inmates decreased to 110,000, more than 100,000 of whom were common criminals.[8]

To expand its powers, the GPU resorted to a linguistic deception in order to increase the number of inmates classified as "incorrigible common criminals." This was no easy task, because leading Bolsheviks believed that there was no such thing as an incorrigible criminal; all such persons could be reformed. This ideological position served Shirvindt's interests, and he hoped that the government would eventually return all common criminals from the GPU to his GUMZ.[9] But the GPU was ahead of everyone on this. In 1923, it merely accepted the view that all criminals could be reeducated and pledged to accomplish this task. It dropped the term "incorrigible" in favor of "most dangerous"; it was, of course, talking about the same criminals, but this tactic kept them under GPU control. A common poster on barracks walls underscored this message: "The Soviet Government does not punish; it reforms."[10] By showing a willingness to participate in the reform of inmates, the GPU challenged the GUMZ's monopoly on educating prisoners.

Mere willingness, however, would have been insufficient had political changes in the Soviet Union not worked to GPU advantage. The First Congress of the Soviets of the USSR approved the formation of the Union of Soviet Socialist Republics on 30 December 1922. There were initially four republics: the Russian Soviet Federated Socialist Republic (RSFSR), the Ukraine, Belorussia, and Transcaucasia. The new constitution of 6 July 1923 separated the GPU offices from the republican-level NKVDs and subordinated them to the newly established Unified State Political Administration (*Ob"edinënnoe gosudarstvennoe politicheskoe upravlenie*, or OGPU). The OGPU and the Commissariats of Defense and Navy, Foreign Affairs, Foreign Trade, Posts and Telegraph, and Communications became All-Union agencies, directly under the USSR Council of People's Commissars. The NKVD continued to function but at the republican level only. Dzerzhinskiĭ was appointed chief of the OGPU and replaced as chief of the NKVD of the RSFSR by his deputy, Aleksandr Georgievich Beloborodov.[11] When Dzerzhinskiĭ died in 1926, Vi͡acheslav Rudol'fovich Menzhinskiĭ took over. (Menzhinskiĭ had belonged to the Russian Socialist-Democratic Labor Party, or RSDRP, since 1902 and had graduated from the law school at Petersburg University.)[12] By that time, the status of the OGPU had become as high as or even higher than that of its predecessor, the Cheka, which had been subordinate to the Council of People's Commissars of the RSFSR. The OGPU was now directly subordinate to the SNK of the USSR.

The share of OGPU inmates grew at an astounding rate. In 1923 the SLON housed 4,000 inmates, or about 70 percent of all OGPU prisoners. The number increased to 7,093 in 1925 and to more than 22,176 during 1927-28. The number of prisoners in all the OGPU camps exceeded 30,000. The number of GUMZ prisoners in all republics arose from 100,000 to 240-270,000 during 1923-28; thus, the OGPU share grew from 6.5 percent to more than 10 percent.[13]

The Special Department or Spetsotdel apparently administered OGPU places of confinement. The Old Bolshevik Gleb Ivanovich Bokiĭ ran the Spetsotdel. His deputy was Ĭa. P. Fel'dman.[14] One of Dzerzhinskiĭ's deputies, Genrikh Ĭagoda, who headed the OGPU after the death of Menzhinskiĭ until May 1934, was apparently also in charge of GPU-OGPU places of confinement. In 1925 Ĭagoda organized the transfer of a group of political prisoners from Solovki to a prison in the Ural Mountains known as the Verkhneural'skiĭ political isolator. The head of the SLON administration (USLON) was an Old Bolshevik named Eĭkhmans. The Solovetskiĭ Archipelago had six divisions, one each for the Muksol'skiĭ, Anzerskiĭ, and Kond islands and three for Solovetskiĭ Island: the Kremlin, the Savvatievskiĭ Hermitage, and Sekirnyĭ Mountain. Sekirnyĭ Mountain was the penal division, perhaps the most infamous in Soviet history for its tortures. The Kremlin was the residence of USLON, which had moved from Arkhangel'sk in 1923.[15]

In the familiar practice to reduce costs, USLON employed inmates as warders, guards, clerical workers, and even supervisory personnel. The last group was made up primarily of former GPU-OGPU operatives who had been convicted of criminal offenses, and former officers and men of the White Army. The USLON staff was small. Solzhenitsyn maintained that it never exceeded forty people in all six divisions of Solovki, though this figure did not include warders, guards, and clerks at the transit camp at Kem' on Popov Island.[16] Solovki, of course, was not the only place to use inmates as guards, but it was the only area where this practice did not create serious security problems. Escape was extremely difficult; many of those who claimed to have gotten away from the islands actually had fled from the transit prison at Kem', which was close to the mainland.[17]

As a result of this exceptional security, the OGPU sent everyone suspected of planning an escape to the islands. Solovki housed counterrevolutionaries and common criminals until 1923. Politicals were kept elsewhere, such as the former Petrominsk Monastery in western Arkhangel'sk province, from which several escaped to nearby Finland. The OGPU was not authorized to transfer political prisoners without government permission, and Moscow refused to send them to Solovki, not wishing to antagonize socialists in other countries. The harshness of the camp was known abroad, and the Soviet government feared any transfers would provoke foreign protests. That situation changed after two socialists escaped from Petrominsk in June 1923. There were rumors that the OGPU had abetted the escapes to force the government's hand, and Moscow subsequently did approve the transfers. Thereafter, politicals were segregated at the Savvatievskiĭ and Muksol'ma Hermitages from other inmates on the Solovetskiĭ Islands. Socialists abroad did protest, as expected, but they were badly organized, and Moscow was able to ignore them.[18]

The Kremlin of the Solovetskii monastery, located on an island in the White Sea. The OGPU transformed the monastery into one of its most infamous prison camps.

Designation as a political prisoner was not a minor matter. Ekaterina Olit̑skaia, a former Eser who from 1924 spent about thirty years in Soviet prisons and camps and in exile, has described the difference in conditions for political prisoners and others:

> The regime of our [political] prisons and camps drastically differed from the general regime: in some ways it was easier, but in others, significantly more strict. Political prisoners received additional portions of food. They were released from forced labor, they had self-government in the political isolators, they elected monitors, through whom they communicated with the administration [as a group]. They retained their belongings, clothes, books, pens, pencils, stationery, watches, knives, forks, and even razors. They had the right to subscribe to magazines and newspapers. But their isolation from the outside world was significantly more strict. Their movements were limited within the camps and prisons. Their correspondence and visits by relatives were also limited.[19]

Men and women political prisoners were not segregated, and politicals received food packages from the Political Red Cross, which continued somehow to function throughout the 1920s. The transfer of a political prisoner to the general regime was regarded as a tragedy that could easily end in death.[20]

A former prisoner described the general regime:

[Every day sleds arrived from the forest] with corpses of prisoner-loggers. Some of them were beaten [by the administration] and some were frozen to death. . . . Because [the Solovki] did not provide prisoners with clothes, they had to work [in the forest] in their own clothes; and some actually had no clothes at all. . . . Behind the sleds there walked a group of loggers who had been injured, frostbitten, or crippled by the administration. . . . some prisoners . . . intentionally cut their own wrists or feet [hoping to get out of the forest]. . . . [Because the prisoners had to produce,] the standing order [of the camp commandant] stipulated that those who intentionally injured themselves might be executed.[21]

Those who transgressed the camp rules were taken to the central penalty division or isolator located in the former church at the Sekirnyĭ or Sekirka Mountain. Although the prisoners there did not work, the conditions were extremely difficult. Their clothes were taken, and "they were supposed to stay there only in ther underwear. . . . One should remember that [the isolator] was in a huge, very high-ceilinged building . . . which actually was not heated . . . in the polar winter. Food was given once a day. It consisted of one pound of bread . . . and a bowl of turbid liquid called soup which hardly contained any nutrients."[22] A song made the isolator at the Sekirka Mountain known to generations of prisoners:

There is a Sekirka Mountain.
Many dead bodies have been buried there.
[Only] wind is free there.
And dear mother will never know
Where her son's grave is.[23]

In general, the conditions in the OGPU places of confinement in the 1920s were better than in the Cheka's during the Revolution, but some prisoners said that the difference was not very significant.

Is it true that they shoot prisoners in the Soviet Union? Yes, they do. Not so often as they did earlier and only with the permission of the center. Nevertheless, they shoot when they want and as many people as they want.
    Physical torture and beating [also] exist in the Soviet Union. I can give you many examples of beating and torture in the Solovki and in prisons. . . . [What is most depressing is not that] they beat or shoot prisoners but that they can do it any time, . . . they can beat you up, torture you, shoot you any time they want [whether you are guilty or innocent]. It is important to remember that everybody is afraid of this possibility, that there are neither [individual] rights nor laws, that arbitrary rule [in the Soviet Union] continues.[24]

Although both counterrevolutionaries and common criminals were nominally on the same regime, the camp administration actually treated counterrevolutionaries more harshly. They "were not protected by any law. . . . When
a criminal was caught in an attempt to escape, he actually received an additional two years, but whenever a counterrevolutionary tried to escape, he was
inevitably executed. Counterrevolutionaries were often executed for a [sim-
ple] transgression of the camp rules, and certainly for disobedience." The life
expectancy for counterrevolutionaries at Solovki was probably less than two
years. It was between two and three years for common lawbreakers, and four
to five for politicals.[25]

Because privileges for political prisoners provoked jealousy among other
inmates, the OGPU used inmate demands for equal treatment to deprive
politicals of their privileges. The politicals responded by refusing to obey
orders and by going on hunger strikes—which were successful only if word
reached socialists abroad and, of course, as long as the Soviet government
cared about foreign opinion. In December 1924 a group comprising mostly
Eser political prisoners at the Savvatievskiĭ Hermitage refused to obey an
injunction to be in their barracks by six o'clock in the evening; they considered
the order a test of wills. The chief of Savvatievskiĭ, a man named Nogtev,
ordered prisoners shot; six were killed, and news of the incident provoked
sufficient outrage among socialists in the West to help the political prisoners
retain their privileges.[26]

The incident also persuaded the OGPU to enforce its will. In 1925 most
political prisoners were transferred from the Solovki to various political isolators on the mainland. The Soviet government characterized this move as a
humanitarian gesture, but socialist prisoners decided that the true motive was
to divide the politicals into smaller, more manageable groups. If so, the
government had indeed acted wisely. Over the ensuing three years, political
prisoners lost their privileges at most of the places of confinement.[27] Nonetheless, for most of the 1920s, the politicals were able to hold their ground and
retain their most valued right—not to work.

As previously mentioned, inmate production was not included in the state
economic plans during the 1920s; it was enough if the places of confinement
were self-sufficient. Both the Spetsotdel and the GUMZ failed to achieve even
this goal, but the Spetsotdel created the impression that its inmates were
more efficient than prisoners at GUMZ facilities—partly because most OGPU
inmates worked in the timber industry, whereas only a negligible portion of
GUMZ laborers were employed as lumberjacks.[28]

Lumber was important to the Soviet government for export. Peasants had
dominated the seasonal industry before the Revolution. They were untrained
and inefficient but produced at least enough to meet the industrial needs of
the country and to provide some surplus for export. Prior to the Revolution,

the major Russian export was grain, which amounted to approximately 50 percent of the total value of exports. Wealthy and middle-class landowners marketed the greater portion; most peasants raised just enough to meet their own needs. When the Bolsheviks redistributed the land of the wealthy and middle-class landowners among the peasants, grain exports stopped abruptly. Despite efforts to restore the grain trade, exports had reached only 20 percent of their pre-Revolutionary level in 1923. [29]

The government decided in 1924-25 that lumber should replace grain as the main export. Arable land actually belonged to the peasants, but the forests belonged to the government; all the state needed was people to cut the trees. But many peasants who had worked as lumberjacks, having now been given land, were no longer interested, and the number of peasants working part time in the lumber industry dropped significantly during the early Soviet period. In the Ural region the number of lumberjacks fell from 50,000-60,000 in 1913 to 30,000 in 1925. [30]

This was happening throughout the countryside. Lumber production in 1925 was half that of 1913. The government needed a dramatic increase in production in order to export lumber profitably, but even with its new source of labor in the GUMZ and the Spetsotdel, there were still too few healthy and strong inmates to make up for the loss of peasant labor. Lumber production grew slowly, and output reached the 1913 level only in 1928. [31]

Forced collectivization changed everything. Thousands of peasants were arrested in 1929-30 for resisting the campaign, and the Spetsotdel was transformed in a most remarkable way.

9 THE OGPU DURING COLLECTIVIZATION & INDUSTRIALIZATION

During the collectivization and industrialization phase of the Soviet Union, the number of inmates in OGPU facilities increased from thousands to millions. Most worked in the lumber industry during 1929-30, the first two years of the expansion of the prison population. Thousands were conscripted for such massive construction projects as the White Sea–Baltic Sea and Moscow-Volga canals, and to work in gold mines in the Kolyma region.

Theory was adjusted to suit practice. The idea prevailed in 1929 that inmate participation in the Five-Year Plan would have beneficial reeducational effects. This notion was modified to suggest that the best effects would be obtained by having inmates work on large construction projects. The theory was propagated by the Main Administration of Corrective Labor Camps and Labor Settlements (soon known as GULAG), the OGPU prison agency responsible for construction. Established in April 1930, the GULAG took over the places of confinement that had belonged to the Spetsotdel, which had operated the OGPU prisons and camps since 1921.

Two other agencies also ran places of confinement. The Main Administration of Corrective Labor Institutions (GUITU) of the Commissariat of Justice (NKIU) assumed responsibility for the facilities of the Main Administration of the Places of Confinement (GUMZ) in December 1930. The GUMZ had been subordinate to the Commissariat of Internal Affairs (NKVD) of the RSFSR. Another prison organization, the Dal'stroĭ (Far Eastern Construction Administration) was organized during the winter of 1931-32. It was legally subordinate to the GULAG but actually was directly responsible to the chief of the Unified State Prison Administration (OGPU). As with previous prison bureaucracies, all three agencies competed for young and healthy inmates.

The GULAG was the most successful. Its power increased in July 1934 when the NKVD of the USSR took over the OGPU. The GULAG became a subagency of this new commissariat. Several months later it absorbed the GUITU. In 1937, after the execution of the head of the Dal'stroĭ for being too independent, the GULAG gained control of its enterprises as well.

No other agency was as profoundly influenced by collectivization and industrialization as the Spetsotdel. The decisions of the fifteenth Party Congress in
December 1927 to collectivize agriculture and to draft the First Five-Year Plan
of economic development did not have an immediate impact on the OGPU
places of confinement, however. During the first half of 1928, only those
agencies whose budgets were reduced felt the effects of the innovations.[1]

The GUMZ was affected, but the Spetsotdel was too small to have its
budget cut. It housed 30,000 inmates (about 10 percent of the total prison
population); it employed no more than 1,000 people; and its budget hardly
exceeded 0.05 percent of state expenditures. By comparison, the GUMZ of
the RSFSR held about 150,000 inmates and consumed 0.25 percent of the
state budget.[2] The government went after the larger target. It proposed
reducing the population of the GUMZ facilities by sentencing more people to
forced labor without deprivation of freedom, a policy that was financially
successful. By 1931, deductions from salaries of persons sentenced in this way
covered the expense of all GUMZ places of confinement.[3]

The practice undermined the GUMZ's competitive edge over the Spetsotdel. The government arrested thousands of peasants for their resistance to
collectivization in 1929-30. Moscow did not particularly want to increase the
population of GUMZ facilities but considered the offenses too serious to sentence the perpetrators only to forced labor without deprivation of freedom. Its
only recourse seemed to be to send them to the OGPU camps and prisons.
During two years (spring 1928-spring 1930), the number of prisoners under
OGPU jurisdiction apparently increased from 30,000 to at least 300,000, or
1,000 percent![4]

The new prisoners were employed in the timber industry and in the
construction of railroads and highways. The increase in lumber production was
dramatic. In 1929, SLON inmates produced 37 times as much lumber as in
1926; in 1930, they increased production another 300 percent. The growth was
attributable not only to the increase in the number of inmates working as
lumberjacks but to a rise in inmate productivity as a result of the USLON's
policy of punishment for inefficient work. Inefficiency had always been a
punishable offense; prison administrations had put inmates with low productivity in punishment cells, reduced their food rations, and occasionally shot
them. But there had been no generally accepted rules governing punishment;
under local discretion, there had been instances where the refusal by a good
worker to perform a certain task was punished severely, whereas refusal by
an inefficient inmate to work for several days met with indifference. The
new rules eliminated these inconsistencies. Systematic refusal to work was
deemed "counterrevolutionary sabotage," punishable by execution. For those

who worked, the Spetsotdel set up four levels of food rations. The more efficiently inmates labored, the more they got to eat. The lowest ration meant certain death by starvation.[5]

Credit for establishing the system of correlating food to work has been attributed to two inmates, Naftaly Frenkel' and Ivan Seletskiĭ. Fellow prisoners have, for this reason, portrayed Frenkel' and Seletskiĭ as the founding fathers of the Soviet camp system, and various researchers have accepted this view.[6] This was certainly not the case. Not even Stalin can be blamed for this idea. Because Frenkel' and Seletskiĭ were associated with the distribution of food, the most important thing in the lives and thoughts of inmates, fellow prisoners understandably remembered them, but their infamy for creating the system must be shared.

The new system, in any case, greatly appealed to the Spetsotdel and its successors, and equating food with work was used intermittently in the camps from 1930 on, particularly in camps associated with the lumber industry. Inmates likewise believed that this sytem was responsible for the growing efficiency of OGPU camps and prisons. Some prisoners later claimed that the practice forced inmates to work harder than free workers, and a few researchers have used these facts to challenge Marx's assertion that slaves were less efficient than free workers.[7] Other researchers have maintained that inmates were actually less productive than free workers.[8] Same data, opposite conclusions.

There is no unassailable answer. In some industries, inmates failed to achieve the level of productivity of free workers; in others, they were more productive. Traditions and working conditions frequently were the decisive factors. Inmates were probably more efficient in cutting trees and mining gold and more productive on large construction projects and at some coal mines, whereas free workers performed more effectively in agriculture and in most manufacturing industries.[9] It was natural that inmate lumberjacks were more productive than their untrained peasant counterparts who worked only during the winter. The government never understood why inmate productivity was greater and gave credit to the Spetsotdel, even though lumberjacks at GUMZ places of confinement were about as productive as Spetsotdel inmates. But most GUMZ prisoners engaged in manufacturing; hence, the reputation of the Spetsotdel as an effective organizer of inmate labor continued to rise.[10]

The Spetsotdel also had political advantages over the GUMZ, which had been publicly accused of supporting Bukharin against Stalin. The OGPU was Stalin's important tool during collectivization, and he certainly supported the Spetsotdel. His confidence was especially important in the distribution of inmates. Until 1929, the Spetsotdel only received political prisoners, counterrevolutionaries, and common criminals in exceptional cases. This traditional distribution changed at the end of 1929, though the new arrangements were not confirmed until April 1930. Under the new rule, the OGPU received healthy inmates whose terms lasted three or more years; elderly and disabled inmates were sent to the GUMZ. The latter naturally protested, but no one in Stalin's government was listening. As a result, Spetsotdel places of confinement rapidly expanded. They had accommodated 10 percent of all inmates in 1928 but housed at least 50 percent in 1930. The OGPU momentarily saw itself gaining a monopoly on the prison system. The government planned to disband the NKVD, which was accused of backing Bukharin at this time, and the OGPU had high expectations of getting the NKVD facilities.[11]

There was a third powerful rival. The old Commissariat of Justice (NKIU) had supported Stalin's views on collectivization, and it had a long history of managing the places of confinement. Its predecessor, the Ministry of Justice, had been responsible for prisons before 1917, and the NKIU had operated a substantial share of these places between 1917 and 1922. The most important Soviet jurists, such as Petr Stuchka and Evgeni Pashukanis, worked in the Commissariat of Justice. The NKIU argued that it could reduce the number of crimes, especially those committed by recidivists, if it inherited the NKVD places of confinement and received the common criminals currently held by the OGPU. The NKIU claimed that crimes had increased because the judiciary had been excluded from the inmate reeducation process. Judges, the most educated and knowledgeable persons in this area, should make decisions regarding inmates. The system would be less liberal than that of the NKVD and less severe than that of the OGPU.[12]

Anyone who has studied the NKVD system can easily refute the allegation that it was too liberal, but criticism of the harshness of the OGPU system was more than justified. The OGPU places of confinement were already overcrowded at the beginning of 1928, when inmates reached 30,000. It is a mystery how the OGPU could have absorbed another quarter-million by the spring of 1930. Most inmates arrested in these years were peasants who were unable to write memoirs. Hence, the major sources of information about conditions at OGPU facilities are inmate songs and stories told to Western interviewers by Russian refugees after World War II.[13] (Conditions appear to have been similar to those in the German camps for Russian prisoners of war in 1941, when millions of Soviet soldiers surrendered. The Germans could not supply sufficient food, clothing, or medicines; housing was inadequate, and many prisoners died during their first months of captivity.)[14] Life expectancy at OGPU camps in 1929-30 hardly exceeded one year. Horror stories circulated throughout the Soviet Union, and eventually abroad. To dispel this negative image, the OGPU invited gullible witnesses to tour selected places where conditions were incomparably better than in ordinary OGPU camps. The best examples of these model facilities were an agricultural colony for adults and the Bolshevo colony for juvenile delinquents in Moscow province.[15]

Juvenile delinquency was especially acute after the Revolution. World War I, the Civil War, and the famine of 1921-22 had left 1.5 million children homeless. Many became criminals and recidivists; some became victims of abuse.[16] The government's struggle against juvenile criminality ironically took on an aura of protecting children, with the OGPU, the NKIU, and the NKVD posing as their benefactors. A celebrated movie, *Putëvka v zhizn'* (A Start in Life), and such books as *Pedagogicheskaia poema* (A Pedagogical Poem) and *Flagi na bashniakh* (Flags on Towers) by A. Makarenko portrayed OGPU officers in a favorable way. The movie preserved for us one of the most lyrical songs of homeless children:

> Forgotten and abandoned
> From my early, young years,
> I became an orphan—
> There is no luck in my life.
> When I die, I die.
> They will bury me,
> But nobody will know
> Where my small grave will be.
> Nobody will know
> And nobody will visit [it].
> Only in early spring
> A nightingale will sing [over my grave].[17]

The problem of juvenile criminality diminished somewhat during the mid-1920s. In 1926 the number of homeless children fell to 100,000. But child homelessness and juvenile criminality increased again in 1929 when the government started its repressive policy against the peasants. The OGPU took the initiative in establishing children's colonies. The Soviet press cloaked the agency in the mantle of the defender and protector of the homeless child, and the OGPU always made the most of this publicity. In the spring of 1929 it transferred juvenile delinquents to Solovki, hoping that the presence of children would make the horror stories about camp conditions less believable. When it invited novelist Maxim Gorky to Solovki in June 1929, he stated publicly that the OGPU had created an environment conducive to inmate reform. How great a fool he was has been hotly debated. We will probably never know whether he had been completely deceived by the OGPU, or whether he was complicitous in deceiving the public. Whatever the circumstances, the tragedy lay in the fact that he endorsed the OGPU system at a time the agency badly needed favorable publicity.[18]

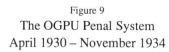

Figure 9
The OGPU Penal System
April 1930 – November 1934

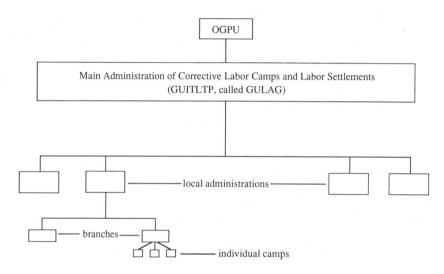

Local offices (administrations and branches) did not correspond to the
administrative divisions of the USSR (republics, provinces, etc.).

Another ploy involved renaming the places of confinement. The SNK of the USSR published "An Act on the Corrective Labor Camps" on 7 April 1930. It announced that all OGPU facilities except for its prisoners would henceforth be called "corrective labor camps." The functions of Spetsotdel, responsible for the OGPU prison networks, were delegated to the new Main Administration of Corrective Labor Camps and Labor Settlements (*Glavnoe upravlenie ispravitel'no-trudovykh lagereĭ i trudovykh poseleniĭ*, or GUITLTP).[19] This acronym, impossible to pronounce, was soon shortened to GULAG (*Glavnoe upravlenie lagereĭ*, which meant merely the Main Administration of Camps), and the agency became known by this name, especially after publication of Solzhenitsyn's trilogy, *The Gulag Archipelago*.

The abbreviation ironically omitted the key words "corrective labor" and "labor settlements." The combination "corrective labor" had been introduced by the People's Commissariat of Justice in 1921 when it sought to emphasize that its places of confinement reeducated inmates. The NKIU prison agency had been named the Central Corrective Labor Department.[20] In 1922, when its places of confinement shifted to NKVD jurisdiction, Shirvindt stopped using the term; after 1922 the NKVD called its prison agency the Main Administration of Places of Confinement.[21] The Council of People's Commissars' decree of April 1930 revived meaningful adjectives, and when the NKĨÜ got control of all of the NKVD places of confinement a few months later, it renamed them "corrective labor colonies."[22] That term stuck after 1930, though the central agencies eliminated the "corrective labor" description in 1936, when the government officially began using the acronym GULAG.

The most remarkable feature of the April 1930 SNK decree was the mere fact of its publication. The Cheka-OGPU had never previously published statutes on their places of confinement, and they never did again. The act was the first and last to describe the structure and regimes at OGPU camps. Its first provision stated that corrective labor camps were to "isolate especially dangerous lawbreakers and to make them conform to the conditions of the society of toiling people." It restated that the OGPU was to house inmates whose terms ran for three or more years and inmates sentenced by OGPU administrative order. Inmates in corrective labor camps were divided into three categories. The first two included prisoners from the toiling classes who were convicted of crimes not involving counterrevolutionary activities. The first category encompassed inmates sentenced to less than five years. Inmates receiving five or more years fell into the second category. The third included all nontoiling "elements" and persons convicted of counterrevolutionary activity.[23]

The decree established three regimens in each camp. All inmates had to begin their terms on the most difficult; good work and approved behavior might get them on a less strict regime. The time an inmate needed to serve before transfer depended on his category. The shortest term was allotted inmates in the first category and the longest in the third. Prisoners in the third group were to be assigned only manual labor; this provision was often violated, however, because qualified inmates in the third category were needed to supervise OGPU construction projects. Food was again dependent upon job performance. He who did not work did not eat. Now this vacuous slogan applied to millions of people. The decree also contained a number of liberal provisions to mislead the public. Prisoners were to work only eight hours a day, but in reality, most worked ten to twelve hours. The decree stated that inmate salaries were to be set jointly by the OGPU and the People's Commissariat of Labor, but the commissariat rarely participated in the process, and the OGPU always exercised complete control over inmate labor.[24]

With the decree came new personnel. Matveĭ Davydovich Berman was appointed head of the GULAG and Semën Firin named his deputy. Bokiĭ and Fel'dman continued to run the Special Department, which lost its role in managing the places of confinement. A man named Zarin replaced Eĭkhmans as chief of the USLON, which was retitled the Administration of the Solovetskiĭ Camps (USLAG).[25] These changes partly reflected OGPU efforts to improve its image: the new people were unconnected with past atrocities.

· At Solovki in September 1930, Zarin formed an organization of juveniles called the Commune (*Kommuna*) to reeducate inmates through labor. This had been an old idea. The first provision of its statute noted that "each inmate should be an active participant in socialist construction," a goal reminiscent of Shirvindt's 1929 article, which had supported Stalin's policies of collectivization and industrialization. However, the statutes also included terminology and ideas which Schirvindt had never expressed about the places of confinement. A second goal, for example, demanded a "struggle for communist morals." Membership was open to all inmates from poor and middle-income families except those convicted of counterrevolutionary activities. This actually limited the membership to common criminals, and the first to join were professional thieves.[26]

Zarin had in mind preserving the current distribution of prisoners, under which the OGPU got most of the healthy inmates, including common criminals, whose terms lasted three or more years. The GUMZ had insisted that it could more efficiently reeducate common criminals, and wanted them consigned to its jurisdiction. By establishing the Commune, Zarin—like his OGPU colleagues A. Makarenko and M. Pogrebinskiĭ elsewhere—was showing that the OGPU was prepared to compete with the GUMZ in reeducating criminals. OGPU efforts were not in vain. When facilities of the Main Administration of Places of Confinement (GUMZ) were transferred from the NKVD to the NKĨU in December 1930, inmate distribution remained unchanged. The NKĨU was disappointed. People's Commissar of Justice Ĩanson complained in January 1931 that the NKĨU had expected to be given responsibility for all common criminals in the country.[27]

Another factor influenced the conditions at the OGPU places of confinement. Beginning in the summer of 1930, Great Britain and the United States were pressured by political and industrial groups to boycott some Soviet exports allegedly produced by "forced labor." The most important item was lumber, which played a huge role in the Soviet government's plan to increase its exports. The boycott has been described elsewhere,[28] but its significance for the camps has never been appreciated.

Fearing that its goods would be boycotted, Moscow replaced some prisoners with non-inmates and invited foreign delegations to inspect the production of lumber. The most likely replacements were people sentenced to a combination of exile and corrective labor. While these people were certainly not free workers, the government hoped they would pass inspection. Exile combined with forced labor had been introduced in January 1930: the OGPU hoped by this means to divert the increasing numbers of peasant counterrevolutionaries from its overcrowded facilities to areas where it could control them without having to feed and house them. Persons sentenced in this way were called "settlers." They were dispatched to wilderness regions, sometimes with their families, to live and work without any deprivation of freedom. To distinguish its settlers from inmates, the OGPU called them "free migrants."[29]

The GULAG was not given much time to substitute settlers for inmates at selected camps. To meet deadlines, camp administrations acted with a cruel efficiency that even shocked persons long accustomed to OGPU methods. George Kitchin, a Finn who spent four years in Soviet camps, has recalled the charade:

> A secret code telegram was received from the head office in Moscow instructing us to liquidate our camp completely in three days, and to do it in such a manner that not a trace should remain. . . . After a short conference [in the camp office], the telegrams were sent to all work posts to stop operations within twenty-four hours, to gather the inmates at evacuation centers, to efface marks of the penal camps, such as barbed-wire enclosures, watchturrets, and signboards; for all officials to dress in civilian clothes, to disarm guards, and to wait for further instruction.

The work posts replied with telegrams protesting the short time allotted to them to execute the order: there were not enough horses; the sick would have to be left in the forest. The camp office responded that whoever failed to fulfill the order on time would be shot.

> From all sides the forest workers were marching in groups to Sol'vychegodsk. They carried government equipment in addition to their own belongings. Those seriously ill were crowded on teamsters' sleds, the sick who could still walk followed in the rear. Some of the sick died en route and were buried in the forest.
>   The situation in Arkhangel'sk was even worse. The evacuation of the thirty thousand prisoners working there required eight hundred railway cars. None was available and the inmates were loaded on old discarded freight and flat cars. Trains picked up groups of inmates at the station to which they had been forced to march from their remote outposts. While waiting for the trains, they spent several nights in the forest, hungry and freezing. Inmates suffering from fever, scurvy, or tuberculosis were no exception, and endured the same privations. Many men died during the mad rush of the evacuation. There were also many attempts to escape, but the cordon of guards had not yet been lifted and most fugitives were caught.

At the end of 1930, it was learned that the evacuation of Arkhangel'sk and Uftug had cost 1,370 lives. There were many similar reports.[30]

The effort was, in a sense, successful. Thousands of inmates were replaced by settlers by the beginning of February 1931. Speaking to the Sixth Congress of Soviets on 8 March, Chairman Viacheslav Molotov of the USSR Council of People's Commissars admitted that the government had used convict labor for the construction of highways and other projects, but he asserted that prisoners had nothing to do with producing exports. Molotov emphasized this was the case in the lumber industry, and invited delegations to visit the Soviet Union. This deception did not defuse the campaign in Britain and the United States, however. The boycott of Soviet goods lasted into 1931, then was undermined by conflicting political and economical interests among the participants. There had been no united front and, basically, no action.[31] Nonetheless, the campaign left its mark on history in a quite unexpected way.

SECOND PHASE, 1931-1934

With the displacement of inmates by settlers, several hundred thousand prisoners lost their jobs. To maintain its image as an economically efficient organization, the GULAG had to find work for its new army of unemployed inmates. Jobs were created.

Molotov mentioned in March 1931 that inmates had already helped in the construction of the Kem'–Ukhta Highway, the Parandovo–Kiksozero Highway, the Syktyvkar–Ukhta Highway, and the Syktyvkar–Piniug Highway, and in building the White Sea–Baltic Sea Canal. The canal was certainly the most important project and the most costly: none of the others required more than 50,000 inmates, but the White Sea–Baltic Sea Canal needed 300,000.

Although Molotov said in March that the inmates' labor had already been used for construction of the canal, the construction had in fact not started. Blueprints were approved only in July, almost four months after Molotov's speech.[32] As a rule, construction projects in the North began in the spring, when the soil was not frozen. This time, the OGPU was in a hurry, and the major construction works started in November, when the soil was rock-hard. Inmates used picks, wedges, and sledgehammers to break it. The OGPU promised that the project would take a year and a half, which would have been a record pace under normal conditions. Incredibly, the GULAG met its goal— at a cost of perhaps 100,000 lives. If anybody had any doubts about the propriety of utilizing inmates in such murderous working conditions they said nothing, and it would have made no difference if they had. It was well known that Stalin had personally approved the project and entrusted it to the OGPU. Fear of being arrested for any criticism of Stalin made writers and journalists repeat and possibly even believe in the OGPU propaganda about the reeducational value of work on the canal.[33]

The Soviet government appreciated OGPU's efficiency. Several months after the canal began, the GULAG was awarded another project, its most profitable enterprise ever, employing 200,000-300,000 inmates. Prisoners would mine gold from the Kolyma region, which, it was believed, held one of the richest deposits in the world. The state needed gold for the same reason it needed lumber—to pay for imported machinery. In 1928, the USSR estab-

Above, inmates breaking rocks at the construction site of the White Sea-Baltic Sea Canal, the first in the series of big projects built by inmate labor. Construction began in November 1931 and ended in May 1933. The canal was named for Stalin. Below, music was supposed to make inmates work harder at the site of the Moscow River-Volga River Canal, 1934. The musicians were inmates who, not surprisingly, preferred this task to the alternative—manual labor.

"The Valley of Death," Kolyma, 1943. A painting by Thomas Sgovio showing an inmate carrying a corpse to a burial site. Sgovio spent ten years in the Kolyma camps, 1938-48. Courtesy of Thomas Sgovio and the Hoover Institution Archives.

lished the *Soiuz-Zoloto* (Gold Trust) to organize mining around Kolyma using free laborers, but a lack of funds and the extreme climatic conditions limited the numbers of people willing to work there. The government had either to find the money to attract free workers or to enlist prisoners. The second alternative seemed easier than the first.[34]

The Dal'stroĭ was established by the OGPU during the winter of 1931-32 to extract gold in the area, using inmate labor. The Dal'stroĭ's position in the OGPU was unique. It was a GULAG subagency, but its chief, Reĭngold Berzin (a Latvian Communist who had experience with Cheka troops, the Red Army, and industrial enterprise) reported directly to OGPU Deputy Chief Iagoda rather than to GULAG Chief Berman. Berzin had unlimited authority within the territory of Dal'stroĭ operations. No other government agencies had representatives in the area. The territory was six times as large as France.[35]

The Dal'stroĭ was given its choice of OGPU inmates to organize enterprises in the sparsely populated region. Before the summer of 1932, when the first prisoners arrived, only some 20,000 people lived there. The Dal'stroĭ sent thousands of inmates to the area every year. They worked as lumberjacks, fishermen, and farmers; they constructed barracks, highways, and buildings and founded and built Magadan, the capital. Their major endeavor, however, was mining gold. Starting in the mid-1930s the Dal'stroĭ produced 200,000 kilograms annually, or 80 percent of total Soviet gold production. As a result of its operations, the Soviet share of world output rose from 12-14 percent to at least 40 percent. The human cost was high, even by GULAG standards. The exact number of those who perished in Kolyma will never be known. Estimates of three to five million seem exaggerated, however; the Kolyma camps existed just over twenty years and housed hardly more than 300,000 inmates at any one time. It is difficult to believe that more than half of the Kolyma camp population died every year.[36]

The formation of the Dal'stroĭ traditionally has been portrayed as an important step in the expansion of the GULAG. This proved true, but during the first five years of existence (1932-37), the Dal'stroĭ was an independent rival of the GULAG. It had first priority in selecting inmates, and it had complete control of its own territory. This resulted in serious friction between the organizations. It was the same old story: both wanted healthy, young prisoners for construction work. Even though the OGPU numbered its charges in the millions, the Dal'stroĭ shipped thousands of inmates to the Kolyma region every year, and with this drain on prison labor the GULAG began to worry that it would not be able to complete its own construction projects on time. The dispute was finally resolved in 1937: Berzin and his associates were arrested and executed. The GULAG absorbed its rival.[37]

In 1932, however, the GULAG definitely did have some labor shortages, and measures were introduced to make inmates work harder. Some camps put them on sixteen-hour shifts.[38] The shortages did not last long, however. The decree of 7 August 1932 increased the OGPU prison population by more than 100,000 during the winter of 1932-1933, and the Dal'stroĭ was unable to transport inmates to the Kolyma region during the winter because of impassable roads. Consequently, all the new arrivals went to GULAG projects.[39]

There were, in fact, so many new arrivals that the GULAG could not handle them; for a time it had to create jobs. At the end of 1932, the GULAG began construction on the Moscow–Volga Canal, a project the government had approved in June 1931. Just as with the Kolyma mining scheme, the Soviet government had initially intended to build the Moscow–Volga Canal using free workers.[40] The GULAG was awarded the project because, at the moment, it had an excess number of inmates. This was an enormously important project for the GULAG. Deputy Chief Firin headed the construction himself. It engaged half a million prisoners, more than the 300,000 who built the White Sea–Baltic Sea Canal and the 200,000-300,000 who worked in the Kolyma region. The government proclaimed the construction completed in July 1937.[40]

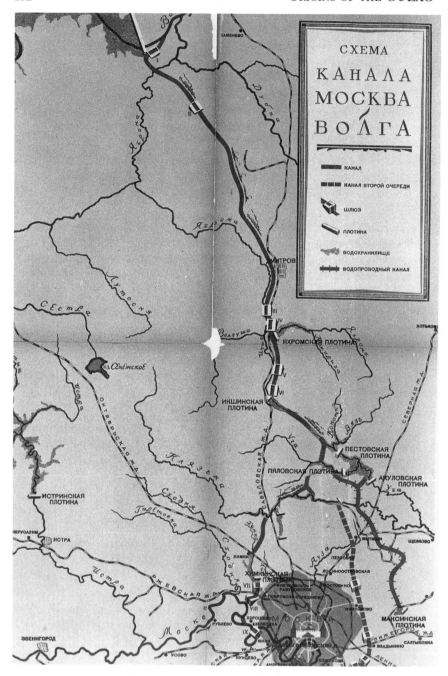

Map of the Moscow River-Volga River Canal. The GULAG completed the canal—its largest construction project ever—in five years, 1932-37, with labor from 500,000 inmates.

These massive projects altered the GULAG theory of inmate reeducation, the theory based on Shirvindt's 1929 idea that inmate participation in the Five-Year Plan would by itself reform prisoners. In 1936 the Institute of Soviet Construction and Law of the USSR Academy of Sciences published *Ot prestupleniĭa k trudu* [From Crime to Productive Labor] by I. L. Averbakh, with an introduction by Andrei Vyshinskiĭ. The book summarized GULAG reeducation theory and practice. Averbakh maintained that large construction projects concentrated in a small area created more opportunities to reform inmates than scattered enterprises. The author argued two major points. First, large projects "captivated the imagination of the country" and made inmates realize the political significance of both their collective contribution to the industrial development of the USSR and their personal contribution to these projects. Prisoners participated in the construction from beginning to end. Averbakh implied that those who survived became personally involved in the projects. Second, the physical and emotional involvement of inmates in these projects were prerequisites for a creative attitude toward work. Big projects provided a variety of jobs, allowing prisoners to act creatively and to experience personal growth. Peasants learned new professions and advanced to managerial positions. Technicians and engineers applied their knowledge and gained new experience.[41]

Averbakh did not stop there. The author cautioned that these conditions alone could not eradicate the old consciousness and hatred of socialism. To suppress these negative attitudes, inmates had to realize that there was no chance to restore the capitalist order, that their survival depended on their willingness to adjust to the socialist reality. To help them understand their circumstances, Averbakh urged the establishment of a strict system of rewards and punishment. Hard-working, obedient inmates would receive better food and clothing. Lazy, recalcitrant inmates would find themselves in punishment cells on starvation rations. Some who committed crimes would be executed.[42]

Of course, Averbakh insisted that material incentives were only a temporary remedy. The public would soon recognize and honor hard work and proper behavior. The administrations of those camps which engaged in building the White Sea–Baltic Sea and Moscow–Volga Canals published daily reports on outstanding workers, introduced insignia for prisoners who consistently fulfilled norms, and convened periodic conferences of the best workers. Conference reports appeared in national newspapers. In 1933, Gorky and other writers visited the White Sea–Baltic Sea Canal and in a widely acclaimed book praised OGPU inmates for their remarkable achievements.[43] (Not surprisingly, when the canal was completed in 1933, it bore Stalin's name.) Averbakh contended that inmates eager to prove they had reformed did not work just well but "heroically." They excelled every day, every minute, as a matter of honor; for them, rewards and punishments were eventually unnecessary. Such people deserved to become members of socialist society.[44]

As previously mentioned, good workers were sometimes released from the camps before finishing their terms, often in large groups. Not previously mentioned was the fact that some were subsequently arrested for new crimes. Averbakh blamed this on the lack of assistance from local governments and from businesses. Many factories refused to hire former inmates, even those released as heroes after the completion of major projects. Inmates' expectations were dashed, and they returned to crime.[45]

Averbakh was right in raising the issue. An untitled prisoners' song describes the difficulties encountered by a released prisoner.

> I am a son of a worker, who was an underground party member
> [before the Revolution].
> He loved me and took great care of me.
> But he got sick with tuberculosis
> And died in a hospital.
> Being left without father's supervision,
> I left my mother and started to live a street life.
> Soon they called me thief
> And I do not remember how I ended up behind bars.
> And then everything went as one could expect:
> I used to serve my time in camps.
> But in 1933, after the completion of the Canal,
> I decided to quit the criminal world.
> I came to a town, the name of which I do not remember,
> And decided to get a job at a factory.
> But they told me that I had been imprisoned
> And therefore should forget their address.
> I went from factory to factory
> But heard the same words everywhere.
> Why have I gained my freedom
> If you regard me a thief as before?[46]

Averbakh was wrong, however, in claiming that the GULAG was more efficient and successful than other agencies in reeducating prisoners. Inmates released from GUMZ and the Dal'stroǐ places of confinement encountered the same difficulties finding jobs. The percentage of GULAG inmates who committed new crimes after being freed was apparently the same as for other agencies; had GULAG inmates achieved a better record, Averbakh would surely have mentioned it.

Nobody challenged the GULAG position in public or in private. Public discussion of these issues had ended by 1930; collectivization imposed strict censorship on many matters, particularly on the places of confinement. Nor is

Above, a newspaper, *Woman Shock Worker*, whose articles encouraged women to fulfill their production quotas on the Moscow River-Volga River Canal and named the best and worst women workers. Below, these women laboring on the canal in 1934 were doing jobs traditionally assigned to young, healthy men.

Заставка из газеты «Перековка».

Above, the logo from *Reforging*, the central newspaper in the Moscow River-Volga River Canal camp. The caption reads, "Please take your seat on the wheelbarrow," reiterating the maxim that no job is degrading and that hard work makes one virtuous. Below, a cartoon from a camp magazine lampooning "The Face of a Refusenik." Although refuseniks were severely punished, some inmates believed they had a better chance of surviving by refusing to work than by submitting to the working conditions in the camp.

«Лицо отказчика»
(Карикатура из журнала «На штурм трассы», 1934 г., № 2).

there evidence that anyone complained in private. The GULAG was the most powerful prison agency in the country during the 1930s. In 1934 the total number of inmates in the country was at least three million. For the sake of comparison, in January 1934, fifty-two other countries had 437,917 inmates whom Soviet penologists called political prisoners; in 1926-1931, the total number of inmates in eight countries (England, France, India, Italy, Japan, Poland, Sweden, and the United States) was 559,082. The GULAG housed 2.5 million inmates, the Dal'stroĭ 200,000 and the GUITU probably 600,000.[47] Although the Dal'stroĭ was economically important and had unlimited power in its territories, it was unable to expand beyond its boundaries. The GUITU and the GULAG were not limited by physical boundaries, but the GUITU was not on the same high political or economical level as the GULAG.

There were rumors in the spring of 1934 that the GUITU would disband. People's Commissar of Justice Krylenko attempted to preserve the agency; he organized foreign visits to a corrective labor colony in Magnitogorsk, and several Soviet newspapers published declarations by the visitors that living conditions there were better than those of free workers in the West.[48] Additionally, the GUITU belonged to the People's Commissariat of Justice, which was regarded as more humane than the OGPU. None of these circumstances, however, was enough to save the organization.

By 1933 the collectivization was finished. Grigoriĭ Zinoviev and Nikolaĭ Bukharin were defeated. They admitted at the seventeenth Party Congress in January 1934 that their opposition to Stalin had been wrong. A few Politburo members who had always supported Stalin now urged that he relax his pressure on the Party and the country. These moderates, Sergeĭ Mironovich Kirov, Valerian Vladimirovich Kuĭbyshev, and Grigoriĭ Konstantinovich Ordzhonikidze, proposed abolishing the OGPU.[49] Stalin yielded to their demand, but only slightly. When a decree of 6 July 1934 established the Commissariat of Internal Affairs (NKVD) of the USSR, it absorbed several agencies, including the people's militia and the OGPU. The OGPU was renamed the Main Administration of State Security (*Glavnoe upravlenie gosudarstvennoĭ bezopasnosti*, or GUGB) and separated from the GULAG and the Main Administration of Frontier and Internal Troops, which became subagencies of the NKVD.[50] Ĭagoda, who had headed the OGPU after Menzhinskiĭ died in April 1934, was appointed chief of the NKVD of the USSR.

This all seemed familiar. The July 1934 reform looked a great deal like the 1922 reform, when the Cheka had become the State Political Administration (GPU) and had been subordinated to the NKVD of the RSFSR. Dzerzhinskiĭ had headed the GPU and simultaneously became the People's Commissar of Internal Affairs: that is, chief of the NKVD. Both the GPU in 1922 and the GUGB in 1934 lost most of their places of confinement by these decrees, and their powers to arrest were significantly curtailed.[51]

Figure 10

The Prison System of the People's Commissariat of Internal Affairs of the USSR, 1934 – 1946

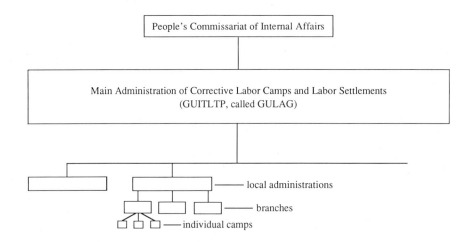

In 1936, GULAG became the official name of the supervising agency.
Local offices (administrations and branches) did not correspond to the
administrative divisions of the USSR (republics, provinces, etc.).

Since the relations among government agencies differed in 1922 from those in 1934, so did the effects of the decrees. Transfer of the security agencies to the NKVD strengthened the commissariats in both cases. During the 1920s, however, other agencies such as the NKIU could challenge the supremacy of the NKVD. The situation had changed completely by 1934, when no one could challenge the NKVD—which, ironically, had been formed by moderates who wished to restrain the OGPU because they felt it had become too powerful.

In the end, the GULAG accomplished under the NKVD what it had always wanted to do under the OGPU. The prolonged rivalry between the Commissariats of Justice and Internal Affairs for the places of confinement in the Soviet Union was finally decided in favor of the NKVD. The GUITU was disbanded in November 1934 and absorbed by a new subagency of the GULAG called the Division of Corrective Labor Colonies.[52] With the execution of Berzin in 1937, the GULAG assumed de facto as well as de jure control of the Dal'stroĭ.[53] The triumph of the GULAG was complete: virtually all the places of confinement had fallen under its supervision.

CONCLUSION

By 1934 the Soviet government had reversed its views on crime and punishment and on the self-sufficiency of the places of confinement. It had modified its position on the reeducation of inmates and on their employment. It had fully implemented its notion of the subordination of the places of confinement to a single agency.

Prior to the October Revolution of 1917, Bolsheviks had believed that crime arose from the injustices of the capitalist system. They denied individual guilt and held society responsible for individual crimes. They thought crime would decrease if the capitalist order were destroyed and disappear completely under socialism.

Of course, it did not happen. Crime increased after the Revolution. It grew as the result of World War I, the Russian Civil War, the famine, and the decision to label opponents of the regime counterrevolutionaries. The Bolsheviks explained this contradiction by asserting that people committed crimes under the influence of the *remnants* of capitalism: the habits they had acquired before the Revolution made them commit crimes after the Revolution. In 1932, however, the number of inmates had reached two million. Ten times as many people were committing crimes under the remnants of capitalism as had done so under capitalism itself.

Stalin claimed in 1930 that the class struggle intensified as the country approached socialism. This view still held that crime would disappear once socialism had been achieved. That day was officially proclaimed in December 1936. The places of confinement then held three to six million inmates. No explanations were proffered or required; the Soviet government accepted—in fact, had created—this new reality. The maximum number of inmates in Imperial Russia never exceeded 184,000. The number of prisoners remained below 300,000 in 1928. After the collectivization in 1933, their numbers exceeded three million. At this time the rest of the world evidently had fewer inmates.

The Bolsheviks were forced to modify their views on inmate reeducation. The Bolshevik system was supposed to reform those who had become habitual

Views of a camp and barracks in Vorkuta, 1945-47. Courtesy of the Hoover Institution Archives.

criminals under capitalism. Those prisoners who showed improvement were granted additional privileges and more food. Once they reached the fifth level of privileges, inmates living conditions were supposed to be similar to those of free workers. Reeducation was not to exceed five years, after which a released inmate would never commit another crime. The Soviet government established the Distributive Commissions to reform prisoners. The commissions were designated the only agencies to receive government subsidies. Inmate labor was supposed to pay for the operation of all other places of confinement.

But prisoner labor acquired more than economic value to bureaucrats and politicians. Labor came to be viewed as part of the reeducational process. To emphasize this connection, the government introduced the term "corrective labor" and called some places of confinement "corrective labor institutions." Then, during the period of the New Economic Policy, the theory of reeducation became less prominent. The goal to reform prisoners completely was no longer mentioned. It was enough for released prisoners to adjust to the conditions outside the places of confinement. Liberal penologists in Imperial Russia could easily have accepted this interpretation of reeducation.

The collectivization and the First Five-Year Plan revitalized interest in inmate reeducation. In 1929 the chief of the prison agency of the People's Commissariat of Internal Affairs, Evseĭ Shirvindt, stated that inmate participation in fulfilling the tasks of the Five-Year Plan of economic development would, by itself, have a reeducational impact on inmates. They would recognize the importance of their labor to society. To encourage prisoners to work harder, the success of an inmate's reeducation was measured by his or her work efficiency. Prisoners who fulfilled their production norms by 120 percent were considered better reeducated than those who achieved only 110 percent.

These notions were slightly modified in the 1930s. The administration of the places of confinement required that inmates work not merely hard but "heroically." Those who worked heroically demonstrated that they believed in socialism and deserved release. There were, in fact, many such heroes among the inmates. After the completion of the White Sea–Baltic Sea Canal, approximately 12,500 of the best workers were freed—though some of the lesser heroes were arrested shortly afterward for perpetrating new crimes. None of this completely daunted proponents of the theory of reeducation until late 1936. By then, the government had given up and accepted the fact that a high crime rate and socialism were compatible.

The idea of universal forced labor at places of confinement was also modified. A 1918 decree of the People's Commissariat of Justice had ordered that all inmates—including suspects, who had traditionally been kept in prison—must work. The Cheka sabotaged the order and forced only those held in concentration camps to be employed. For security reasons, suspects in Cheka prisons were not permitted to work. Many prisoners escaped from their work places in or near cities. The concentration camps presented a different situation. Most were located outside urban areas, often in remote regions, where escape was extremely difficult. Cheka inmates were considered the most dangerous enemies of the regime, and flight was prevented by strict security. Demands for security eventually prevailed in the system, and after the mid-1930s, suspects were not required to work.

The hope that inmate labor would cover the expense of the prison facilities proved infeasible. The People's Commissariat of Justice first proposed the idea and was the first to doubt its viability. It was often asserted that many places of confinement had become self-sufficient and some even profitable, but there was never any evidence to support these claims. After 1931, when inmates began laboring on large construction projects, the whole idea of self-sufficiency lost its meaning. The projects were entirely financed by the government; inmates did not have to work to pay for their maintenance.

The Soviets fully implemented only one idea that had originated in 1918. In Imperial Russia, most places of confinement were under the Ministry of Justice, although some other agencies, such as the Ministries of the Interior and War had their own facilities. In November 1917, the new government put everything under one agency, the People's Commissariat of Justice. It was unable to prevent inmates from escaping, so two more systems were organized: the Cheka (which dealt with the most dangerous enemies of the regime) and the People's Commissariat of Internal Affairs.

The government attempted to unify the system once again in 1922. The People's Commissariat of Internal Affairs was granted a monopoly on the places of confinement. The Cheka was to retain just two of its 300 places, and the People's Commissariat of Justice lost all its camps and prisons. Feliks Dzerzhinskiĭ, who headed both the NKVD and the Cheka, managed to sabotage part of the plan. The Cheka retained about 30 camps and prisons with 7,000 inmates, or about 6.5 percent of the total prison population.

The People's Commissariat of Internal Affairs was disbanded at the end of 1930 after its prison agency had been accused of siding with Bukharin. The Cheka, which had staunchly supported Stalin's idea of rapid industrialization and collectivization, did not gain by its rival's loss. Another ally of Stalin, the People's Commissariat of Justice, received the places of confinement formerly under Internal Affairs. By 1934, things had gone round again, and Internal Affairs got everything, including the camps and prisons that had been under the Cheka and the People's Commissariat of Justice. The Soviet prison system had become unified for the first time since 1918.

The Soviet penal system had expanded under Lenin, but near the end of his life he acted to limit the power of the Cheka. He failed as his mind and body failed. Stalin did not interfere with the operation of the camps and prisons, but he dramatically altered the system indirectly by collectivizing agriculture and by implementing the First Five-Year Plan, during which inmate labor contributed to the national economy for the first time. Without these campaigns, the Soviet prison population might well have decreased; prisoners who had belonged to the White Army or to pre-Revolutionary political parties eventually would have died, and the number of common criminals might have leveled off as economic and social stability returned. This, of course, is not what happened. Stalin filled the camps with peasants who were labeled "counterrevolutionary" for killing their cattle and hoarding their grain rather than surrender them to the state.

All the while, prison agencies and their officials used abstruse arguments about self-financing and reeducation to protect and expand their bureaucracies. Who can say whether anyone actually believed these arguments, or whether there was any thought of the human costs? The prison agencies looked efficient in the production of lumber only because the peasant lumberjacks had been unproductive. One construction success of the GULAG led to another; no one was counting the lives. The brutality was obscured by the argument that labor on large projects reeducated prisoners. The GULAG, in effect, had offered inmates the choice between work and starvation, then congratulated itself that so many chose to live—to live only a bit longer, as things turned out.

Although the Soviet prison system was evil, its origins, development, and intentions were, to a considerable measure, banal. Bureaucrats pursued unattainable goals of prison self-sufficiency and inmate reeducation. Officials sought manpower and funds, expanded their bureaucracies, and tried to meet unrealistic goals. Administrators and warders dutifully enforced rules and regulations. Theorists rationalized and justified. Eventually, everything was reversed or modified or abandoned.

The vast scale of evil, the GULAG Archipelago, emerged directly from the collectivization of agriculture. The origins of the Soviet prison system have been attributed to Marxism, to Leninism, to the October Revolution, the Civil War, and Stalin. Their degree of responsibility was as much or as little as each was responsible for the collectivization. Perhaps no other single event so changed the lives of the majority of the Russian people since the Tartar conquest in the thirteenth century.

The institutions to change most dramatically were the labor camps, the most important component of the Stalinist system. The dreadful image of the camps persuaded people to obey government orders, to work long hours with great intensity at factories and collective farms, to participate in mass demonstrations supporting the most heinous actions of the Soviet Union, and to die in the Great Patriotic War with Stalin's name on their lips. Fear made them believe what they said and what they did. This is a simple explanation, but under these horrendous circumstances, it seems sufficient.

Abandoned railroad tracks at Syktyvkar-Igarka. Construction was begun in 1948 and halted in 1952. Although thousands of inmates died during its construction, the railroad was never completed because it was judged useless. Courtesy of Alexander Vologodsky of the Second World Center, Amsterdam.

To disband the camps, then, would have meant an end to the Stalinist system, and Stalin could not take such a step. His own existence ultimately depended on total control of society, and this totalitarianism depended on the existence of the camps. People believed that they had to obey Stalin to survive. In the final analysis, perhaps everyone in the country, including Stalin himself, became a prisoner of the system. As a prison song of 1948 lamented, "All Russia is a big concentration camp."

A large reduction in the number of prisoners in 1956 cracked the foundation of Stalinist system. Khrushchev may have released the prisoners to win popular support in his struggle against the old hard-line Stalinists in the Presidium. Whatever his reasons, the population lost its fear and ceased to be obedient and industrious. The government faced its first serious dissent in 1958. It began to open to the West and even to import grain in 1963. Labor productivity started to decline and reached alarmingly low levels in the 1980s. To repair decades of damage, Mikhail Gorbachev had to choose between introducing a market economy and political democracy or reestablishing the labor-camp system. He proved unable to make the choice. Recent events have overtaken him and nearly eliminated the possibility that the camp system will be reestablished. It had developed by certain ironies of history and collapsed, along with the whole totalitarian system, with other ironies. Mercifully, the GULAG is past. That fear is over.

Appendix
The Major Agencies in Brief

Cheka. *See* Vecheka

GPU. *Gosudarstvennoe politicheskoe upravlenie* (State Political Administration), 1922-23. Soviet secret police. The GPU succeeded the Vecheka and was replaced by the OGPU. The GPU was under the NKVD of the Russian Soviet Federated Socialist Republic (RSFSR); its prison agency was apparently called the Spetsotdel. The GPU preserved only some of the Cheka places of confinement and housed only less than 10 percent of the inmates.

GTU, *Glavnoe tiuremnoe upravlenie* (Main Prison Administration), 1879-1917. Major prison agency in Russia before February 1917. The GTU was transferred from the Ministry of the Interior to the Ministry of Justice in 1895; it was renamed the GUMZ after the February Revolution of 1917.

GUITLTP. *Glavnoe upravlenie ispravitel'no-trudovykh lagereĭ i trudovykh poseleniĭ* (Main Administration of Corrective Labor Camps and Labor Settlements), 1930-36. Prison agency of the OGPU, 1930-34, and of the People's Commissariat of Internal Affairs of the Union of Soviet Socialist Republics (USSR), 1934-36. The GUITLTP succeeded the Spetsotdel and was renamed (at first informally and then officially) the GULAG.

GUITU. *Glavnoe upravlenie ispravitel'no-trudovykh uchrezhdeniĭ* (Main Administration of Corrective Labor Institutions), 1931-1934. Prison agency of the People's Commissariat of Justice. It succeeded the GUMZ and was disbanded when its places of confinement were transferred to the NKVD of the USSR.

GULAG. *Glavnoe upravlenie lagereĭ* (Main Administration of Camps), 1936-56. Prison agency of the People's Commissariat of Internal Affairs, USSR, 1936-46, and of the Ministry of Internal Affairs after 1946 (the People's Commissariats were renamed Ministries in 1946). The GULAG succeeded the GUITLTP.

GUMZ. *Glavnoe upravlenie mest zakliucheniia* (Main Administration of Places of Confinement), 1917-18 and 1922-31. Prison agency of the Ministry of Justice after the February Revolution and of the People's Commissariat of Justice after the October Revolution of 1917 until April-May 1918 (The Ministries were renamed People's Commissariats in October 1917). The GUMZ succeeded the GTU and was replaced by the TSKO. Prison agency of the People's Commissariat of Internal Affairs, RSFSR, 1922-30, and of the People's Commissariat of Justice, 1930-31. This second GUMZ succeeded the TSITO and was succeeded by the GUITU.

GUPR. *Glavnoe upravlenie prinuditel'nykh rabot* (Main Administration of Forced Labor), 1920-22. Prison agency of the People's Commissariat of Internal Affairs,

RSFSR. The GUPR succeeded the OPR and was disbanded when the TSITO of the People's Commissariat of Justice was transferred to the People's Commissariat of Internal Affairs in October 1922.

Komendatura, 1918-21. Probably a title of the Vecheka prison agency. The Komendatura was apparently succeeded by Spetsotdel.

NKIU (RSFSR). *Narodnyĭ kommissariat iustitsii* (People's Commissariat of Justice of the Russian Soviet Federated Socialist Republic), 1917-46. Succeeded the Ministry of Justice in 1917 and was replaced by the Ministry of Justice in 1946. The NKIU was under the Council of People's Commissars of the RSFSR. The NKIU had a monopoly on the places of confinement from October 1917 to July 1918, when the Cheka prison system was established. It still housed roughly one-third of the inmates from 1912 to 1922, then lost all its prison facilities to the People's Commissariat of Internal Affairs, RSFSR. The NKIU regained some places of confinement in 1930 when all the People's Commissariats of Internal Affairs of the union republics, including that of the RSFSR, were disbanded. From 1930 to 1934, the NKIU's share of the inmates decreased from one-half to one-sixth. In 1934, everything was reversed once more: the NKIU lost its remaining places of confinement to the newly established People's Commissariat of Internal Affairs, USSR. The NKIU prison agency was successively called GUMZ, 1917-18; TSKO, 1918-21; TSITO, 1921-22; GUMZ, 1930-31; GUITU, 1931-34. Other union-level republics (Belorussia, Transcaucasia, and the Ukraine, established in 1923; Turkmenia and Uzbekistan, established in 1925; and Tadzhikistan, established in 1929) had their own NKIUs, with the same structures as the NKIU (RSFSR).

NKVD (RSFSR). *Narodnyĭ kommissariat vnutrennikh del* (People's Commissariat of Internal Affairs of the Russian Soviet Federated Socialist Republic), 1917-30. Succeeded the Ministry of Internal Affairs in October 1917, was disbanded in 1930 and its places of confinement transferred to the People's Commissariat of Justice. The NKVD was under the Council of People's Commissars of the RSFSR. The commissariat ran some places of confinement from 1919 to 1930, housing one-third of the republic's inmates from 1919 to 1922, and 90 percent from 1923 to 1928. By 1930, after thousands were arrested and sent to OGPU facilities, the NKVD's proportion had shrunk to 50 percent. The NKVD's prison agency was successively called the OPR, 1919-20; the GUPR, 1920-22; the GUMZ, 1923-30. Other union-level republics (Belorussia, Transcaucasia, the Ukraine, established in 1923; Turkmenia and Uzbekistan, established in 1925; and Tadzhikistan, established in 1919) had their own NKVDs with structures identical to that of the RSFSR.

NKVD (USSR). *Narodnyĭ kommissariat vnutrennukh del* (People's Commissariat of Internal Affairs of the Union of Soviet Socialist Republics), 1934-46. Established four years after the People's Commissariats of Internal Affairs of all seven union republics had been disbanded. The new commissariat was directly under the Council of People's Commissars of the USSR. The NKVD of the USSR was renamed the Ministry of Internal Affairs in 1946, when all commissariats were renamed accordingly. The NKVD of the USSR controlled all the inmates in the Soviet Union. Its prison agency was called the GUITLTP, 1934-36, and GULAG, 1936-46.

OGPU. *Ob'edinënnoe gosudarstvennoe politicheskoe upravlenie* (Unified State Political Administration), 1923-34. Soviet secret police. The OGPU succeeded and united the GPUs of four union republics and was in turn absorbed by the NKVD (USSR). The OGPU was under the Council of People's Commissars of the

USSR. It housed about 10 percent of all inmates in the country until 1928; its share of inmates had increased to 50 percent by 1930 and 80 percent in 1933. The OGPU prison agency was apparently called Spetsotdel, 1923-30, and GUITLTP, 1930-34.

OPR. *Otdel prinuditel'nykh rabot* (Department of Forced Labor), 1919-20. Prison agency of the People's Commissariat of Internal Affairs. The OPR was succeeded by the GUPR.

Spetsotdel (Special Department), 1921-30. Apparently the name of the prison agency of the Cheka, GPU, and OGPU. The Spetsotdel succeeded the Komendatura and was succeeded by the GUITLTP.

TSITO. *Tsentral'nyi ispravitel'no-trudovoi otdel* (Central Corrective Labor Department),1921-22. NKIU prison agency during 1921-22. The TSITO succeeded the TSKO and was replaced by the GUMZ after its transfer to the NKVD.

TSKO. *Tsentral karatel'nyi otdel* (Central Penal Department), 1918-21. Prison agency of the NKIU. It was succeeded by the TSITO.

Vecheka. *Vserossiiskaia chrezvychainaia komissiia po bor'be s kontrrevoliutsiei i sabotazhem* (All-Russian Extraordinary Commission for Combatting Counterrevolution and Sabotage), 1917-22. Soviet secret police, succeeded by the GPU. The Vecheka was directly under the Council of People's Commissars of the RSFSR. In July 1918, the Vecheka established its prisons and prison camps, called concentration camps. The Vecheka prison agency was apparently called Komendatura (or possibly Operational Department), 1918-21, and Spetsotdel, 1921-22.

Figure 11
The Penal System of the RSFSR, 1917 – 1922

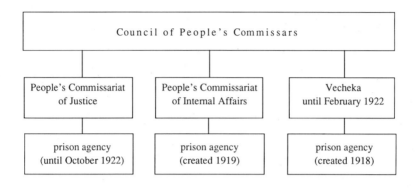

Figure 12
The Penal System of the RSFSR, 1922

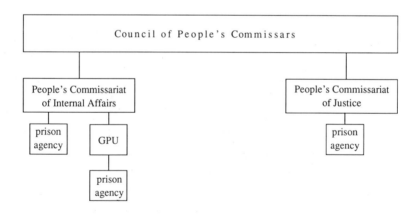

Figure 13
The Penal System of the USSR, 1923 – 1934

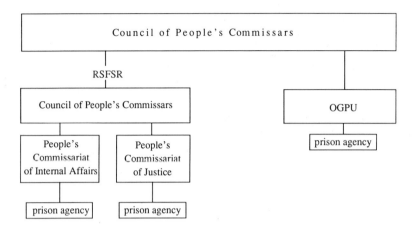

Other soviet socialist republics (Belorussia, Transcaucasia, and Ukraine, established in 1922; Turkmenia and Uzbekistan, 1925; and Tadzhikistan, 1929) had their own NKI͡Us and NKVDs, structured like those of the RSFSR. The NKVDs in all the republics ceased to exist in 1930. Their NKI͡Us had no prisons until 1930.

Figure 14
The Penal System of the USSR, 1934

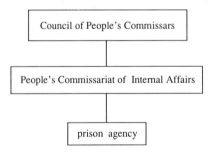

Figure 15

The Chronology of Prison Responsibility

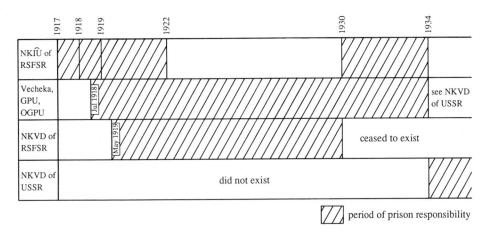

Figure 16

The Prison Agencies

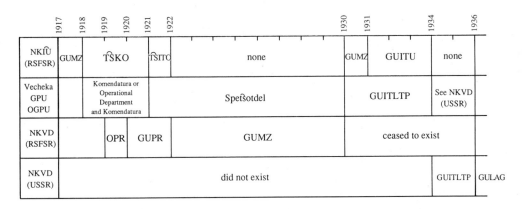

NOTES

INTRODUCTION

1. M.N. Gernet, *Istori͡a t͡sarskoĭ t͡iur'my*, 5 vols. (Moscow, 1960-63).

2. Vi͡acheslav P. Artem'ev, *Rezhim i okhrana ispravitel'no-trudovykh lagereĭ* (Munich: Institut po izucheni͡iu SSSR, 1956).

3. *Zur Geschichte der deutschen Kriegsgefangenen des zweiten Weltkrieges*, 15 vols. (Munich: Verlag Ernst & Wener Gieseking Biefeld, 1965-67).

4. David Dallin and Boris Nicolaevsky, *Forced Labor in Soviet Russia* (New Haven, Conn.: Yale University Press, 1947).

5. A.I. Solzhenitsyn, *Arkhipelag-Gulag*, 4 vols. (Paris: YMCA Press, 1973-74).

6. George Legget, *The Cheka: Lenin's Secret Police* (Oxford: Clarendon Press, 1981); Jacques Rossi, *Spravochnik po GULAGu* (London: Overseas Publications Interchange, 1987).

7. *The Modern Encyclopedia of Russian and Soviet History* (Gulf Breeze, Fla.: Academic International Press, 1976-1990), s.v. "Labor Camps in the Soviet Union." Here are examples of these mistakes. The article states that "the first decree on forced labor and camps appeared only in April 1919"; actually, on 24 January 1918 the People's Commissariat of Justice, decreed that all able-bodied prisoners should work. According to the article, the decree of the Central Executive Committee on 17 May 1919 established both concentration and forced labor camps; in fact, the decree did not mention the concentration camps at all. The following sentence contains three errors: "In 1922, when the Cheka became the OGPU (The All-Union State Political Administration), the GUMZAK and the Central Corrective Labor Department merged into a new GUMZAK, or Chief Administration of Places of Detention subsequently renamed GUITI (Chief Administration of Corrective Labor Institutions) under the OGPU." In 1922, however, the Cheka became not the OGPU but the GPU; the OGPU was not established until 1923. The GUMZAK (better GUMZ) was not united with the Corrective Labor Department; these two agencies never coexisted. And neither GUMZAK nor GUITI (should be GUITU) were under the OGPU; the GUMZ was an agency of the Commissariat of Internal Affairs, the GUITU of the Commissariat of Justice.

8. I.L. Averbakh, *Ot prestupleni͡ia k trudu* (Moscow: OGIZ, 1936).

1. THE IMPERIAL RUSSIAN PRISON SYSTEM

1. B.S. Khorev and V.M. Moiseenko, *Sdvigi v razmeshchenii naseleniia SSSR* (Moscow: Statistika, 1976), 6.

2. Gernet, *Istoriia*, 4:23.

3. Khorev and Moiseenko, *Sdvigi*, 8.

4. Gernet, *Istoriia*, 4:22-23.

5. Ibid., 4:21, 24-25.

6. *Svod zakonov Rossiiskoi Imperii* (St. Petersburg: Zakonovedenie, 1911), 2:3458-59, 3461-65.

7. Ibid., 2:3479, 3472, 3452-57; Gernet, *Istoriia*, 4:25, 4:20-21.

8. Gernet, *Istoriia*, 3:24-25; 4:24.

9. *Svod zakonov*, 2:3479-82.

10. "Kak zhivët katorga i ssylka," *Vestnik katorgi i ssylki* 1 (February 1914): 12; B.S. Utevskii, *Sovetskaia ispravitel'no-turdovaia politika* (Moscow: Gosizdat, 1934), 149-50.

11. *Svod zakonov*, 2:3481.

12. *Entsiklopedicheskii slovar'* (St. Petersburg: Brokgauz-Efron, 1890-1904), s.v. "Tiur'ma."

13. *Svod zakonov*, 2:3482; Gernet, *Istoriia*, 4:25.

14. Dallin and Nicolaevsky, *Forced Labor*, 299.

15. Gernet, *Istoriia*, 4:26.

16. *Svod zakonov*, 2:3435-39.

17. Ibid., 2:3433-43.

18. Gernet, *Istoriia*, 4:19-21.

19. *Svod zakonov*, 1:255; 2:3435-52.

20. *Entsiklopedicheskii slovar'*, s.v. "Tiur'ma."

21. P.I. Stuchka and I. Apeter, "Perekhod ot prinuditel'nogo truda po prigovoru suda k dobrovol'nomu trudu," *Sovetskoe gosudarstvo i revoliutsiia prava* 7 (1931): 124.

22. *Svod zakonov*, 1:255-56, 2:3433-36.

23. Ibid., 2:3425-36, 3439-43.

24. Ibid., 2:3428-34.

25. Ibid., 1:254-56.

26. Ibid., 2:3443-53.

27. *Entsiklopedicheskii slovar'*, s.v. "Tiur'ma."

28. *Proposed Budget of the Russian Empire* (Petrograd: Ministry of Finance Publishing House, 1917), 93, 119.

29. Ibid., 95-96.

30. *Svod zakonov*, 2:3428-52.

31. *Proposed Budget of the Russian Empire*, 94.

32. *Sovetskaia istoricheskaia entsiklopediia* (Moscow: Sovetskaia entsiklopediia, 1961-1973), s.v. "Zasulich, Vera."

33. Gernet, *Istoriia*, 4:24.

34. "Kak zhivët katorga i ssylka," *Vestnik katorgi i ssylki* 1 (February 1914):12; *Tiuremnyi vestnik* (1915): 872, quoted in Gernet, *Istoriia*, 4:37; V.S. Voitinskii, "Pravda ob Orlovskom tsentrale," Boris I. Nicolaevsky Collection, 277:10, Hoover Institution Archives, Stanford University, California.

35. *Ustav vspomogatel'nogo fonda russkim politicheskim prestupnikam* [Geneva,

1875]; "Letter by Frenk to Tkachev," Nicolaevsky Collection, 271:12; "Societies for Aid to Political Prisoners and Exiles," Nicolaevsky Collection, 98:2.

36. Gernet, *Istoriia*, 4:45; Klimyshkin, "K amnistii," *Katorga i ssylka* 1 (1921): 8-20; Sandmoirskiĭ, "Na poslednеĭ stupeni," *Katorga i ssylka* 1 (1921): 41-44.

37. Nikolai Podvoĭskiĭ, "Krasnaia gvardiia v Oktiabr'skie dni v Moskve," *Proletraskaia revoliutsiia* 11 (1927): 79-80; L.D. Trotskiĭ, *Istoriia Russkoĭ revoliutsii* (Berlin: Granit, 1933), 2:360.

38. Utevskiĭ, *Sovetskaia*, 84.

39. Trotskiĭ, *Istoriia*, 1:163.

40. "Telegramma Narodnogo Komissara iustitsii," *Administrativnyĭ vestnik* 10 (1928) in P.M. Losev and F.I. Ragulin, eds., *Sbornik normativnykh aktov po sovetskomu ispravitel'no-trudovomu pravu (1917-1959)* (Moscow: Gosudarstvennoe izdatel'stvo iuridicheskoĭ literatury, 1959), 10.

41. Untitled report re Political Prisoner Aid Society, Nicolaevsky Collection, 782:1.

2. THE BOLSHEVIK JUDICIAL SYSTEM, 1917-1922

1. O. Lidak, "Iiul'skie sobytiia 1917g.," in *Ocherki po istorii Oktiabr'skoĭ revoliutsii*, ed. M.N. Pokrovskiĭ (Moscow: Gosizdat, 1925), 2:281.

2. Trotskiĭ, *Istoriia*, 1:344, 2:362.

3. A. Stanchinskiĭ, "Ocherki tiuremnogo byta," *Katorga i ssylka* 4 (1922):17-34; biographical materials on Grigoriĭ Ivanovich Kotovskiĭ and Aleksandr Mikhaĭlovich Lbov in Nicolaevsky Collection, 747:10-11. Maxim Gorky, *Sobranie sochinenii* (Moscow: Gosudarstvennoe izdatel'stvo khudozhestvennoĭ literatury, 1961), 1:108-32.

4. Borisov, "Mertvyĭ dom nashikh dneĭ," *Nasha zaria* 6 (1913).

5. V.I. Lenin, "Gosudarstvo i revoliutsiia," in *Polnoe sobranie sochinenii*, 5th ed. (Moscow: Gospolitizdat, 1962), 33:91.

6. Dallin and Nicolaevsky, *Forced Labor*, 149.

7. *Sobranie uzakonenii i rasporiazhenii Rabochego i krest'ianskogo pravitel'stva* (Moscow: Iuridicheskaia literatura, 1919), 66:590.

8. Ibid., 1917, 5:71.

9. V.R. Iakubson, "Ugolovnaia repressiia v pervye gody revoliutsii," *Ezhenedel'nik sovetskoĭ iustitsii* 4 (1922): 4.

10. *Sobranie*, 1918:589, 605.

11. N.I. Krylenko, "Tri proekta reformy ugolovnogo kodeksa," *Sovetskoe gosudarstvo i revoliutsiia prava* 1 (1931): 103; B.S. Utevskiĭ, *Vospominaniia iurista* (Moscow: Iuridicheskaia literatura, 1989), 271.

12. *Sobranie*, 1918, 53:597, 605.

13. F.I. Dan, *Dva goda skitanii* (Berlin: Sklad Izd. Russische Bucherzentrale Obrazowanje, 1922), 177-78.

14. *Sobranie*, 1919, 66:590.

15. "Clippings from Menshevik newspapers," Nicolaevsky Collection, 663:4-7.

16. *Sobranie*, 1919, 66:590.5-16.

17. Krylenko, "Tri proekta reformy," 101-3.

18. D.A. Chugaev et. al, eds., *Petrogradskiĭ Voenno-revoliutsionnyĭ komitet: Dokumenty i materialy* (Moscow: Navka, 1966), 1:10.

19. *Sobranie*, 1917, 4:50, 12:170; 1919, 66:590.

20. E.G. Gimpel'son, "Stroitel'stvo mestnykh organov gosudarstvennoĭ vlasti," in *Istoriia SSSR* (Moscow: Navka, 1967), 7:269.

21. *Sobranie*, 1917, 12:180; G.A. Belov et al., ed., *Iz istorii Vserossiĭskoĭ Chrezvyzhaninoĭ komissii 1977-1921 gg.: Sbornik dokumentov* (Moscow: Gospolitizdat, 1958), VI.

22. N. Zubov., *F.E. Dzerzhinskiĭ: Biografia* (Moscow: Politizdat, 1971), 56-57.

23. *Sobranie*, 1918, 65:70.

24. Ibid., 1919, 12:130.

25. I.P. Makintsian, ed., *Krasnaia kniga VCHK* (Moscow, 1920), 1:107-8, 127, 157-58, 194-96, 365-66 (typescript in Nicolaevsky Collection, 143:1-3; "O solovetskikh kontsentratsionnykh lageriakh," Records of the Russian Embassy in the USA, 26:11, Hoover Institution Archives, Stanford University, California; *Tiuremnoe delo v 1921 godu* (Moscow, 1921), 10-12; M.Ia. Latsis, *Dva goda bor'by na vnutrennem fronte* (Moscow, 1920), 74-76.

26. G. Portugalov, "Administrativnye vzyskaniia," *Vlast' sovetov* 3 (1922): 15.

27. Nikolai Erdman, *Mandat* (Berlin: J. Ladyschnikov Verlag, 1926).

28. Portugalov, "Administrativnye vzyskaniia," 16.

29. Solzhenitsyn, *Arkhipelag-Gulag* 3-4:89-90.

30. *Tiuremnoe . . . 1921*, 16.

31. Legget, *The Cheka*, 181-82.

32. *Tiuremnoe . . . 1921*, 8.

33. Gernet, *Istoriia*, 4:23.

34. *Sobranie*, 1922, 53:675.

35. Gernet, *Istoriia*, 4:26.

36. E. Tarnovskiĭ. "Sudebnaia repressiia v tsifrakh za 1919-1922," *Ezhendel'nik sovetskoĭ iustitsii* 44-45 (1922): 43-44.

37. Makintsian, *Krasnaia*, 1:9, 107-8, 127, 157-58, 194-96, 365-66; "O sovetskikh kontsentratsionnykh lageriakh"; *Tiuremnoe . . . 1921*, 10-12; Latsis, *D'va goda bor'by*, 74-76; Legget, *The Cheka*, 200; Iakubson, "Ugolovnaia," 3-4.

38. Stuchka and Apeter, "Perekhod," 125; *Sobranie*, 1918, 53:598; 1921, 23-34:141.

39. *Tiuremnoe . . . 1921*, 10.

40. E. Tarnovskiĭ, "Dvizhenie prestupnikov v 1920-1921 g.g.," *Ezhenedel'nik sovetskoĭ iustitsii* 19-20 (1922): 10; V.R. Iakubson, "Golod i tiuremnoe naselenie," *Ezhenedel'nik sovetskoĭ iustitsii* 11-15 (1922):11.

41. *Letters from Russian Prisons* (New York: Albert & Charles Boni, 1925), 214; Ekaterina Olitskaia, *Moi vospominaniia* (Frankfurt am Main: Posev, 1971), 216-17, 231-34.

42. Olitskaia, *Moi vospominaniia*, 216-17, 231-34.

43. Partiia sotsialistov-revoliutsionerov, *Cheka* (Berlin: Orfeĭ, 1922), esp. 91, 97, 102.

44. V.R. Iakubson, "Kul'turno-prosvetitel'naia rabota v tiur'me," *Ezhenedel'nik sovetskoĭ iustitsii* 19-20 (1922): 11.

45. Solzhenitsyn, *Arkhipelag-Gulag*, 3-4:31; Stanchinskiĭ, passim.

46. Ibid., 174, 427, 415-33.

47. Legget, *The Cheka*, 176, 178, 181.

48. Gernet, *Istoriia*, 4:19-20.

49. "Telegramma," in Losev and Ragulin, *Sbornik*, 10.

3. THE NKĨŨ's RISE TO POWER

1. Lenin, "Zadacha proletariata v nasheĭ revoliutsii," in *Polnoe*, 31:162.
2. For discussion of the Soviet judicial system, see Chapter 2.
3. "Telegramma," in Losev and Ragulin, *Sbornik*, 10.
4. *Sobranie*, 1918, 53:598.
5. Stuchka and Apeter, "Perekhod," 124.
6. *Sobranie*, 1917, 9:127.
7. Solzhenitsyn, 3-4, *Arkhipelag-Gulag*, 22; Legget, *The Cheka*, 175; Rossi, *Spravochnic po GULAGu*, 417.
8. *Sobranie*, 1917, 12:171, 9:146; 1918, 15:222.
9. *Dekrety sovetskoĭ vlasti* (Moscow: Gospolitizdat, 1957) 1:401-2, in Losev and Ragulin, 14.
10. *Sobranie*, 1918, 15:223.
11. Ibid., 19:284.
12. Ibid.
13. *Svod zakonov*, 2:3481; *Sobranie*, 1918, 19:284.
14. *Tiuremnoe . . . 1921*, 22.
15. Gernet, *Istoriia*, 4:25.
16. Solzhenitsyn, *Arkhipelag-Gulag*; Dallin and Nicolaevsky, *Forced Labor*.
17. Stuchka and Apeter, "Perekhod," 124.
18. *Sovetskaia iustitsiia* 1 (1919), quoted in I. Apeter, "15 let sovetskoĭ ispravitel'no-trudovoĭ politiki," *Sovetskaia iustitsiia* 33 (1932):18.
19. Stuchka and Apeter, "Perekhod," 124.
20. *Rezoliutsii i postanovleniia I i II vserossiĭskikh s"ezdov partii levykh sotsialistov-revoliutsionerov* (Moscow, 1918), 15-18, 25-26; B.D. Kamkov, *Kto takie sotsialisty-revoliutsionery* (Petrograd, 1918); both these pamphlets are in the Nicolaevsky Collection, 781:6, 10.
21. *Sobranie*, 1918, 53:598.1. For Lenin's view on crime and punishment, see the opening pages of Chapter 2.
22. *Sobranie*, 1918, 53:598.2-5.
23. Ibid., 1920, 82:399.
24. Ibid., 1918, 53:598.7-10.
25. See Ibid., 598.7.
26. Ibid.
27. Ibid., 598.9-14, 16-20.
28. Ibid., 598.16-20, 26.
29. Ibid., 598.24.
30. Ibid., 598.10-11.
31. See Chapters 1 and 2.
32. *Sobranie*, 1918, 53:598.12, 23.
33. Ibid., 33:598.21-27 19:284; *Svod zakonov*, 2:3481.
34. *Sobranie*, 1918, 53:598.27.
35. Ibid., 598.27.
36. *Tiuremnoe . . . 1921*, 22.
37. James Bunyan, ed., *The Origin of Forced Labor in the Soviet State* (Baltimore, Md.: John Hopkins Press, 1967), chap. 1.
38. *Sobranie*, 1918, 53:598.28, 31, 5.

39. *Tiuremnoe . . . 1921*, 21; "IV Vserossiĭskiĭ s"ezd deĭateleĭ sovetskoĭ iustitsii," *Ezhenedel'nik sovetskoĭ iustitsii* 6 (1922): 9.

40. *Tiuremnoe . . . delo v 1921*, 18-19; Vladimir Alekseevich Nekrasov, untitled memoirs, in Nicolaevsky Collection, 414:7; Stuchka and Apeter, "Perekhod," 125.

41. *Sobranie*, 1917, 9:146.

42. Lenin, *Polnoe*, 50:143-44; Makintsian, *Krasnaia*, 1:86.

43. Legget, *The Cheka*, 100-101; *Sobranie*, 1918, 66:728; "Instruktsiia Chrezvychaĭnym komissiiam na mestakh," Nicolaevsky Collection, 143:7; E.V. Dumbadze, *Na sluzhbe Cheka i Kominterna* (Paris: Izdatel'stvo Mishen', 1930), 40; G.S. Agabekov, *G.P.U.: Zapiski chekista* (Berlin: Izdatel'stvo Strela, 1930), 14-15, 41, 43.

44. Partiia sotsialistov-revoliutsionerov, *Cheka*, 14, 19, 42, 88, 93, 173, 196, 227, 141.

45. "O Solovetskikh kontsentratsionnykh lageriakh"; *Tiuremnoe . . . 1921*, 11-12; *Vlast' sovetov* 1-2 (1922): 42.

46. *Tiuremnoe . . . 1921*, 4, 18-19.

47. Partiia sotsialistov-revoliutsionerov, *Cheka*, 112, 155, 242.

48. Ibid., 75, 92-95, 102, 117; Olitskaia, *Moi vospominaniia*, 1:216-27.

49. *Sobranie*, 1918, 53:598, 2-5; Partiia sotsialistov revoliutsionerov, *Cheka*, 117.

50. Dallin and Nicolaevsky, *Forced Labor*, 168; Solzhenitsyn, *Arkhipelag-Gulag*, 3-4, 17-28; *Sobranie*, 1918, 19:284.

51. B. L., "O strakhovanii lesorubov," *Voprosy truda* 4 (1925): 140-41; I.V. Pervozvanskiĭ, "Ekspluatatsiia lesa v Severnoĭ Karelii vo vtoroĭ piatiletke," *Sovetskaia Kareliia* 1-2 (1932): 59-60.

52. Partiia sotsialistov-revoliutsionerov, *Cheka*, 119; Solzhenitsyn, *Arkhipelag-Gulag*, 3-4, 54-55.

53. Lennard D. Gerson, *The Secret Police in Lenin's Russia* (Philadelphia: Temple Univ. Press, 1976), 149; Voĭtinskiĭ, "Pravda," Nicolaevsky Collection, 277:10.

54. Partiia sotsialistov-revoliutsionerov, *Cheka*, 242-47.

55. Ibid., 85, 94.

56. Ibid., 80-81.

57. Ibid., 150.

58. Ibid., 198.

59. Ibid., 209-10.

60. See Chapter 2.

61. Solzhenitsyn, *Arkhipelag-Gulag*, 3-4, 18; *Sobranie*, 1922, 53:675.

62. *Tiuremnoe . . . 1921*, 22.

63. Stuchka and Apeter, "Perekhod," 124; Peter H. Solomon, Jr., "Soviet Penal Policy, 1917-1934: A Reinterpretation," *Slavic Review*, June 1980, 197-98.

64. *Sobranie*, 1918, 53:598, 19:284.

65. Ibid., 1918, 75:813; Stuchka and Apeter, "Perekhod," 125.

66. *Sobranie*, 1918, 53:598.5; 52:598.2.

67. Ibid., 1919, 12:124, 20:235.

68. Ibid., 12:124.5; 20:235.5.

69. I.I. Kizilov, *NKVD RSFSR 1917-1930* (Moscow: Nauchno-issledovatel'skiĭ i redaktsionno-izdatel'skiĭ otdel, 1969), 89; "O perekhode vsekh mest zakliucheniia v vedenie Narkomvnudela," *Ezhenedel'nik sovetskoĭ iustitsii* 37-38 (1922), in Losev and Ragulin, *Sbornik*, 106-7.

70. *Sobranie*, 1919, 12:124.1, 20:235.1.

71. Legget, *The Cheka*, 210-11.
72. Partiia sotsialistov-revoliutsionerov, *Cheka*.
73. Legget, *The Cheka*, 210-11.
74. Agabekov, *G.P.U.*, 14-15.
75. For the GTU prison system, see Chapter 1.
76. *Sobranie*, 1918, 53:598; 1919, 20:235.
77. Ibid., 1918, 53:598.6; 1919, 20:235.6.
78. Ibid., 235.8, 10, 3.
79. Legget, *The Cheka*, 178; Tarnovskiĭ, "Dvizhenie," 9-10.
80. *Sobranie*, 1919, 20:235.1, 9-10.
81. Ibid., 1918, 53:598.11; 1919, 20:235.11.
82. Ibid., 1919, 20:235.12-19; *Tiuremnoe . . . 1921*, 18-19.
83. *Sobranie*, 1919, 20:235.20-24.
84. Ibid., 1918, 53:598.5; 1919, 20:235.29-31.
85. For the NKIU view on self-sufficiency, see Chapter 4.
86. *Sobranie*, 1919, 20:235.31-34; 1918, 53:598.21.
87. Ibid., 1918, 53:598.27, 5; 1919, 20:235.27.
88. Ibid., 1919, 20:235.44.
89. Ibid., 1918, 53:598.3; 1919, 20:235.26; Olitskaia, *Moi vospominaniia*, 1:212-13.
90. *Sobranie*, 1919, 20:235.37-40.
91. Gernet, *Istoriia*, 4:42-44.
92. Olitskaia, *Moi vospominanaia*, 217.
93. *Statisticheskiĭ ezhegodnik RSFSR, 1918-1920*, 2 (1921): 59.
94. *Vlast' sovetov* 1-2 (1922): 41-42; Legget, *The Cheka*, 178.

4. REEDUCATION VERSUS FINANCIAL SELF-SUFFICIENCY

1. *Sobranie*, 1919, 20:235.
2. Ibid., 1918, 53:598.17-20; 1919, 27:300.
3. Ibid., 48:462.
4. Ibid., 53:515.
5. Michael Jakobson, "Literary Censorship in the USSR," in John L. Scherer, ed., *USSR Facts and Figures Annual* (Gulf Breeze, Fla.: Academic International Press, 1981), 329-30.
6. *Sobranie*, 1920, 65:283.
7. Ibid., 1922, 77:649.
8. Ibid., 1921, 23-24:141.
9. Ibid., 23-24:141.4.
10. Ibid., 141.10; 1920, 65.238.
11. *Tiuremnoe . . . 1921*, 8.
12. *Sobranie*, 1918, 53:598.5; 1921, 23-24:141.11.
13. Ibid., 1921, 23-24:141.13-25.
14. *Tiuremnoe . . . 1921*, 4-9.
15. *Sobranie*, 1921, 23-24:141.17, 24.
16. Ibid., 1918, 53:598.11-13; 1921, 23-24:141.6-9; 1919, 20:235.10-11.
17. Ibid., 1921, 23-24:141.46-60.

18. Ibid., 23-24:141.49-56.
19. For further discussion of this point of view, see Chapter 5.
20. *Sobranie*, 1918, 52:598.1, 26; 1919, 20:235.43.
21. Ibid., 53:598.21; 1921, 23-24:141.111-127.
22. Ibid., 1918, 53:598.27; 1919, 20:235.27; 1921, 23-24:141.64-67.
23. Ibid., 1918, 53:598.5; 1919, 20:235.35; 1921, 23-24:141.
24. Stuchka and Apeter, "Perekhod," 127.
25. T͡iuremnoe . . . *1921*, 3.
26. Solzhenitsyn, *Arkhipelag-Gulag* 3-4:73.
27. T͡iuremnoe . . . *1921*, 3-6.
28. Ibid., 18-19, 5.
29. Ibid., 19-20.
30. Ibid., 6.
31. Ibid., 8-9.
32. Ibid., 10.
33. Ibid., 1, 17; *Sobranie*, 1918, 53:598.26; 1919, 20:235.69-83.
34. T͡iuremnoe . . . *1921*, 17-18, 19.
35. Ibid., 5.
36. *Sobranie*, 1919, 23:300; 1920, 65:283; T͡iuremnoe . . . *1921*, 7-8.
37. *Sobranie*, 1918, 53:598.5; 1921, 23-24:114.112.
38. T͡iuremnoe . . . *1921*, 3, 20.
39. Ibid., 21, 22-23.
40. Ibid., 22, 23-24.
41. Ibid., 15, 25-31.
42. Legget, *The Cheka*, 339.
43. Lenin, "L.B. Kamenevu," in *Polnoe*, 54:39; Lenin, "Nabrosok proekta postanovleniia Politbi͡uro TSK RKP(b) o VCHK," in *Polnoe*, 44:261, 567-68; Lenin, "O vnutrenneĭ i vneshneĭ politike Respubliki," in *Polnoe*, 44:327-29; *Sobranie*, 1922, 4:42. See also Legget, *The Cheka*, 341-46.
44. B.P., "Ob organizat͡sii ti͡urem na nachalakh samookupaemosti," *Ezhenedel'nik sovetskoĭ i͡ustit͡sii* 14-15 (1922): 8-9; M.K.-F., "Nova͡ia ėkonomicheska͡ia politika i lageri prinuditel'nykh rabot," *Vlast' sovetov* 3 (1922): 18; P.N., "O revoli͡ut͡sionnoĭ zakonnosti i organizat͡sii bor'by s prestupnost'i͡u," *Ezhenedel'nik sovetskoĭ i͡ustit͡sii* 13 (1922): 2-4.
45. C.A. Savrasov, "O sovremennoĭ karatel'noĭ politike (vidy i rody nakazani͡ia v svi͡azi s novoĭ ekonomicheskoĭ politikoĭ)," *Ezhenedel'nik sovetskoĭ i͡ustit͡sii* 4 (1922): 9-10.
46. Ibid.
47. "IV Vserossiĭskiĭ," 9.
48. S. Rav'ich, "Vserossiĭskiĭ s'ezd zavedui͡ushchikh otdelami upravleni͡ia," *Vlast' sovetov* 3 (1922): 6-7; "Rezoli͡ut͡si͡ia po karatel'noĭ politike," *Vlast' sovetov* 3 (1922): 65; M.K.-F., "Nova͡ia ekonomicheska͡ia," 18.
49. B.P., "Ob organizat͡sii," 8-9; "Rezoli͡ut͡si͡ia," 65.
50. *Sobranie*, 1922, 53:675.
51. Ibid., 28:136.28-34.
52. Ibid., 136.1.
53. B.P., "Ob organizat͡sii," 8-9; S. Narkevich, "Sud i zhisn'," *Ezhenedel'nik sovetskoĭ i͡ustit͡sii* 37-38 (1922): 23-26.
54. "O peredache," in Losev and Ragulin, *Sbornik*, 106-7.

5. THE NKVD MONOPOLY, 1922-1930

1. B.P., "Ob organizatsii," 8-9; M.K.-F., "Novaia ėkonomicheskaia," 18; P.N., "O revoliutsionnoĭ," 2-4; "Rezoliutsiia," 65.

2. *Sobranie*, 1918, 53.598.5; see also Chapter 4.

3. "O peredache," in Losev and Ragulin, *Sbornik*, 106-7.

4. "Glavnoe upravlenie mestami zakliucheniia," *Vlast' sovetov* 11-12 (1922): 60-62; Utevskiĭ, *Vospominaniia*, 219, 231.

5. "Glavnoe upravlenie," 60-62; "Evseĭ Gustavovich Shirvindt," *Sovetskoe gosudarstvo i pravo* 12 (1958): 130.

6. "Glavnoe upravlenie," 61-62.

7. Ibid.

8. Ibid.

9. Ibid.

10. Stuchka and Apeter, "Perekhod," 132-33; Dallin and Nicolaevsky, *Forced Labor*, 163; "Glavnoe upravlenie," 62.

11. *Sobranie*, 1923, 62:587.

12. Ibid., 1924, 53:552.

13. S. Faĭnblit, "Sudebnyĭ prigovor i dosrochnoe osvobozhdenie," *Ezhenedel'nik sovetskoĭ iustitsii* 3 (1928): 61-69.

14. Kadin, "Sovetskoe stroitel'stvo i vopros o NKVD," *Vlast' sovetov* 2 (1924): 69-77; G. Lobanov, "K voprosu o NKVD," *Vlast' sovetov* 5 (1924): 98-99; Zaĭtsev, "Organizatsionnaia putanitsa v voprose o NKVD," *Vlast' sovetov* 2 (1924): 62-68.

15. *Sobranie*, 1924, 83:870.

16. S. Faĭnblit, "Tiuremnyĭ rezhim i dosrochnoe osvobozhdenie," *Ezhnedel'nik sovetskoĭ iustitsii* 11 (1928): 328; Utevskiĭ, *Vospominaniia*, 269-74.

17. *Sobranie*, 1924, 83:870.7; V. Iakubson, *Ispravitel'no-trudovoĭ kodeks RSFSR: Populiarnoe izlozhenie i postateĭnyĭ komentariĭ* (Moscow: Izdanie NKVD, 1926), 7-15.

18. Utevskiĭ, *Vospominaniia*, 232-34.

19. N.A. Popov, "K voprosu o bor'be s detskoĭ presupnost'iu," *Vlast' sovetov* 1-2 (1923): 54.

20. F. Traskovich, "Ispravitel'no trudovaia politika," *Ezhenedel'nik sovetskoĭ iustitsii* 7 (1929): 155; Faĭnblit, "Tiuremnyĭ," 326; Utevskiĭ, *Vospominanaia*, 269-70.

21. *Sobranie*, 1924, 83:870.7.

22. Ibid., 1918, 53:598; 1924, 83:870.46-47.

23. "Telegramma," in Losev and Ragulin, *Sbornik*, 10-11; "Glavnoe upravlenie," 60-62.

24. *Sobranie*, 1924: 870.11-12; 1918, 53:598; *Svod zakonov*, 1:255-56, 2:3433-36; "Telegramma," in Losev and Ragulin, *Sbornik*, 10.

25. *Sobranie*, 1924, 83:870.11-12, 23-43; 1918, 53.598.

26. Ibid., 1924, 83:870.23-32; Dallin and Nicolaevsky, *Forced Labor*, 162; Utevskiĭ, *Sovetskaia*, 98-101.

27. V. Klokova, "Prekratit' shtampovanie prigovorov k prinuditel'nym rabotam," *Sovetskaia iustitsiia* 28 (1930): 20.

28. *Sobranie*, 1924, 83:870.13-18; 1919, 27:300; 1929, 81:795.

29. Ibid., 1924, 83:870.19-22; *Svod zakonov*, 2:3439-43.

30. *Sobranie*, 1924, 83:870.19-22; Iakubson, *Ispravitel'no-trudovoi*, 44-45.

31. *Sobranie*, 1918, 19:784; 1924, 83:870.52, 70; Iakubson, *Ispravitel'no-trudovoĭ*, 72-73; "Kak zhivët katorga i ssylka," *Vestnik katorgi i ssylki* 1 (February 1914): 12.

32. *Svod zakonov*, 2:3482; *Sobranie*, 1917, 9:146; Iakubson, *Ispravitel'no-trudovoĭ*, 62-63, 72-73, 80.

33. Iakubson, *Ispravitel'no-trudovoĭ*, 50; *Vedomosti Verkhovnogo Soveta SSSR* 1 (1959).

34. *Sobranie*, 1924, 83:870.79. For inmates' productivity, see Chapter 9.

35. *Sobranie*, 1923, 16:202; Stuchka and Apeter, "Perekhod," 127; Chernysh-Cherner, "Reforma ispravitel'no-trudovogo dela," *Sovetskaia iustitsiia* 1 (1930): 23.

36. Tolmachëv, "Ocherednye zadachi v oblasti raboty administrativnykh organov," *Ezhenedel'nik sovetskoĭ iustitsii* 22 (1928): 645; Gernet, *Istoriia*, 4:25.

37. Dallin and Nicolaevsky, *Forced Labor*, 160-61, 163; *Sobranie*, 1925, 25:181.

38. V. Radus-Zen'kovich, "Sudebnaia sistema i prokuratura," *Ezhenedel'nik sovetskoĭ iustitsii* 30 (1928): 830; Dallin and Nicolaevsky, *Forced Labor*, 162; Utevskiĭ, *Vospominaniia*, 247.

39. S. Faĭnblit, "Liberal'naia boltovnia," *Ezhenedel'nik sovetskoĭ iustitsii* 35 (1928): 954-56; N. Lagovier, "Nabolevshie voprosy ugolovno-sudebnoĭ i ispravitel'no-trudovoĭ praktiki," *Ezhenedel'nik sovetskoĭ iustitsii* 40-41 (1928): 1077-78; Dallin and Nicolaevsky, *Forced Labor*, 161-63.

40. "Programma pravogo opportunizma v ugolovnoĭ politike: K proektu UK tovarishcha Shirvindta," *Sovetskoe gosudarstvo i revoliutsiia prava* 11-12 (1930): 106-29; A. P. and N. L., "Pravyĭ uklon v karatel'noĭ politike," *Ezhenedel'nik sovetskoĭ iustitsii* 3 (1930): 14-17; Dallin and Nicolaevsky, *Forced Labor*, 202-3.

41. Stuchka and Apeter, "Perekhod," 125; Boris Skvirskiĭ, "Economic Progress under Soviet Rule," *Current History* 23, no. 2 (November 1927): 174; *Proposed Budget of the Russian Empire*, 93, 119.

42. "O karatel'noĭ politike," *Ezhenedel'nik sovetskoĭ iustitsii* 14 (1928), in Losev and Ragulin, *Sbornik*, 202-7.

43. *Sobranie*, 1930, 22:248; V.P. Danilov and N.V. Teptsov, "Kollektivizatsiia: Kak èto bylo," *Pravda*, 26 August 1988.

44. "O karatel'noĭ politike," in Losev and Ragulin, *Sbornik*, 202-3.

45. Ibid., 203-4.

46. Ibid., 205-6.

47. "Programma pravogo opportunizma v ugolovnoĭ politike," 106-29; A.P. and N.L., "Pravyĭ uklon," 14-17; Dallin and Nicolaevsky, *Forced Labor*, 202-3.

48. "Tsirkuliar Verkhovnogo Suda RSFSR no. 7 ot 29 avgusta 1928 goda," *Sudebnaia praktika RSFSR* 17 (1928): 3; "Rech' t. Iansona na 3em soveshchanii sudebno-prokurorskikh rabotnikov," *Sovetskaia iustitsiia* 24-25 (1930): 1-2.

49. K. Galis, "Prinuditel'nye raboty i drugie mery sotsial'noĭ zashchity vmesto kratkosrochnogo lisheniia svobody," *Ezhenedel'nik sovetskoĭ iustitsii* 7 (1929): 158-61; "Instruktsiia po primeneniiu prinuditel'nykh rabot bez soderzhaniia pod strazheĭ," *Ezhenedel'nik sovetskoĭ iustitsii* 9-10 (1929): 233-39; "Na mestakh," *Ezhenedel'nik sovetskoĭ iustitsii* 25 (1929): 590; 26 (1929): 614.

50. "Rech' t. Iansona," 1-2.

51. Dallin and Nicolaevsky, *Forced Labor*, 162.

52. V.R. Iakubson, "Ispravitel'no-trudovoĭ rezhim i dosrochnoe osvobozhdenie," *Administrativnyĭ vestnik* 8 (1928), quoted in N. Lagovier, "Nabolevshie," 1078.

53. Tolmachev, "Ocherednye zadachi," 643-47.

54. Ibid., 645.

55. Faĭnblit, "Liberal'naia boltovnia," 955.

56. Lagovier, "Nabolevshie," 1078.

57. E.G. Shirvindt, "Protiv iskazheniĭ i izvrashcheniĭ," *Ezhenedel'nik sovetskoĭ iustitsii* 48 (1928): 1225.

58. Ibid.

59. Ibid.

60. Traskovich, "Ispravitel'no-trudovaia politika," 152; A. Konovalov, "Sistema Ugolovnogo kodeksa i nasha ugolovnaia politika," *Ezhendel'nik sovetskoĭ iustitsii* 6 (1929): 136.

61. Traskovich, "Ispravitel'no-trudovaia politika," 153-55.

62. "Prodolzhenie preniĭ po dokladu t. Traskovicha," *Ezhenedel'nik sovetskoĭ iustitsii* 9-10 (1929): 228.

63. "Preniia po dokladu t. Traskovicha," *Ezhendel'nik sovetskoĭ iustitsii* 9-10 (1929): 228.

64. Tolmachev, "Ocherednye zadachi," 645; B.S. Utevskiĭ, "K voprosu ob organizatsii koloniĭ v otdalënnykh mestnostiakh," *Administrativnyĭ vestnik* 6-7 (1929): 39-43; Stuchka and Apeter, "Perekhod," 127.

65. E. Shirvindt, "K dvenadtsatiletiiu sovetskoĭ ispravitel'no-trudovoĭ politiki" *Ezhenedel'nik sovetskoĭ iustitsii* 46 (1929): 1087-89.

66. Ibid., 1087-88.

67. Ibid.

68. Ibid., 1089.

69. Averbakh, *Ot prestupleniia k trudu*, 21-31.

70. E.B. Pashukanis, *Sovetskiĭ gosudarstvennyĭ apparat v bor'be s biurokratizmom* (Moscow: Izdatel'stvo Kommunisticheskoĭ akademii, 1929), 8; Ia. Vitbaum, "Neobkhodimo sobliudat' klassovuiu liniiu v mestakh zakliucheniia," *Ezhenedel'nik sovetskoĭ iustitsii* 46 (1929): 1090.

71. Gurevich and Tikhomirov, "Nuzhny li narkomvnudely," *Pravda*, 30 December 1929; V.Z., "Narkomvnudely ne nuzhny," *Ezhenedel'nik sovetskoĭ iustitsii* 3 (1930): 6-8.

72. "T., Nuzhny li narkomvnudely?," *Ezhenedel'nik sovetskoĭ iustitsii* 6 (1930): 22-23.

73. *Sobranie*, 1930, 60:640.

74. Ibid.

6. The NKIU's Last Chance, 1930-1932

1. "Doklad tovarischa Iansona," *Sovetskaia iustitsiia* 3 (1931): 13-14; Krylenko, "Tri proekta reformy," (1931) 100-101; Shirvindt, "K dvenadtsatiletiiu sovetskoĭ," 4-5; Stuchka and Apeter, "Perekhod," 131-35.

2. "Doklad tovarishcha Iansona," 13-14.

3. *Sovetskaia iustitsiia* 3 (1931): 30; Utevskiĭ, Vospominaniia, 269-74.

4. "Doklad tovarishcha Iansona," 13.

5. "V soveschanie rukovodiashchikh rabotnikov iustitsii kraev i oblasteĭ RSFSR," *Sovetskaia iustitsiia* 21 (1931): 31.

6. "Doklad tovarishcha Ĭansona," 13-14; Stuchka and Apeter, "Perekhod," 130; B.S. Utevskiĭ, "Ob ukreplenii Narkomvnudela po linii mest zakliucheniia," *Administrativnyĭ vestnik* 7 (1930): 30-32; Dallin and Nicolaevsky, *Forced Labor*, 84-87; Oĭtskaia, *Moi vospominaniia*, 306-7.

7. N. Stogov, "Tiuremnaia pechat', 1921-1935 godov," in *Pamiat'* (Moscow: Khronika Press, 1976), 1:542-49; Stuchka and Apeter, "Perekhod," 139. See also Chapter 5.

8. "Doklad tovarishcha Ĭansona," 13.

9. Stuchka and Apeter, "Perekhod," 130-31.

10. Shirvindt, "K dvenadtsatiletiiu sovetskoĭ," 4-5; Stuchka and Apeter, "Perekhod," 129-32.

11. Ibid., 136-38.

12. *Sovetskaia istoricheskaia èntsiklopediia*, s.v. "Sotsialisticheskoe sorevnovanie."

13. Stuchka and Apeter, "Perekhod," 137, 140-41.

14. Ibid., 135; "Ispravitel'no-trudovaia politika rekonstruktivnogo perioda," *Sovetskaia iustitsiia* 25 (1931): 25-28.

15. "Doklad tovarishcha Ĭansona," 13-14.

16. Men'shatin, review of E. Shirvindt and B. Utevskiĭ, *Sovetskoe ispravitel'no-trudovoe pravo* (Moscow: Gosudarstvennyĭ institut po izucheniiu prestupnosti i prestupnika, 1931), in *Sovetskoe gosudarstvo i revoliutsiia prava* 4 (1931): 173-74.

17. Beri-Slavskiĭ, "Likvidirovat' proryvy v ispravitel'no-trudovoĭ politike na Severnom Kavkaze," *Ezhenedel'nik sovetskoĭ iustitsii* 17 (1931): 27-28.

18. Stuchka and Apeter, "Perekhod," 129-32, 137; "Ispravitel'no-trudovaia politika," 25-28.

19. Ibid., 28.

20. *Sobranie*, 1933, 50:294; E. Timoshenko, "Kanalarmeĭtsy: Ikh zhizn' i sud'ba," in *Vozvrashchenie k pravde* (Moscow: Iuridicheskaia literatura; 1989), 2:313.

21. Utevskiĭ, *Vospominaniia*, 288-95.

22. *Sobranie*, 1932, 53:237; 1934, 36:283; *Tiuremnoe . . . 1921*, 3.

23. Stuchka and Apeter, "Perekhod," 128.

24. "Ispravitel'no-trudovaia politika," 25.

25. Stuchka and Apeter, "Perekhod," 129.

26. Viktor Kravchenko, *I Choose Freedom* (New York: Charles Scribner's Sons, 1950), 335-36; Naum Jasny, "Labor and Output in Soviet Concentration Camps," *Journal of Political Economy* 4 (1951): 416-18.

27. Dallin and Nicolaevsky, *Forced Labor*, 54.

28. *Sovetskaia iustitsiia* 8 (1933): 11; Bulatov, "Ispravitel'no-trudovaia politika RSFSR," *Sovetskaia iustitsiia* 2 (1934): 18.

29. Dallin and Nicolaevsky, *Forced Labor*, 162-63.

30. Stuchka and Apeter, "Perekhod," 138-41.

31. Ibid., 128.

32. *Sobranie*, 1918, 19:284.

33. Stuchka and Apeter, "Perekhod," 129; "Tsirkuliar NKIU No. 36," *Ezhenedel'nik sovetskoĭ iustitsii* 11 (1931); Beri-Slavskiĭ, "Likvidirovat' proryvy," 27.

34. "Tsirkuliar NKIU No. 40," *Ezhenedel'nik sovetskoĭ iustitsii* 12 (1931).

35. "Tsirkuliar NKIU No. 36."

36. Galkin, "Kak rabotaiut nashi organy iustitsii," *Ezhenedel'nik sovetskoĭ iustitsii* 14 (1931): 23; "Ustranit' politicheskie nedochëty," *Sovetskaia iustitsiia* 13 (1932):

15-18; Kostin, "Rabota organov i͡ustit͡sii AKSSR i proizvodstvenno-tovarishcheskie sudy na lesozagotovkakh," *Sovetskai͡a i͡ustit͡sii͡a* 12 (1932): 22; Zinin, "Organy i͡ustit͡sii i rabota po lesnym zagotovkam," *Sovetskai͡a i͡ustit͡sii͡a* 14 (1932): 9-13; Dallin and Nicolaevsky, *Forced Labor*, 194.

37. Dallin and Nicolaevskky, *Forced Labor*, 193-97.

38. "V soveshchanie rukovodi͡ashchikh rabotnikov organov i͡ustit͡sii kraëv i oblasteĭ RSFSR. Doklad Apetera," *Ezhenedel'nik sovetskoĭ i͡ustit͡sii* 18 (1931): 24, 26-27.

39. Merle Fainsod, *Smolensk under Soviet Rule* (Cambridge, Mass.: Harvard University Press, 1958), 207.

40. Ibid., 208; Stuchka and Apeter, "Perekhod," 138-41.

41. "V soveshchanie rukovodi͡ashchikh rabotnikov organov i͡ustit͡sii kraëv i oblasteĭ RSFSR," 31.

42. P.P. Postyshev, "Osnovnye zadachi sovetskoĭ i͡ustit͡sii na sovremennom étape," *Sovetskoe gosudarstvo i revoli͡ut͡sii͡a prava* 2 (1932): 9-10.

7. THE GUITU UNDER SIEGE, 1932-1934

1. Dallin and Nicolaevsky, *Forced Labor*, 149; Robert Conquest, *The Great Terror* (New York: Oxford University Press, 1990), 311.

2. Stuchka and Apeter, "Perekhod," 131-33; "Ispravitel'no-trudovai͡a politika," 27.

3. I.V. Stalin, "Political Report of the Central Committee to the Sixteenth Congress of the CPSU," in *Works* (Moscow: Foreign Languages Publishing House, 1955), 12:311, 313.

4. Postyshev, "Osnovnye zadachi," 1-8.

5. Shepilov, *Alkogolizm i prestupnost'* quoted in Aminov, "Ret͡senzii͡a knigi Shepilova 'Alkogolizm i prestupnost'," *Sovetskoe gosudarstvo i revoli͡ut͡sii͡a prava* 5-6 (1932): 235.

6. Aminov, "Ret͡senzii͡a," 235-36.

7. Stuchka and Apeter, "Perekhod," 130.

8. O.Ia. Gurevich, "Na bor'bu za okhranu i ukreplenie osnovy sovetskogo stroi͡a—obshchestvenoĭ (sot͡sialisticheskoĭ) sobstvennosti," *Sovetskai͡a i͡ustit͡sii͡a* 6 (1933): 13.

9. N.I. Krylenko, "Okhrana sot͡sialisticheskoĭ sobstvennosti," *Sovetskoe gosudarstvo i revoli͡ut͡sii͡a prava* 7-8 (1932): 18-23.

10. O. Benediktov, "Itogi senti͡abr'skogo plenuma i voprosy ugolovnoĭ politiki," *Sovetskoe gosudarstvo i revoli͡ut͡sii͡a prava* 11-12 (1932): 74.

11. "Ocherednye zadachi organov i͡ustit͡sii," *Sovetskai͡a i͡ustit͡sii͡a* 7 (1933): 6-10; Akimov, "Reshenie XVII parts'ezda i zadachi organov i͡ustit͡sii," *Sovetskai͡a i͡ustit͡sii͡a* 13 (1934): 1-8.

12. Stalin, "The Results of the First Five-Year Plan," *Works*, 13:213.

13. Gurevich, "Na bor'bu," 13.

14. Danilov and Tept͡sov, "Kollektivizat͡sii͡a; Iu.A. Shchetinov, "Rezhim lichnoĭ vlasti Stalina: k istorii formirovanii͡a," *Vestnik Moskovskogo universiteta* 4, ser. 8, Istorii͡a (1989): 25. For conditions in the first years after the October Revolution of 1917, see Chapter 2.

15. Quoted in Fainsod, *Smolensk*, 185.

16. Ibid., 187; D. Volkogonov, *I.V. Stalin* (Moscow: Izdatel'stvo Agenstva pechati Novosti, 1989), 1-2: 240.

17. Fainsod, *Smolensk*, 187.

18. Bulatov, "Ispravitel'no-trudovaia politica RSFSR," 18.

19. Ibid., 20: Rybakov, "Za kachestvo i svoevremennoe vypolnenie khozdogovorov v sisteme ITU na 1933 g.," *Sovetskaia iustitsiia* 2-3 (1934): 35; Apeter, "15 let vospitatel'no-trudovoĭ politiki," 19.

20. "V soveshchenie rukovodiashchikh rabotnikov organov iustitsii kraëv i oblasteĭ RSFSR," 23-24.

21. "VIII rasshirennoe soveshchanie rabotnikov iustitsii RSFSR," *Sovetskaia iustitsiia* 8 (1933); 11; O. Gempfler, "Vyshe tempy po vypolneniiu programmy ITU po vypusku predmetov shirportreba," *Sovetskaia iustitsiia* 30 (1932): 19.

22. For OGPU propaganda methods, see Chapter 9.

23. Bulatov, "Ispravitel'no-trudovaia politika RSFSR" *Sovetskaia iustitsiia* 2 (1934): 21; "Na soveshchanii agronomov sel'skokhoziaĭstvennykh ispravitel'no-trudovykh koloniĭ," *Sovetskaia iustitsiia* 6 (1934): 10-14; "Vyshe kachestvo raboty sel'skokhoziaĭstvennykh ITK," *Sovetskaia iustitsiia* 7 (1934): 2-3; S. Muranov, "Lesnoe delo v sisteme sotsialistichekogo stroitel'stva," *Sovetskoe stroitel'stvo* 3 (1934): 29-37.

24. Dallin and Nicolaevsky, *Forced Labor*, 84-87.

25. "Na soveshchanii agronomov," 10, 13.

26. Ibid., 10.

27. "Vyshe kachestvo," 2-3.

28. "Sovety v bor'be za les," *Sovetskoe stroitel'stvo* 12 (1934): 19-28.

29. I. Apeter, "Novyĭ ispravitel'no-trudovoĭ kodeks," *Sovetskaia iustitsiia* 18 (1933): 1-2.

30. *Sobranie*, 1933, 48:208.1, 20.

31. Ibid., 208.28-35.

32. Apeter, "Novyĭ ispravitel'no-trudovoĭ kodeks," 1-2.

33. "Inostrannye rabochie—gosti udarnikov Magnitogorskoĭ ispravitel'no-trudovoĭ kolonii," *Sovetskaia iustitsiia* 15 (1934): 3.

34. N.I. Krylenko, "Osonovnye printsipy ispravitel'no-trudovoĭ politiki," *Sovetskaia iustitsiia* 15 (1934): 1-2.

35. "Vtianut' vse ITU v sotssorevnovanie na luchshuiu organizatsionnuiu rabotu," *Sovetskaia iustitsiia* 25 (1934): 20; Madevosian, "Ispravitel'no-trudovye kolonii massovykh rabot v bor'be za perevospitanie osuzhdënyykh," *Sovetskaia iustitsiia* 32 (1934): 7.

36. *Sobranie*, 1934, 56:421.

8. THE GPU-OGPU PLACES OF CONFINEMENT, 1922-1928

1. *Sobranie*, 1922, 53:675.8; 16:160.

2. "Sud i zhizn'," *Ezhenedel'nik sovetskoĭ iustitsii* 21-22 (1922): 25.

3. "O peredache," in Losev and Ragulin, *Sbornik*, 106-7.

4. Lenin, *Polnoe*, 54:569; Legget, *The Cheka*, 343-44; S.S. Khromov, *Po zadaniiu Lenina: deiatel'nost' F.E. Dzerzhinskogo v Sibiri* (Moscow: Izdatel'stvo Moskovskogo universiteta, 1964), 14, 18, 23, 131.

166 NOTES TO PAGES 112-120

5. Solzhenitsyn, *Arkhipelag-Gulag*, 3-4:18-19; Oliṯskaía, *Moi vospominaniía*, 1:217, 220; Volkogonov, *Stalin*, 1-2; photo of Solovki camp between pp. 64 and 65.

6. Averbakh, *Ot prestupleniía*, 16; *Sobranie*, 1930, 22:248.

7. Dallin and Nicolaevsky, *Forced Labor*, 169-75; Oliṯskaía, *Moi vospominaniía*, 1:217; Bezsonov, *Dvadṯsat' shest' tiurem i pobeg s Solovkov* (Paris: Imprimerie de Navarre, 1928), 165-67.

8. Dallin and Nicolaevsky, *Forced Labor*, 173; L. Skliar, "Prestupnost' v RSFSR za 1920-23 g.g.," *Vlast' sovetov* 6-7 (1923); Tarnovskiĭ, "Dvizhenie," *Vlast' sovetov* 10 (1923): 110-19; L. Skliar, "Statistika Ukrainy," *Vlast' sovetov* 10 (1923): 119-22; V. Iakubson, "Naselenie v mestakh zakliucheniía do i posle vvedeniía Ugolovnogo Kodeksa," *Vlast' sovetov* 4 (1923): 132-34.

9. *Sobranie*, 1924, 86:870.3-9.

10. Dallin and Nicolaevsky, *Forced Labor*, 172.

11. *Sobranie*, 1923, 66:640.

12. *Sovetskaía istoricheskaía enṯsiklopediía*, s.v. "Menzhinskii, V.R."

13. See Chapter 2; Dallin and Nicolaevsky, *Forced Labor*, 173; N. Ṯsipurenko, "Slon-Khronika terrora," *Vospitanie i pravoporiadok* 2 (1991): 60.

14. Agabekov, GPU 14-25, 41, 43. On the prison agency's title, see Chapter 3.

15. Oliṯskaía, *Moi vospominaniía*, 1:220; Dallin and Nicolaevsky, *Forced Labor*, 173-74; Solzhenitsyn, *Arkhipelag-Gulag*, 3-4, 43-46.

16. Solzhenitsyn, *Arkhipelag-Gulag*, 3-4, 41, 43-46.

17. Dallin and Nicolaevsky, *Forced Labor*, 174; N. Ṯsipurenko, "Slon-Khronika terrora," 63.

18. Dallin and Nicolaevsky, *Forced Labor*, 170, 172-73; Oliṯskaía, *Moi vospominaniía*, 1:216-17.

19. Oliṯskaía, *Moi vospominaniía*, 1:217.

20. Ibid., 219, 225-28, 231-34; *Letters from Russian Prisons*, 197.

21. I.M. Zaiṯssev, *Solovki* (Shanghai: Slovo, 1928), 21-22.

22. Ibid., 147, 149.

23. Rossi, *Spravochnik po GULAGu*, 353.

24. Bezsonov, 169.

25. Ibid., 165-67.

26. Ibid., 167; *Letters from Russian Prisons*, 159, 192-208, 214; Oliṯskaía, 1:218, 220-24.

27. Dallin and Nicolaevsky, *Forced Labor*, 188-89.

28. "Ispravitel'no-trudovaía politika," 29.

29. B.L., "O strakhovanii lesorubov," 141; Pervozvanskiĭ, "Ekspluataṯsiía," 60; M.F. Zamengof, "Vneshniaía torgovliá i narodnoe khoziaĭstvo v 1923/1924 g.," in V.G. Groman, N.A. Koval'skiĭ, P.E. Vaĭsberg, *Narodnoe khoziaĭstvo SSSR v 1923-1924 g.* (Moscow: Rossiĭskaía assoṯsiaṯsiía nauchno-issledovatel'skikh institutov obshchestvennykh nauk, 1925), 251, 242.

30. B.L., "O strakhovanii lesorubov," 141-42.

31. *Narodnoe khoziaĭstvo SSSR za 60 let* (Moscow: Statistika, 1977), 173.

9. THE OGPU DURING COLLECTIVIZATION AND INDUSTRIALIZATION

1. See Chapter 5.

2. Dallin and Nicolaevsky, *Forced Labor*, 53, 54, 173; Solzhenitsyn, *Arkhipelag-Gulag*, 3-4:41; *Sobranie*, 1922, 53:675.

3. "O karatel'noĭ politike," in Losev and Ragulin, *Sbornik*, 202-6; Stuchka and Apeter, "Perekhod," 128.

4. Dallin and Nicolaevsky, *Forced Labor*, 53-54; Conquest, *Great Terror*, 311.

5. Solzhenitsyn, *Arkhipelag-Gulag*, 3-4:53, 75-76; Bezsonov, *Dvadtsat'*, 172-76.

6. Solzhenitsyn, *Arkhipelag-Gulag*, 73-76; Dallin and Nicolaevsky, *Forced Labor*, 181-82.

7. Statement by Eduard Martynovich Dune in Nicolaevsky Collection, 236:15.

8. Dallin and Nicolaevsky, *Forced Labor*, 144-46.

9. Ibid.; Gempfler, "Vyshe tempy," 11; "Na soveshchanii agronomov," 10-14.

10. Shirvindt, "K dvenadtsatiletiiu sovetskoĭ," 1088; Gempfler, "Vyshe tempy," 11; "Na soveshchanii agronomov," 10-14; "Ispravitel'no-trudovaia politika," 29.

11. *Sobranie*, 1930, 27:248; "Doklad tovarishcha Iansona," 13-14; Dallin and Nicolaevsky, *Forced Labor*, 52-53, 57, 173; T., "Nuzhny li narkomvnudely," 23.

12. "Doklad tovarishcha Iansona," 13-14.

13. Harvard University Russian Refugee Interview Project, Russian Research Center, Cambridge, Massachusetts; Michael Jakobson, "Prisoners' Songs as a Historical Source," unpublished manuscript, 1975.

14. "Letter from Alfred Rozenberg to General Keitel on Nazi Treatment of Soviet Prisoners of War, 28 February 1942," in Yury Boshyk, ed., *Ukraine during World War II: History and Aftermath* (Edmonton: Canadian Institute of Ukranian Studies, 1986), pt. 3, doc. 4; Kromiadi, "Polozhenie russkikh voennoplennykh v Germanii v 1941 g.," Nicolaevsky Collection, 409:11.

15. *Khronika presledovaniĭ v Sovetskoĭ Rossii* 2 (1925): 1-4; *Letters from Russian Prisoners;* Stuchka and Apeter, "Perekhod," 140-41.

16. "K voprosu o bor'be s detskoĭ prestupnost'iu," *Vlast' sovetov* 1-2 (1923): 54.

17. *Pesennik* (Paris: Iunosheskiĭ otdel Russkogo studencheskogo khristianskogo dvizheniia, [1970]), 7.

18. Men'shatin, review of Shirvindt and Utevskiĭ, 174; G.A. Bordiugov, "Sotsial'nyĭ parazitizm ili sotsial'nye anomalii," *Istoriia SSSR* 1 (1989): esp. 61; Solzhenitsyn, *Arkhipelag-Gulag*, 3-4:61-62, 65; Dallin and Nicolaevsky, *Forced Labor*, 189.

19. *Sobranie*, 1930, 22:248; 1934, 56:421; Robert Conquest, *Inside Stalin's Secret Police* (Stanford, Calif.: Hoover Institution Press, 1985), 14.

20. *Tiuremnoe . . . 1921*, 3.

21. "O peredache," in Losev and Ragulin, 106.

22. *Sobranie*, 1932, 53:237.3.

23. Ibid., 1930, 22:248.2, 14-15.

24. Ibid., 248.16; Solzhenitsyn, *Arkhipelag-Gulag*, 3-4:76; *Sobranie*, 1930, 22:248.21, 27-28.

25. Dallin and Nicolaevsky, *Forced Labor*, 217-30; Solzhenitsyn, *Arkhipelag-Gulag*, 63.

26. Averbakh, *Ot prestupleniia*, 112; Shirvindt, "K dvenadtsatiletiiu sovetskoĭ," 1087-88.

27. "Doklad tovarishcha Iansona," 13-14.

28. Dallin and Nicolaevsky, *Forced Labor*, 217-30.

29. Ibid., 40.

30. George Kitchin, *Prisoner of the OGPU* (London: Longmans, Green, 1935), 267-70; Vladimir Cherniavin, *I Speak for the Silent: Prisoners of the Soviets* (Boston: Ralph T. Hale, 1935), 251-53; M.Z. Nikonov-Smorodin, *Krasnaia Katorga* (Sofia: NTSNP, 1938), 274.

31. Dallin and Nicolaevsky, *Forced Labor*, 222-26.

32. Ibid.,224, 212-13; Timoshenko, "Kanalarmeitsy," 2:308.

33. Solzhenitsyn, *Arkhipelag-Gulag*, 3-4, 102; Rossi, *Spravochnik po GULAGu*, 26; Averbakh, *Ot prestuplenia*, 23-32; *Belomoro-Baltiiskii Kanal imeni Stalina* (Moscow: OGIZ, 1934).

34. Dallin and Nicolaevsky, *Forced Labor*, 113.

35. "Deiatel'nost' prezidiuma TSIK Soiuza SSR," *Sovetskoe striotel'stvo* 8 (1934): 112; Dallin and Nicolaevsky, *Forced Labor*, 116-17; Robert Conquest, *Kolyma* (New York: Viking Press, 1978), 214-31.

36. Dallin and Nicolaevsky, *Forced Labor*, 145-46; S. Swianiewicz, *Forced Labor and Economic Development* (London: Oxford University Press, 1965), 292-93; Volkogonov, *Stalin*, 2-2:64-65; B. Piskarev, "Arkhiv sovesti," *Sotisalisticheskaia industriia* 10 (October 1989): 7.

37. Solzhenitsyn, *Arkhipelag-Gulag*, 3-4:127; Ronald Hingly, *The Russian Secret Police* (New York: Simon & Schuster, 1970), 176-77; Dallin and Nicolaevsky, *Forced Labor*, 130-31.

38. Averbakh, *Ot prestupleniia*, 148.

39. Fainsod, *Smolensk*, 185-87; "Ocherednye zadachi organov iustitsii," 6-10; I. Donets, "O faktakh nechestnoi raboty sudebnykh organov," *Sovetskaia iustitsiia* 8 (1933): 14-15; Danilov and Teptsov, "Kollektivizatsiia." Shchetinov, "Rezhim lichnoi vlasti Stalina," 25.

40. Averbakh, *Ot prestupleniia*, 21; Solzhenitsyn, *Arkhipelag-Gulag*, 3-4, 102; Dallin and Nicolaevsky, *Forced Labor*, 58; Conquest, *Kolyma*, 214-31; Swianiewicz, *Forced Labor*, 290.

41. Averbakh, *Ot prestupleniia*, 19-24.

42. Ibid., 24-27.

43. *Belomoro-Baltiiskii kanal imeni Stalina*.

44. Averbakh, *Ot prestupleniia*, 148-66, 26-27.

45. *Sobranie*, 1933, 50:294; Averbakh, *Ot prestupleniia*, 201-3.

46. Boris Efimov, *Zhertva kul'ta lichnosti* (London: Fredon Press).

47. Dallin and Nicolaevsky, *Forced Labor*, 54-58; Swianiewicz, *Forced Labour*, 37; Volkogonov, *Stalin*, 1-2:239-41; Utevskii, *Sovetskaia*, 30; see also Chapter 7.

48. "Inostrannye rabochie," 1.

49. M. Ibragimov, untitled article, Nicolaevsky Collection, 638:25.

50. *Sobranie*, 1934, 36:283.

51. Ibid., 1922, 16:160, 53:675; 1934, 36:283.

52. *Sobranie*, 1934, 56:421.

53. Dallin and Nicolaevsky, *Forced Labor*, 130-31.

INDEX

Administration of Northern Special Purpose Camps (USLON), 38, 125

Administrative Commission of Petrograd, 24

Administration of Solovetskiĭ Camps (USLAG), 125

Administration of Solovetskiĭ Special Purpose Camps (USLON), 38, 125

Agabekov, G., 37-38

agricultural colonies: in the 1920s, 62; and financial self-sufficiency of prison-camp system, 64-65; in the 1930s, 107-8

All-Russian Central Executive Committee (VTSIK), 37, 71-72, 75; and forced labor camps, 45-52; and corrective labor camps, 59; and concentration camps, 68; and reform of prison-camp system, 81-83; and People's Commissariat of Internal Affairs, 89-90; and GPU facilities, 111

All-Russian Extraordinary Commission for Combating Counterrevolution and Sabotage (Vecheka), 3, 22-27, 36, 38, 148, 149, 151; occupies former prisons, 32; receives places of confinement, 37; functions of, 39, 51, 65; establishes forced labor camps, 44-47; disbanded, 111

All-Union conference of various agencies: on subordination of places of confinement, 89

Aminov, I., 103-4

Apeter, P., 92-93; on reeducation of inmates, 95; reduces budget of prison-camp system, 99

Artem'ev, Viacheslav, 1

Averbakh, I.L., 5, 132-34

Bachulis, 41

Baehrens, Kurt, 1

Bekhterev, Iu., 97

Beloborodov, A.G., 113

Berman, M.D., 7, 125, 130

Berzin, Reĭngold, 130, 131, 138

Board of Places of Confinement, 55

Bogdanov, A.A., 54

Bokiĭ, G.I., 7, 47, 114

Bolsheviks, 16, 18; on crime and punishment, 5, 19, 139; as former political prisoners, 18

Breshkovskaia, Ekaterina, 16

budget of places of confinement: in Imperial Russia, 11; in 1920s, 67, 81-82; in 1931, 97-98

Bukharin, N.I., 5, 81, 87, 89, 122, 137; Shirvindt accused of supporting, 92; GUMZ accused of supporting, 94, 121-22; Utevskiĭ accused of supporting, 97

Bureau of Corrective Labor without Deprivation of Freedom, 97

Bureau of Forced Labor without Deprivation of Freedom, 77, 97

Burlachenko, 73

Main Administration of Frontiers and Internal Troops, 157

Main Administration of Places of Confinement (GUMZ): established by Provisional Government, 2, 17, 27, 28, 146, 151; and local offices and places of confinement, 16-17, 27-31; ignored by Bolsheviks, 28-29; disbanded, 31

Main Administration of Places of Confinement (GUMZ): established by Soviet Government, 69, 72, 91, 93, 96, 119, 146, 151; structure, 71-72; All-Russian conference of, 72-73; and local offices, 77; social origins of guards and warders of, 89

Main Administration of State Security (GUGB), 137

Main Prison Administration (GTU), 13, 146; structure, 12-13; under Provisional Government, 16; compared with Soviet prison agencies, 47

Makarenko, A., 126

Marxist view of crime and punishment. *See* Bolsheviks

Men'shatin, V., 96

Menzhinskiĭ, V.R., 6, 113

Military Revolutionary Committees, 21-23, 37

Ministry of the Interior, 3, 12, 13, 17; cooperation with Ministry of Justice, 14

Ministry of Justice, 3, 13, 17, 26; cooperation with Ministry of the Interior, 14-15; budget of, 14-15

Ministry of the Marine, 12, 13, 31

Ministry of War, 12, 13, 31

Molotov, V.M., 89; on forced labor, 127-28

Moscow-Volga Canal, 119, 129, 131-32, 136

Mundshtukmakher, 80

Narkompros. *See* People's Commissariat of Education

Nekrasov, 36

Nicolaevsky, B.I., 1

NKIU. *See* People's Commissariat of Justice

NKVD. *See* People's Commissariat of Internal Affairs

Nogtev, 117

Northern Special Purpose Camps (SLON), 38, 40-41, 43, 68, 112

Observation Commissions: in Imperial Russia, 14; under Provisional Government, 16-17; under Soviet Government, 78-79, 82

officials and employees: and inmates, 36, 39, 41, 56, 60, 74, 101; living and working conditions of, 39, 54, 60, 66, 74; training of, 56, 60, 101; statistics, 60; social origins of, 89. *See also officials by name*

OGPU. *See* Unified State Political Administration

Olit̂skai̇a, Ekaterina, 115

Operational Department and Komendatura. *See* Komendatura

Ordzhonikidze, G.K., 137

orphans. *See* homeless children

overcrowding: in 1918-21, 29, 43, 61; in 1925-28, 80, 84-85

Pashukanis, Evgeniĭ, 122; on Main Administration of Places of Confinement, 89

People's Commissariat of Food Supply, 23, 29, 62

People's Commissariat of Education, 54-56

People's Commissariat of Internal Affairs (NKVD) of RSFSR, 1, 3, 5, 26, 46, 65, 72, 147, 149, 150, 151; periodicals of, 2; has rights to arrest and execute, 23-24; statistics, 24; controls former police stations, 32; reduces subsidies to places of confinement, 67; nearly disbanded, 74-75; encourages harsh treatment of inmates, 84; disbanded, 89-90; controls all places of confinement, 111

People's Commissariat of Internal Affairs (NKVD) of USSR, 5, 147, 150, 151;